Feminist Social Work Theory and Practice

Also by Lena Dominelli

Love and Wages

*Anti-Racist Social Work

*Feminist Social Work (with Eileen McLeod)

Women and Community Action

Women Across Continents: Feminist Comparative Social Policy

Gender, Sex Offenders and Probation Practice

Anti-Racist Probation Practice (with Lennie Jeffers, Graham Jones,
    Sakile Sibanda and Brian Williams)

*Sociology for Social Work

Community Approaches to Child Welfare: International Perspectives

Beyond Racial Divides: Ethnicities in Social Work (with Haluk Soydan
    and Walter Lorenz)

*Social Work: Themes, Issues and Critical Debates (with Robert Adams
    and Malcolm Payne)

*Also published by Palgrave

Feminist Social Work Theory and Practice

Lena Dominelli

Consultant Editor: Jo Campling

palgrave

First published 2002 by
PALGRAVE
Houndmills, Basingstoke, Hampshire RG21 6XS and
175 Fifth Avenue, New York, N.Y. 10010
Companies and representatives throughout the world

PALGRAVE is the new global academic imprint of
St. Martin's Press LLC Scholarly and Reference Division and
Palgrave Publishers Ltd (formerly Macmillan Press Ltd).

ISBN 978-0-333-77154-9   ISBN 978-0-230-62820-5 (eBook)
DOI 10.1007/978-0-230-62820-5

This book is printed on paper suitable for recycling and
made from fully managed and sustained forest sources.

A catalogue record for this book is available
from the British Library.

10   09   08   07   06   05   04   03   02   01
11   10   09   08   07   06   05   04   03   02

To my father

Contents

Acknowledgements

Writing a book is never the activity of a single individual. Knowledge is created through interaction between people. Even the author locked away in a garret relies on knowledge acquired, created and disseminated by others. Also, the act of writing becomes meaningless if no reader engages with the written words. But writing a book within an academic context has a further set of conditions that impact upon the author–reader relationship and place it on a more formal footing: the requirements of academia.

I wish to thank many unnamed people who have assisted me in the creation of this book: the people who have agreed to be interviewed; the students who have engaged with me in a mutual exchange of information in the teaching and learning relation; and colleagues who have shared their knowledge with me. However, there are individuals who have made specific contributions that I would like to acknowledge by giving my sincerest thanks: Marilyn Callahan for her invaluable support and feedback after reading the draft manuscript; my parents for the endless love and wisdom that saw me through the physical process of writing; my brothers and sisters for their emotional succour when I felt lost; and David and Nicholas for the love, wit and sympathy in responding to my many absences. Thank you all. Without your contributions, this book would have been much poorer.

Summer 1999   Lena Dominelli

Introduction

Feminism seems an old-fashioned word in today's allegedly postmodern world. The media in Western countries has confidently asserted that feminism is passé by claiming that we have entered the post-feminist era. To women like me, this is a strange paradox. For as women experience the feminisation of poverty, increasing levels of sexual violence, the loss of welfare state benefits which women have accessed in the recent past, the threatened loss of livelihood and statehood, I marvel at the idea that feminist claims have been realised and need consume the energies of women and girls no longer.

The absurdity of this position is even more evident when the realities of everyday life for women in industrialising or low income countries are considered. There, poverty is endemic and many children, women and men struggle to secure the basic necessities of life such as food, water and shelter (UNDP, 1998). In industrialised countries, numerous communities have lost their manufacturing bases. With these have gone employment opportunities for young women to earn their economic independence and strike out on their own. The chances for young men to acquire highly paid skilled manufacturing jobs have also disappeared. With the resultant loss of status and purpose, young men drift into crime and social isolation (Young, 1999). And, the possibility of engaging with them to facilitate their assuming an equal share of the responsibilities of family life including the care of children and dependent older people has also retreated.

Without a lot of hard work, most of it undertaken by women working in their homes and communities, the sense of alienation and hardship would be even more overwhelming. Through ceaseless work, women have managed to keep body and soul together, at least for the time being, in the hopes that a brighter day will dawn. And then, maybe then, women and the people they love will be free to savour the lives they choose. At least, this dream keeps women optimistic in periods of despondency and despair when there is not enough food in the cupboard to feed the baby and no money in her purse to buy grandma's medicine. Women's determination to survive bleak social situations and create new visions for a better world is what inspires me to promote feminist social work as one way of contributing to women's desire to improve the welfare of all. However, this task cannot be undertaken in a naïve and deterministic manner, but through a process of engaging with others and their concerns.

1

Caring is hard work. It is also socially necessary work. Yet, it has been consistently devalued and taken for granted. Something women do 'naturally'. None the less, women are constantly engaged in servicing its circuitous motions, often at the expense of looking after their own needs as they pour their efforts into ensuring that the lives of their loved ones are a little easier. Social workers collude with the seeming effortlessness of women's endeavours and thereby negate the recognition of how much effort they put into basic survival (Callahan, 2000). Moreover, they tend to focus on the woman as an autonomous island whose energies create an oasis in a harsh social desert. In traditional social work practice in impoverished communities where everyone suffers from rising levels of poverty, women practitioners pay little attention to the structural causes of women's predicament. Though critical of women's best efforts and aware of the commonalities which bind them across the gender divide, women social workers, no less than their male counterparts, expect women to manage in the most obdurate social conditions and berate them when they fail.

Holding women personally responsible for the socio-economic and political forces which wreak havoc with their best laid plans, professionals intervening in their lives can pathologise them mercilessly and in doing so risk crushing the fragile blooms of self-sufficiency that women display. All this happens in the name of encouraging independence and ensuring that a dependency on the welfare state or the charity of others does not materialise. What they must be offered is 'a hand up, not a handout', women have been told by leading politicians (Blair, 1999). But a hand up without resources is like being given a straw to bridge a yawning crevice. It breaks with the slightest exertion and lands the unsuspecting holder with an even greater range of problems to solve.

Feminist social work purports to address these issues by placing women and the elimination of structural gender inequalities at the centre of its practice. I explore its tenets in this book. In doing so, I question the relegation of feminism into the annals of history and consider its usefulness in a social work practice that is embedded within a (de)industrialising and globalising planet. The current scene has diverged substantially from that evident when Eileen McLeod and I wrote *Feminist Social Work*. But, I have retained one element from those days – an optimism that feminists continue to envision a world in which people and the environment they live in matter.

There are a number of feminist viewpoints which need to be considered, for feminism has always contained within its ranks a wide range of divergent and diverse opinions. It is more appropriate, therefore, to speak of feminisms, of which my particular interpretation and construction is only one. My own perspective is an amalgamation of elements I borrow from a broad range of feminist views. Despite feminisms' fragmentation and diversity, there are a number of principles that feminists share, regardless of their overall analyses and calls for action. These include integrating the personal and political dimensions of life (Millet, 1969); respecting the diversity encompassed by women (hooks, 2000); seeking more egalitarian forms of social relationships (Collins, 1991); and transforming the existing social order (Adamson *et al.*, 1988) for it serves badly the needs of men, women and children. I use these commonalities to explore the differences encapsulated by the range of voices emanating from women's lives and expressed through women's activities. Then, I go on to examine how social workers can utilise feminist principles of theory and practice to work more effectively with 'clients' than they would have done had they followed more orthodox social work ideologies.[1] Although I write primarily as one embedded within a British cultural context, feminism seeks to transcend exclusionary approaches to difference through self-reflective critiques and reaching out, so I hope that what I say resonates with women elsewhere.

Feminists Envisage the Creation of Egalitarian Social Relations

Feminists, as women who have sought to improve the conditions in which women live from their own point of view, have challenged unjust social relations that have oppressed women for centuries in different ways in every country in the world (Basu, 1997). In places such as Britain, the 'second wave' of feminism became the term applied to women who have been demanding an end to the injustices that have oppressed women in modern society since the 1960s (Banks, 1981; Tong, 1989). In industrialising countries, feminists have focused on different issues, but their commitment to ensuring justice for women has galvanised their energies in these parts of the globe (Jayawardna, 1986; Basu, 1995).

Feminists involved in mobilising women have not had a single view of either the causes of women's oppression, or of the ways for ending it. Diversity has been an important feature of contemporary feminism although the Western media's coverage of its activities has focused on the preoccupations of white middle-class women in the United States and characterised the women's movement as a monolithic one. This attitude disparages the issues that have taken up the energies of marginalised groups of women, particularly those living in poor working-class and ethnicised communities for equally long periods of time (Dominelli, 1997a). The media's approach has more to do with the politics of subverting feminism's appeal to a wide range of women world-wide, an outcome achieved by not acknowledging that although different struggles preoccupy different categories of women, there are also concerns that women hold in common (Basu, 1997).

Women activists have continued to work on their own issues regardless of the media's representation of their activities, the 'differences' that have divided one group of women from another, and their uneven successes in achieving their goals. Women have persevered in searching for ways of symbolically and practically emphasising their commitment to 'unity in diversity' (Collins, 1991) through sustained critiques of the silencing of different voices. Older women have raised issues of ageism (Doress and Siegal, 1987); lesbian women have called for the celebration of women's diverse sexual orientations (Forster and Hanscombe, 1982; Basu, 1997); disabled women have demanded recognition of their concerns across the range of women's groupings (Morris, 1991; Begum, 1993); and women with mental health problems have insisted on the right to mental well-being (Bayess and Howell, 1981; Ashurst and Hall, 1989).

The fragmentation of the women's movement has meant that there are a variety of voices being raised in relation to their overall vision of a society in which the oppression of women is no longer practised. Some of these have sought to ensure that women's diversity is not ignored by a narrowly focused form of women's social action. So, for example, black women[2] have sought to broaden analyses by insisting that women's experience of oppression is racialised, gendered and classed (hooks, 1984, 2000). They have criticised many white women theorists of excluding black women from their analyses (Bryant *et al.*, 1985; Bhavani, 1993). Their writings have addressed the specificities of opppression through slavery, colonialism and genocide (Maracle, 1996), and argued powerfully for not indulging in a hierarchy of oppressions that prioritises one form of oppression over another (Collins, 1991).

Women's critiques of the positions adopted by other women have been rooted in feminists' commitment to being self-reflective, aware of and responsive to the distinctive needs identified by different groups of women (Collins, 1991; Dominelli, 1991). Critiques have provided opportunities for feminists to: grow in their awareness of other women's life experiences; deepen their analyses; recognise the presence of other women as equally legitimate occupiers of public spaces; and respect the wide range of voices through which women portray their stories and aspirations for a better life.[3]

Besides focusing on different matters than their predecessors, 'second wave' feminists in the West have differed in their approach to liberation from their earlier counterparts in that they have insisted that the 'personal is political' (Millet, 1969). For them, power relations are expressed in everyday life in private or family-based relationships as much as those occurring within the public arena. They have also believed in the integration of theory and practice, a stance that has sought to eliminate the binary division between the ends that are being sought and the means whereby these are to be achieved (Brandwein, 1991). In this, they have insisted that there is a direct connection between the processes whereby activities are conducted and the goals they seek to realise (Cook and Kirk, 1983). Women's hopes for a better future are prefigured in the relationships in which they engage today (Dominelli, 1991b). Moreover, feminists no longer simply want to sit at the same table as men. They have aspirations for a different social order (Basu, 1997). It is one that is based on the notion that the well-being of people should be at the heart of the social agenda. Although ideas that will put substance to these hopes are taking a while to assume their shape, feminists' new visions for the world endorse egalitarian relations, the recognition of mutual interdependencies and inter-generational solidarities and the creation of an economic system that is geared to meeting people's needs rather than subverting them (Dominelli, 1991, 1997c). In short, the traditional way of doing things is no longer adequate and its continued reproduction cannot be assumed.

Feminist Theory and Practice has Implications for Men and Children

Feminists have highlighted the gendered nature of social relations in all spheres of public and private life. Their analyses have revealed men as privileged at the expense of women in many dimensions of social existence, including their exclusion from the waged labour domain when men collar high-paying jobs (Armstrong, 1984; Coyle, 1989). Feminist research has also demonstrated that men exert social control over women through the exercise of emotional, physical and sexual forms of violence (Rush, 1980; Dworkin, 1981). Although they have argued that women have rights of access to the same public domains as men if they wish, some feminists have also wanted men to take responsibility for many tasks which women have traditionally undertaken within the domestic realm (Segal, 1983). These include housework, child care and elder care (Walby, 1990). However, other feminists have found the inclusion of men in feminist activities extremely problematic and have chosen to resolve the matter by insisting that feminists should not work with men under any circumstances (Solanas, 1971; Jo, 1981; Frye, 1983).

So, a substantial ingredient in feminist critiques of the *status quo* calls for an end to the privileging of men for it occurs at the expense of women. And, that is unjust. Sadly, the realisation of the implications of this stance has engendered fear in conservative men who wish to retain their privileges

(Brooks, 1996). Instead of welcoming an enterprise through which even their own lives can be enriched, these men remain myopically fixed in a mythologised past that has accorded them unchallenged governance (see Bly, 1985). And, they devote their energies to an anti-feminist attack to reverse feminist gains that they deem undermine their spheres of influence (see Lyndon, 1992; Farrell, 1994).

A further group of feminists have argued that for women to be truly free, men have to liberate themselves from the shackles imposed upon them by their adherence to patriarchal social relations (Dominelli and McLeod, 1989; Collins, 1991). And, they have sought to include children and men as beneficiaries of their social action. With regard to children, this has meant the recognition of children as individuals with their own set of inalienable rights (Clinton, 1996; Dominelli, 1999). Some feminist authors have attempted to find ways of responding to women's interests without pitting these against those of children (Dominelli and McLeod, 1989). Other feminists have found it difficult to reconcile women's needs for liberation with those of children for the same, and have continued to struggle with reconciling the contradictions in which women live (Wise, 1985). Some feminist scholars have identified the role of the state in using women caring professionals to control other women (Wilson, 1977). This too, has been considered unacceptable (Marchant and Wearing, 1986; Dominelli and McLeod, 1989). Although its realisation remains elusive, feminists have sought to be inclusive without being oppressive. That is, feminists have not sought to overcome one set of oppressions – that of women by men, by merely replacing it with another, that of men by women, or even by one group of women dominating other women.

Feminist Social Work

Feminist social work arose out of feminist social action being carried out by women working with women in their communities (Dominelli and McLeod, 1989). Their aim has been to improve women's well-being by linking their personal predicaments and often untold private sorrows with their social position and status in society. This has meant that private troubles have been redefined as matters of public concern. Although other social workers have insisted that society creates personal ills, e.g., Attlee (1920), feminist social workers have been first to root women's troubles in their social positions and roles as women. In creating feminist social work, women activists have drawn on feminist insights more generally and woven these into their own unique patterns of theory and practice, thereby setting up an interactive relationship by which feminist social work also contributes to feminist scholarship, research and practice.

I define feminist social work as a form of social work practice that takes women's experience of the world as the starting point of its analysis and by focusing on the links between a woman's position in society and her individual predicament, responds to her specific needs, creates egalitarian relations in 'client'–worker interactions and addresses structural inequalities. Meeting women's particular needs in a holistic manner and dealing with the complexities of their lives – including the numerous tensions and diverse forms of oppression impacting upon them, is an integral part of feminist social work. Its focus on the interdependent nature of social relations ensures that it also addresses the needs of those that women interact with – men, children and other women.

In giving women pride of place in their analyses, feminist social workers have challenged gender-blind theories and practices that have treated women as offshoots of men (Harding, 1990) under the guise of the universal human being that although ungendered resounds to men's ways of thinking, living and working. In social work, these have been replaced with woman-centered approaches (Hanmer and Statham, 1988) that advocate sensitive gendered responses to the needs of women 'clients' and women workers. More recently, feminist social work has incorporated men more fully into its theory and practice (Dominelli, 1991; Cavanagh and Cree, 1996; Orme *et al.*, 2000).

However, these conceptualisations of women's position have not been unchallenged. Ramazanoglu (1989) has questioned the validity of approaches that treat women as a singular, uniform category. She terms these 'essentialist' for ignoring the impact of 'race', disability, age, sexual orientations and other social divisions upon gender relations, despite their commitment to examining women in their social situations. Additionally, postmodern feminism has critiqued feminist practice and placed greater emphasis on language and power in the interactive processes between individuals, including those in the 'client'–worker relationship (Lloyd, 1998).

Charges of essentialism has been levelled against 'classical' texts on feminist social work (Brook and Davis, 1985; Marchant and Wearing, 1986; Burden and Gottlieb 1987; Hanmer and Statham, 1988; Dominelli and McLeod, 1989; Langan and Day, 1992). It is difficult to construct a case that applies equally to all of them. Some have highlighted the wide range of social divisions that are apparent in the lives of women in any given locality to a greater extent than others: Dominelli and McLeod (1989: 3–4, 27–30) have argued for the adaption of their analysis to this diversity. Langan and Day's (1992) solution has been to examine each social division separately in its own chapter.

Women do have differentiated experiences of their oppression. So, while I accept the postmodern caution of not confusing the part for the whole, the charge of essentialism is wide of the mark. Ordinary discourses are replete with 'essentialist' constructions of reality, as people in different situations seek to identify commonalities and tactical bases on which to build unity for particular purposes and signify common understandings about systemic problems that they wish to address – an everyday version of Hartsock's (1987) and Harding's (1990) 'strategic essentialism'. These are partial and temporary creations. In making blanket assertions, post-modern analyses also fail to acknowledge the diversity that exists in both feminism and feminist social work. Alongside this diversity, I argue that feminists must not lose the continuities in or specificities that distinguish between patterns of discrimination that emerge from women's experiences. Thus, it is difficult to sustain the view that 'essentialism' is a major failing in critical feminist social work.

As a profession, social work is committed to the uniqueness of every individual within his or her social situation. The opportunity to respond without essentialising the person or treating them as a member of a homogeneous category is unparalleled. In linking this to feminism's commitment to social change through individual and collective action that enhances the lives of children, women and men, feminist social work has strengths that transcend postmodern theorists' support for fragmented, individual identities. Feminist social workers can affirm collective solidarities that have been unhelpfully dismissed and sacrificed to individualism (Dominelli and Jonsdottir, 1988). One's individual identity can be retained within the remit of a broader collective (Haber, 1994).

A further strength of feminism that is indispensable to social workers is its commitment to social change to better the lives of men, women and children. This arises from feminists' concern to understand and eradicate *patterns* of inequality that impact on some groups more than others and make some sense of the continuities and discontinuities encompassed within the history of any particular group. Yet, postmodernists have consigned these features to the dustbin of history as an obsolete modernist project.

Relocating Social Work

By placing gender on the social work map, feminist social workers have challenged the gender neutrality regarding this social division usually upheld in traditional professional social work theories and practice. Feminists have questioned traditional practitioners' reliance on a universalist discourse that uses (white) men as the yardstick for measuring (all) women's experiences because locating women in these spaces denies women's specific experiences in the routines of daily life and presupposes their dependent status (Pascall, 1986). Feminist activists have also queried social workers' failure to consider the social situations in which women live and have rejected the assumption that social work is simply concerned with individuals and their functioning. In doing this, feminist social workers have problematised practitioner responses to women's needs. Their critiques have identified the grounds on which this occurs as: turning women into passive victims (Hester *et al.*, 1996); imposing various forms of social control on women seeking liberation from the drudgery of their position (Ashurst and Hall, 1989); extracting heavy emotional penalties from women who are locked into unfulfilling and inappropriate relationships (Marchant and Wearing, 1986; Thorpe and Irwin, 1996); and denying women the right to choose their own futures (Dominelli and McLeod, 1989). Feminist social workers have also examined the contexts in which social work practice is undertaken (Swift, 1995) by both relocating social work within a patriarchal capitalist global social structure (Dominelli, 1998) and focusing on the gendered nature of social relations which are locality specific and differentiated across multiple social dimensions (Dominelli, 1998). In other words, a woman is more than a woman.

Whilst social work is understood within its legislative frameworks and specific national and cultural contexts, feminists attempt to identify those elements that women share with other women. Hence, feminist social workers seek to bridge gaps amongst women by examining the commonalities they share with each other alongside the specificities of their particular positions. Their focus on similarities between women has been criticised by postmodernists (Rojek *et al.*, 1988; Ramazanoglu, 1989).

A monetarist agenda imposed by rightwing ideologues and politicians has undermined the social consensus over publicly-supported welfare and driving changes in the profession. Social work as part of the welfare state has been drawn into politicians' search for a new accommodation between the competing needs of capitalist entrepreneurs seeking capital accumulation and working people demanding social resources including healthcare and education (Dominelli, 1999). Feminists have questioned the social construction of the welfare state (Showstack Sassoon, 1987) through scholarship and social actions that seek to produce alternative services catering to the needs of women as women as the structural conditions in which social work is embedded deteriorate (Dominelli, 1991; 1998).

Macro-level changes have involved globalisation and the internationalisation of the welfare state (Dominelli and Hoogvelt, 1996). The ensuing dynamics have restructured mainstream agencies in unproven ways and are evident in the details of everyday social work practice. In England, the traditional division of statutory social work practice into 'client' groupings has been jettisoned in favour of a separation between working with children and families and working with adults. This two-fold division has ignored the location of both 'client' groups within families and the overlaps between them. It has also rendered less visible other needy 'clients' such as disabled people of all ages. At the same time, the government has severed the links between work with offenders and social work, removed probation training from university settings and siphoned it off to work-places that can contract a range of other university disciplines to provide the necessary knowledge base (Sone, 1995; Ward and Lacey, 1994).

The final outcome of market-driven measures remains unclear, but a number of concerns have been expressed about decoupling probation from its social work origins. These include: the loss of social work's interest in changing behaviour (Ward and Lacey, 1994); disregard for the rehabilita-tion of the offender (Williams, 1995); failure of probation to respond to peo-ple's needs as they define them; and deprofessionalisation of social work (Dominelli, 1996). State measures linked to globalisation have also whittled away professional power by devaluing its expertise. Taken in their totality, these developments have placed the dilemma of the replacement of the professional social worker by the 'streetwise granny' at the centre of public debates. Also, feminisms' preoccupation with women's needs while neglecting men's has been questioned (Cahn, 1995). The unfolding of these developments is of crucial importance to social work at this historical con-juncture, providing themes I explore in this book to give it a topicality that will exercise social workers for some time.

Social work has been implicated in these changes on a number of other levels, some of which operate in contradiction to others. One of these requires practitioners to ensure that people seeking welfare assistance become self-sufficient citizens by being claimants for as short a period as possible (Blair, 1999). This draws on the social work role that has women, as the majority of basic grade workers, controlling other women in their homemaking, child nurturing and elder caring capacities whilst holding out the carrot of retraining for an elusive job (Millar, 1999). Another change questions the need for professional social workers to intervene in people's lives under any circumstances, seeking instead to relegate their activities to the unpaid voluntary and domestic realms in the anticipation that women will fill the gaps left by withdrawn state services. This re-orienta-tion of service provision has relied on the role of women as compensating mechanisms responsible for making good the inadequacies of public wel-fare resources. A third change has been the restructuring of service provi-sions so that those not provided by either the state or the household can be purchased in the marketplace. This has resulted in women becoming con-sumers of services that have become increasingly evasive if they lack financial resources for purchasing them (Neysmith, 1998).

For some women, these restructuring measures have been beneficial in encouraging them to become successful private entrepreneurs occupying a niche in which they provide welfare services that other women are will-ing to purchase (Lloyd, 1996). Though poorly paid, these opportunities are particularly relevant to black women excluded from the labour market by racism. A fourth aspect involves the transferal of welfare resources to private entrepreneurs through enforced sales of public provisions (Dominelli and Hoogvelt, 1996). The combined effect of these developments has been that women have lost jobs in the public welfare state and become subjected to re-employment in the private sector at lower rates of pay than previously and under more insecure conditions (Clarke and Newman, 1997). Restructuring public sector jobs has removed some of women's security and reliance on the welfare state as the source of their financial emancipation and resulted in women workers subsidising privatisation initiatives (Ralph *et al.*, 1997).

Publicly-funded provisions have also targeted those most in need, leaving a large swathe of people without recourse to alternatives because they lack the wherewithal to purchase their own or reside in circumstances that make it impossible for them to rely on impoverished others to help. For example, the loss of access to welfare benefits provided by the British state for young people between the ages of 16 and 18 has increased the numbers of homeless young people roaming the streets without links to their families (Bishopp *et al.*, 1992). Here, as in other countries, this has exacerbated their vulnerability as they have become victims of other people's crimes or involved in prostitution and drug-taking (Reitsma-Street, 1993). Similar dynamics of state neglect have been set in motion for young lone mothers who are encouraged to seek training and paid employment even when children are small and dependent on them for daily care (Zucchino, 1997).

The restructuring of welfare has intensified the vulnerability of those most in need of state services and increased the likelihood of their requirements being ignored. These actions will produce innumerable problems that the state as the holder of the collective desire to help others will have to solve in future. Meanwhile, those most at risk and those who interact with them will pay the price for this neglect. The policies of retrenchment can be redefined as short-termism that stores up foreseen human misery. The predictability of these outcomes makes neo-liberal approaches to the welfare of human beings outrageous in wealthy societies that consider themselves civilised (Teeple, 1995).

The hardening of state attitudes regarding people in need has impacted upon their formal rights of citizenship, intricately intertwined as they have been, with access to welfare benefits. Formal citizenship has been re-affirmed for women who have challenged their former exclusion on the bases of segregated employment careers (Pascall, 1986) and an enforced dependency on men (Dale and Foster, 1986; Showstack Sassoon, 1987), by permitting women with male partners to seek assistance for their families, but full citizenship remains elusive. So, children and women living with men, whether married or not, have their resources aggregated in a family unit despite the unequal distribution of resources within the family (Pahl, 1980; Walby, 1990; Dominelli, 1999).

In other areas, women have lost out to men in the name of equality. For example, in Britain, the equalisation of pensionable ages, has meant that women previously entitled to retire at age 60 now have to wait until 63, whilst men previously retiring at 65 can do so at 63. In effect, this equality measure has been one in which the state compels women to subsidise men. Meanwhile, the rise in the numbers of women and children living in poverty continues unabated world-wide (UNDP, 1998).

At the same time, the importance of social workers responding to men's needs, particularly in relation to assisting men in the tasks of improving their psycho-social functioning and re-education regarding the formation of non-abusive intimate relationships with less socially powerful women and children, has been identified and acted upon (Dominelli and McLeod, 1989; Cavanagh and Cree, 1996; Wild, 1999). Yet, even this can become a contradictory move for it can pit men's and women's organisations against each other in a scramble over resources (Stoltenberg, 1990).

These changes in the welfare state have been crucial in calling for a rethinking of social work responses to people in need. Applicable to all social workers, reconceptualising practice requires a particularly complex response from feminist social workers. This is because feminists have to take as their starting point the gendered nature of social relations that divide men and women, while simultaneously not disregarding other forms of oppression and differences that divide women from each other. Achieving this goal requires that feminist social work theory and practice transcends additive approaches to oppression and seeks ways of working with children, women, and men that establish egalitarian relations amongst them. This is a tall order, but a challenge to be faced if existing unequal power relations are not to be reproduced in perpetuity. It is a concern that guides the writing of this book.

Researching Feminist Social Work Practice

Gathering information for this book has entailed analysing documents of various kinds and interviewing men and women. I have interviewed six women and two men as 'clients' and six women and two men as practitioners about each of the sections I cover in this book to ask about their experiences of social work. I chose these practitioners because they had particular expertise in working with the issues I wished to examine. The 'clients' invited to be interviewed had been recommended by practitioners as being articulate about their own experiences. The interviewees have been willing to have me retell their stories to others, but did not wish to be identified. Hence, I quote them anonymously and refer to their case materials where it seems appropriate by using fictitious names. The criterion I employ to do this is that their words convey their views more powerfully than mine. I do not claim this approach to have produced representative findings. Nor have I presented these in empirical tables.

I adopt this stance for it is in keeping with feminist participative research principles. It enables me to listen carefully to the respondents' experiences as they tell them, try to understand what they are saying, reflect more closely on their lives as they lead them, and theorise from that (Reinhartz, 1992). That theorisation represents my interpretation of their accounts (Stanley and Wise, 1993). Each narrative that I have collected highlights some aspect of the relationship between the person and social environment. The belief that the 'personal is political' provides an intersubjective framework for my consideration of their life stories, and underpins my relationship with the research participants.

Talking to women 'clients' about their encounters with social work professionals and to practitioners about their work helps to develop feminist insights about social work theory and practice. This adds to theoretical developments in feminism more generally and constitutes part of the research process. A sharing of interpretive understandings between the researcher and subjects of the research helps to give meaning to the conclusions reached. The emphasis of this research approach is as much about how data on women is collected as it is about what is obtained, for whom, and why. Feminist principles guide the entire research process – its design, conduct, analysis, and use (Reinhartz, 1992).

Enabling women to tell their own stories and speak of their experiences is integral to feminist ways of gathering knowledge and understanding the world (Reinhartz, 1992). Engaging with women for the purposes of building knowledges rooted in women's practices is an interactive participatory process in which: power imbalances are brought out into the open, scrutinised and equalised as far as possible; the active construction of stories through the processes of listening and interpreting their significance is acknowledged; and the commitment to using research to improve women's well-being is actively pursued (Reinhartz, 1992; Belenky *et al.*, 1997). My research aims to contribute to the further development of feminist social work and extend the formulation of its theories, practice and teaching materials for practitioners in the field and academy.

The approach I used resembles grounded theory (Glasser and Strauss, 1967) in allowing women and men research participants to speak for themselves, but lacks the systematic pursual of themes that grounded theory requires to prove their generalisability. Expenditure of research resources in the exhaustive way propounded in grounded theory is not necessary in a study that examines, deliberates upon and extends data already in the public domain. I also have misgivings about grounded theory's capacity to decontextualise and depoliticise people's stories because it requires a negation of the values of the researcher, something which is methodologically impossible for feminist researchers to achieve. Another reason for my choice is that all research, however rigorous, can only be partial (Harding, 1990). Empirical data is no more than the systematic collection of anecdotes as selected and interpreted by the collector. Thus, although distanced from their stories, I do not claim impartiality in my approach to them, I simply seek to make my own value system evident so that readers can interpret what I say and judge for themselves the extent to which they share my perspective.

The Structure of the Book

In this book, I argue that feminism as a body of thought consisting of a number of diverse strands, has had a considerable impact on social work theory and practice in the past decade. It has done so by changing the gender-blind aspects of both theories and practice and offering alternative ways of delivering services. And, it has more to offer. Despite this, feminist social work has remained a form of practice that is undertaken largely by individuals (although they may come together to form support groups and network with one another) working in social services departments, private enterprises and voluntary organisations, rather than providing a method formally adopted by a wide range of mainstream agencies and collective ventures.

I consider this development in light of the new challenges posed by postmodernism and the insistence of diverse groups of women that the range of oppressions that impinge upon them be taken on board and their different voices be recognised as legitimate expressions of their realities. I examine how feminist social workers can respond to these critiques and formulate forms of theory and practice more appropriate to the needs of individuals and groups seeking welfare assistance at the beginning of the 21st century. Despite the gains in women's position over the past 20 years, I argue that the need for women to continue mobilising around gender-based actions to foster their well-being persists. Because many feminists are concerned about changing the nature of masculinity, feminism is also pertinent to men. And its vision of more egalitarian social relations between men and women, remains relevant. Feminist social work theory and practice is important in promoting the welfare of men, women and children.

This book is structured to revisit feminist social work theory and practice in the hopes of providing new insights that will enable practitioners to work with difference in ways that go beyond the idea that they are experts who exercise power over those they seek to help. People's aspirations for recognition of who they are and the handling of identity politics by different schools of feminist thought will be considered as I explore how to transcend dualism in Chapter one. Chapter two focuses on the significance of social work as a gendered profession within the mixed economy of care at a point in time when public caring activities are being relegated to the private realm of the home and re-asserted as women's responsibilities. In Chapter three, I consider challenges to elitist notions of professionalism emanating from the new social movements and seek to re-orient social work activities in more egalitarian directions. The importance of working with men from a feminist perspective becomes the subject matter of Chapter four, and I consider the appropriateness of feminist action in this area.

In Chapter five, I examine a key area of practice – social work with children and families – and ask the extent to which the tensions which exist between women's rights to self-fulfilment and their responsibility to care for others can be reconciled. As the population continues to age, caring for older people is also becoming a major area in which women are expected to exert their energies. Caring for children and caring for older people will therefore tax women's nurturing skills, and under neo-liberalism, will have to be enacted with minimal state support. Chapter six considers the state's commitment to community care in terms of the demands it is making on women within the context of the community as the site for the explication of a particular kind of gender politics whether the women are unpaid carers in the home or paid employees in the community care system. This chapter focuses on older people because they constitute the largest group covered by community care policies. Other 'client' groups, e.g., disabled people, who are also covered by these, I consider in case study materials throughout the book, where the specific points applying to them can be made. Chapter seven argues the case that working with offenders is a social work task that requires particular skills and initiatives if feminist approaches to probation practice are to be realised. Chapter eight reiterates the view that feminist social work is central to future practice and highlights how it can contribute to creating a better world with women at the centre of social life instead of at its margins (hooks, 1984).

Notes

1   Language is embedded in power relations which are often implicit in its usage. I use 'client' in quotes to indicate the problematic nature of this term and question the assumption that those who engage in 'client' relationships with social workers are dependent beings with no capacity to shape the world to their own liking. I consider both 'clients' and workers as agents capable of influencing the social relationships in which they participate.

2   Language difficulties arise when referring to different groups of women. Identifying only their uniquenesses can obscure shared commonalities. The problematics of terms such as 'black women' or 'white women' are obvious. However, there is merit in using them to point out that although experienced differently, racism impacts on the relationships enacted between them. This does not mean that either category is homogeneous or made up of women who are the same as each other. Heterogeneity of the population is important when discussing matters of identity. When I refer to particular attributes of identity, I will use other terms.

3   The narrator's voice is also problematic. I am both part of the broader feminist movement and an individual woman within it. I use the distancing device of the third person plural to indicate that although I share elements of my experience and viewpoint with other women, I cannot assume who they are and, therefore, desist from using 'we'. I have chosen this option to signal my particular position without appropriating these other voices through inclusivity.

1

Theorising Feminist Social Work Practice

Introduction

Social work has been criticised for being an oppressive part of the modernist project of the nation state (Pierson, 1991). Leftwingers have criticized it for imposing bureaucratic forms of social control upon poor people living in working-class communities (Corrigan and Leonard, 1978). Those in the 'new' social movements have noted its capacity to reproduce oppressive social relations under the guise of providing care (Dominelli and McLeod, 1982; Dominelli, 1988; Hanmer and Statham, 1988; Oliver, 1990; Morris, 1991). Rightwing ideologues have complained about social workers' capacity to throw money at social problems without producing the desired results. These they have identified as preventing families from breaking up, ensuring that parents take proper care of their children, keeping older people safe within the bosom of their families and controlling delinquent behaviour amongst juveniles (Murray, 1990, 1994).

Women have been at the centre of the struggle to define the appropriate role for social work in rapidly changing societies. Although crucial policies and legislation are formulated by men, women undertake the bulk of the caring tasks carried out within the home, and dominate the basic grades of paid professionals doing such work. Thus, arguments about the purpose of social work are intricately wound up with disputes over women's position in the social order.

Feminist social work has shed important insights on this issue because it takes women's well-being as the starting point, though not necessarily the end of its analyses and has made creating egalitarian social relations an integral part of practice. Feminist debates have provided conceptual frameworks with a fluidity and capacity to respond to criticisms and theorise the changing nature of women's lives. Key in feminists' rethinking of social work has been the questioning of positivist epistemological and ontological paradigms (Harding, 1990). These have included:

17

1. challenging men's experiences as the yardstick for measuring women's;

2. unpacking universalist standards and exposing their failure to describe, understand or value women's diverse lifestyles and contributions to society;

3. critiquing dualist thinking and the concepts that formulate knowledge as binary categories operating in opposition to each other;

4. recognising identity politics as a central dynamic in how social relations are organised and reproduced;

5. respecting women's multiple and fluid identities;

6. acknowledging the significance of gendered power relations in shaping the opportunities available for men and women to build their lives in accordance with their views of their needs; and

7. recognising the capacity of women to take action on their own behalf and to demonstrate solidarity across a range of social divisions.

These points become themes I explore throughout this book for these have given rise to what I consider crucial features that differentiate feminist social work from other forms of social work. Although I examine these in greater detail in subsequent chapters, I would summarise them here as the following:

1. assessing and working with the impact of patriarchal gender relations on men, women and children;

2. examining the impact of public and private patriarchy on women, men and children;

3. reconceptualising dependency;

4. avoiding false equality traps when building egalitarian relationships;

5. celebrating differences;

6. celebrating women's strengths and abilities;

7. valuing caring work and reforming the conditions under which it is carried out;

8. deconstructing community;

9. unpacking motherhood;

10. challenging monolithic descriptions of 'the family' and expanding the definition;

11. considering the social construction of gender;

12. separating the needs of women, children and men;

13. working as an insider/outsider;

14. mediating the power of the state; and

15. understanding agency and the capacity of the powerless to resist oppression.

In this chapter I focus on feminist contributions to knowledge and skill building in social work, drawing on different perspectives and controversies that rage over the range of social divisions that divide women from each other. I also consider ways of furthering feminist social work by drawing on feminist insights from the social sciences, particularly sociology, because these contribute to understanding social work.

Creating New Understandings of Women's Lives

Feminist social work theory and practice is a fairly new theoretical construct, appearing formally on the academic social work scene in a significant way during the late 1970s and early 1980s. It originally sought to highlight the differing nature of women's experience in social work – the invisibility of it on the theoretical front where the 'universal' male personae held sway (Wilson, 1977); and identify the inadequacy of a practice that operated within the confines of a view of women as predominantly carers of others – their husbands, children and dependent older relatives (Dominelli and McLeod, 1989). Traditional social work practice has reflected the dominant social order which assumes women's dependency within the family (Segal, 1983) and fails to recognise women's struggles to be themselves through their daily work regardless of setting. Defining women as dependent has devalued their ability to act as agents who shape their lives in different directions by interacting with others (Dominelli, 1986a).

Feminist practitioners and scholars have drawn on feminist theories and practice to place gender on the social work map by drawing upon and validating women's experiences as women. Early feminist analyses identified the gendered nature of social work profession where frontline work was undertaken predominantly by women working with other women (Wilson, 1977). The theorisation of social work as 'women's work' with a segregated division of labour characterised by women working with 'clients' and men in management making decisions about policies that impact on practice and allocate resources, came later (Hallet, 1991). Moves towards professionalisation and the centrally controlled reorganisation of social work within the British welfare state shifted it from being primarily a voluntary activity run on a shoestring to a large bureaucratic empire that has attracted men to its ranks, particularly at the top echelons (Walton, 1975).

In the academy, social work has persistently struggled to maintain its claim as a sound academic discipline (Amann, 1996). Its successes on this score in Britain have been varied, depending on its ability to attract government and public support as well as that of academic colleagues (1). At the same time, social work has become established as a discipline recognised world-wide (Kendall, 1998). Feminist scholars have scrutinised the learning and teaching processes in education and exposed gendered differentials in experiences and practices (Malina and Maslin-Prothero, 1998). In social work, women academics who had worked with women in the field and shared their concerns, brought insights about women's lives and ways of working into their teaching (Dominelli, 1981; Dominelli and McLeod, 1982, 1989) and scholarship (McLeod, 1982). Consequently, feminist pedagogic processes have included students as creators of their own educational experiences in the classroom (Malina and Maslin-Prothero, 1998).

These developments have not proceeded in a straightforward and easy manner. Many of the changes feminists have wanted to introduce into the profession have been and remain hotly contested (Dominelli, 1988). Resistance to their spread has emanated from both conservative colleagues and liberal academics who have felt threatened by both its implicit and explicit critiques of practices that are deeply ingrained in normal teaching (Malina and Maslin-Prothero, 1998). Feminists aim to confirm reciprocity in their relations with others, whether the object of their actions has been: the introduction of gender sensitive language aimed at including both men and women in academic discourses (Spender, 1970); the attempt to equalise relationships between the teacher as the one who does the teaching and the student as the one who undertakes the learning to expose how mutuality and interdependence contribute to the learning and teaching environment; and making visible hitherto forgotten voices (Richardson and Robinson, 1993). Feminists have been ridiculed and ostracised for their pains, and refused promotion opportunities despite more than meeting the formal criteria (Kettle, 1998).

These responses gave rise to a peripatetic, marginalised group of academic staff who have had to move constantly to different institutions to work in the manner that befits their aspirations for the recognition of feminism as a legitimate discipline worthy of study in its own right. Students have also suffered when they have given a high profile to feminist insights in their written work and practice (Malina and Maslin-Prothero, 1998). Black women's position was almost untenable. The few black academics, administrative support staff or students located in the academy, found their existence ignored in most of the white feminists' writings (Thompson, 1998).

Even materials written to explore black students' experience of academia have seldom made visible the specific forms of isolation and suffering endured by black women (see De Sousa, 1991; CCETSW, 1989; Pillay, 1995). In the United Kingdom, the first black woman professor of social work has yet to be appointed. One black man is in this position.

Despite such opposition, feminist principles and educational processes have taken root in a number of areas in the academy and some institutions now teach courses that are labelled either women-centered or feminist. From its tentative beginnings, a strong tradition of feminist scholarships has grown. This has brought innovations into research, theory develop-ment and practice (Dominelli, 1992; Malina and Maslin-Prothero, 1998). Although these have reflected the diversity within feminist ranks, a com-mon feature has been the commitment to bring women's voices in their multiplicity from the margins into the centre of the classroom (hooks, 1984). These have told women's stories from their point of view, highlight-ing their strengths rather than focusing solely on their weaknesses, letting the richness and complexity of women's experiences shine through. Women's narratives have covered awkward areas such as prostitution, physical violence, sexual abuse, as well as joyful ones including the expression of women's sexualities, and the range of emotions featuring in women's lives. Childhood, daughterhood, motherhood, wifehood, mid-dle-age, old age and death have been interrogated from feminist stand-points. Every aspect of women's lives throughout the life cycle has began to be theorised anew (Ashurst and Hall, 1989) and has implications for social work.

Central to women's redefinition as a group different from men has been a re-examination of the division between public and private life (Gamarnikov *et al.*, 1983). Feminists have exposed women's exclusion from the former and demonstrated the close connection between the two. Caring work whether paid or not, has bridged the divide between them. White middle-class femi-nists have revealed how married women's (private) domestic labour enables their husbands to devote themselves to their careers (Gavron, 1966) and rise within the (public) hierarchical structures of the workplace. The price women have paid for undertaking this invisible private work has been incalculable (see Friedan, 1963).

In the West, the costs have been reflected in higher levels of depression (Rowe, 1988), lack of fulfilment, stymied aspirations (Brown and Harris, 1978), and rising levels of physical (Mama, 1989; Newburn and Stanko, 1995) and sexual (Wilson, 1993) violence sustained by women. In low income countries, women have paid with their lives when running away to escape confined existences within particular arrangements in the pri-vate domain (Kassinjda, 1998), committing suicide (Croll, 1978), or being killed by upholders of patriarchal norms (Basu, 1997). At the same time, substantial numbers of women have enjoyed their nurturing roles and gained satisfaction from successfully meeting these demands. They have been proud of their children's achievements and delighted to see their husbands' progress in a competitive world. For although visible as reflected glory, the accomplishments of the people that women have supported represent thousands of hours of hard work, love and devotion that have been energetically and willingly poured into sustaining the activities of loved ones.

In some feminists' eyes, women's nurturing values have been exalted (Davion, 1994) to the extent of being deemed the harbingers of a new world order. If only men could become more like women, violence could be diminished and peace would be realised not only within intimate relationships but on the planet more generally (Cook and Kirk, 1983). At one point, their musings gave rise to an androgeny where men would become more like women, while women acquired some of the more desirable characteristics of men, particularly those of independence and self-assertion (Millet, 1969). The best in masculine and feminine features were to be drawn upon to realign the genders closer to each other. This approach has attracted some people to its precepts, but androgeny has not caught on in any significant way. Women have insisted on celebrating 'difference' and questioned the notion that liberation can be achieved either by women becoming like men or one group of women becoming like any other group of women. Instead, they have discredited and rejected homogenising tendencies (Nicholson, 1990; Collins, 1991).

In social work, feminist understandings of the public–private divide have been central to redefining social problems so as to: encourage women to see private troubles as public issues; involve women in collective action that improves their position; assist women in overcoming isolation and 'learned helplessness'; and create alternative forms of practice that respond to women's needs (Dominelli and McLeod, 1989). To achieve these goals, feminists have argued for the: integration of theory and practice; promotion of egalitarian social relations amongst women; valuing of women's responsibilities in the home and recognising their impact on women's capacity to engage in waged labour; awareness of gendered power relations in disadvantaging women; and acknowledgment of women's capacity to take action themselves (Wendall, 1996). Social workers' relationships with 'clients', colleagues in the workplace and employers have come under scrutiny and been accompanied by demands for changes (Benn and Sedgley, 1984). These seek to meet women's needs for respect; value their contributions to other people's lives; provide services women need; and promote their careers in paid employment. By openly discussing the links between public and private behaviours, feminists have highlighted the interdependent nature of the public and private domains. Their demands for change have impacted upon every aspect of women's lives and undermined a neat division between domestic and (waged) working lives.

Feminist Theories Encompass a Range of Positions

Feminists have developed a wide range of theories to understand gender oppression over many years, centuries even (Wollstonencraft, 1975). The resultant analyses have not been uncontentious, even amongst those who accept that at a very general level of abstraction, women are oppressed. Women simply do not agree about the sources of their oppression (Basu, 1997). Nor do they share the same views as to how to terminate their oppression. A number of women have argued that women can themselves oppress other women, if not along gender lines, along other social divisions. These include 'race', ethnicity, age, disability (Collins, 1991). More fundamentally, some women believe that even creating the category 'woman' is erroneous because it essentialises women and denies the specifics and constantly changing nature of their experiences (Ramazanoglu, 1989). Additionally, actions that are considered radical and appropriate for women to undertake at one historical conjuncture may lose their potency over time and become incorporated into dominant power relations that subject women to further oppression (Banks, 1981). This has happened with regard to women's entry to the political arena. Securing the right to vote has not ended women's exclusion from political power and discriminating structures (Lovenduski and Randall, 1993). I examine central elements within different feminist positions to draw insights that progress the task of developing further feminist social work theory and practice. The results can only be aids to comprehension, for they are incomplete, contested and subject to continuous development.

Banks (1981) has identified the key bodies of 'second wave' feminist thought as liberal, radical, Marxist and socialist. Tong (1989) has added black feminism, although a number of black feminists reject the feminist label and call themselves 'womanist' (Brown, 1990; Phillipson, 1992). I find these categorisations inadequate (Dominelli, 1997c) because they fail to address the overlaps between them and the multiplicity of positions that any individual feminist or group may adopt, e.g., black feminists can be liberal, Marxist or socialist. I prefer to see the label feminist reclaimed to reflect the diversity evident in the realities of women's lives. Yet, these categories are useful descriptors of the different traditions feminists have developed to depict their particular take on the world, underline their egalitarian aspirations, and promote further developments in feminist theory and practice. Feminists have learnt to live with the intricacies of their position whilst working on the problematics of language, the articulation of complexities through linear words and a resolution of the tensions embedded within and amongst them.

Liberal Feminism

Liberal feminism has focused on women becoming free by gaining access to the same opportunities as men (Friedan, 1963). Their value system includes independence, equal opportunities and individualism. Liberal feminists have attacked limitations on women's educational and employment chances and demanded policies that can be realised by individual women – enhancing equal opportunities and insisting upon women's right to their share of social resources. In following this tack, liberal feminists individualise problems that women share as a group. Their recent concerns have focused on women's activities outside the home. In engaging primarily with the public sphere, liberal feminists maintain the division between the public and private domains (Jaggar, 1983).

Liberal feminists deem women's exclusion from the public domain a phenomenon perpetrated by men who refuse to acknowledge women as their equals and by women who do not make the most of their talents (Wollstonecraft, 1975). Their analyses do not challenge the basic power structures of society but take these as sound. Policies that promote women's access to power, resources and education to enhance women's skill levels have been central planks in changing social relations that devalue women's contributions to society. Liberal feminists do not take the view that men cannot be involved in supporting women's struggles for liberation. Liberal men have, at times, been instrumental to formulating policies that have argued the public case in favour of and getting a better deal for women, e.g., John Stuart Mill.

Liberal feminist struggles have been central in achieving workplace equality and recognition for the work that women do as mothers through transfer payments such as child benefits or family allowances paid by the state directly to women (Pascall, 1986). Securing recognition for women's contributions to the family, particularly its caring work within the context of a familial ideology has been a crucial plank in liberal feminist strategies for action (Pascall, 1986). This approach does not question the gendered division of labour either within or outside the family, and their efforts have reinforced private patriarchy in the public domain (Walby, 1990). On a more historical note, suffragettes were liberal feminists who in succeeding to get women the vote, brought the public domain, especially that involved with the body politic, into women's private lives. Later, they demanded women's rights to family allowances, education and paid work on an equal basis with men. Women can be liberal feminists and still be militant!

Social work's professional beginnings fit the liberal feminists' framework for it has focused on women's capacities to mother – how to improve the mothering skills of 'clients' and how to mother the mothers if they are workers. Women's struggles to transform working relations, especially those around equal pay for equal work, belong to this tradition. Women practitioners' attempts to break the glass-ceiling and secure more managerial positions, also exemplifies liberal feminism as applied to the workplace. Social work has yet to meet liberal feminist demands for equal pay for equal work or for having women fully involved at the top echelons of its labour hierarchy.

Liberal feminist precepts applied in social work with 'clients' aim to encourage women to gain financial independence through waged work as is indicated in the extract below:

> Anna, a young woman on probation, asked her woman probation officer to introduce her to a range of educational opportunities so that she could break the cycle of offending and do something useful with her life. This wish became incorporated into her individual plan.

Liberal feminism's inability to critique the overall structure of society and anticipate the consequent fragility of its gains is a major weakness (Tong, 1989). Another is its failure to acknowledge the relevance of 'race' and other social divisions in differentiating women from one another (Jagger, 1983). As they accept working within the *status quo*, there is considerable debate about the extent to which liberal feminists can be considered feminists (Jaggar, 1983). My view is that their achievements have to be judged in the context of the times that they actively promoted their vision and the risks they ran to secure women's place in the public arena. Then, they have to be considered feminists like any other group of women claiming the label. For albeit framed within men's view of the world, they are committed to changing social relations between men and women.

Radical Feminism

Patriarchy is the concept that radical feminists utilise to describe the systematic subjugation of women by men. Patriarchy, as a form of social organisation that advantages men, has been used by men to dominate the world and privilege their interests over those of women (Epstein and Ellis, 1983). Patriarchy is configured as the oppression from which other types stem. In radical feminist theory, men, rather than the social organisation of masculinity or the processes whereby men become men are problematised. Radical feminist analyses view women's oppression as caused by men's control over women, particularly their reproductive capacities (Firestone, 1970). Sexuality becomes a key arena in which men's control of women is played out. This arrangement is deemed to frame women as a 'sex-class' (Firestone, 1970).

Radical feminists claim violence plays a crucial role in men's system of domination. They have taken a central role in highlighting men's use of violence to control women and redefined its physical and sexual forms as assaults calculated to give men the upper hand in a societal power game that favours them. Men's abuse of power through violence against women is a major feature of the radical feminist worldview (Brownmiller, 1976; Dworkin, 1988; MacKinnon, 1993). Radical feminists have identified the importance of sexual politics within the family and exposed the unequal power relations that oppress women within it (Millet, 1969).

There is a broad range of positions within radical feminism. These vary from the separatist ones in which women have no contact with men (Solanas, 1971), devoting their energies instead to living and working for and with other women (Firestone, 1970; Echols, 1989) to those which permit social contact with boys and men in particular contexts (hooks, 1982). The diversity of radical feminism has been credited for giving rise to a number of offshoots within the feminist movement, including lesbian feminism and cultural feminism. Radical feminists have criticised cultural feminism for its exclusive emphasis on personal self-fulfilment within an individualistic and apolitical stance that ignores the plight of other women (Echols, 1989).

Some mothers found certain stances adopted by radical feminists difficult, e.g., the exclusion of boy children over a certain age from their circles (Donovan, 1985). Radical feminists' contention that all men benefit equally from patriarchy has been rejected by black feminists (hooks, 1982). Additionally, radical feminists' insistence on holding men responsible for the violence they perpetrate against women, has alienated black feminists. They have felt radical feminism does not give due weight to the impact racism has in black men's lives (Collins, 1991), and reinforces their portrayal in the media as the main perpetrators of violence (Bryant *et al.*, 1985).

Radical feminists have been criticised for falsely universalising white Western middle-class women's condition; having a colour-blind approach to 'race' and ethnicity; and failing to address homophobia by not identifying heterosexuality as a dominant motif in power relations between men and women (Echols, 1989). Engaging with these critiques, radical feminists have incorporated these insights into their analyses (Jaggar, 1983). Radical feminism on social work has highlighted the serious implications of a violent environment on the emotional development of women and children, established the significance of addressing sexuality as a matter of women's welfare, and created a range of resources capable of responding to women's specific needs. Radical feminists have also been key players in developing alternative resources for women to heal themselves, gain confidence in their own capacities to act and assume control of their lives (Jaggar, 1983). The emphasis on empowering women has meant that the services that they have developed have been created by women, for women (Dominelli, 1992). These are also controlled by women, e.g., shelters, rape crises centres, incest survivor groups. Social workers have referred many women to facilities popularised by radical feminists and utilised their understandings in work with women and children, particularly around issues of domestic violence (Mullender, 1997) and sexual abuse (Kelly, 1988).

Women-only spaces and facilities have formed a radical feminist legacy that social workers have utilised in both practice and management. These secure autonomous bases from which women can strategise and support one another, e.g., women in management groups, women in social work groups (Donnelly, 1986). Many are self-help initiatives that occur in the workplace and draw heavily on women's unpaid labour. That is, they are created and sustained by women donating their time, resources and energies rather than being promoted by employers. However, the aim of many feminists has been to mainstream these activities wherever possible as part of a commitment to changing relationships between them and their 'clients' and transforming working relations in the office. Women have found woman-only resources advantageous even if they have used them for only short periods as is indicated in the vignette below:

> Eileen, whose mother had been beaten regularly by her father, recalled a short stay in a women's shelter. She said it was the first time that she had felt safe. The family was later dragged back home by her father who had scoured the city looking for them and found them in a fish and chip shop.

This outcome highlights an inadequacy in radical feminist approaches to solving women's problems – not addressing other structural issues. Refuges, like other women-only resources, are unable to offer more than palliative responses to domestic violence because they do not deal with the inegalitarian social relations that expose individual women to the vagaries of individual men's power (Jaggar, 1983). This is a surprising weakness given the structural elements embedded in the concept of patriarchy. But, it can be seen as stemming from the personalisation of social issues on a category called 'men'.

Marxist and Socialist Feminists

Marxist feminists and socialist feminists have ontological views that overlap. Patriarchy and capitalism have come under scrutiny in their analytical frameworks (Adamson *et al.*, 1976; Segal, 1987) as they seek to deal with economic forms of power and its use by men to control women. I have placed these two categories together because the boundaries between them are blurred, although socialist feminists have a less well-articulated economic analysis than do Marxist feminists. Both have been critical of Marxism's failure to deal with patriarchy and women's equality. As a result of this critique, some Marxist–Leninist men have accused socialist feminists of 'corrupting' Marx's writings by highlighting their gender implications and interpreting them from a feminist perspective (see Burnham and Louie, 1985).

On the economic front, Marxist and socialist feminists' scholarship has been central to theorising the social importance of the domestic work undertaken by women to the processes of capitalist reproduction (Benston, 1969; Dalla Costa and James, 1972; Rubin, 1974; Coulson, Magas and Wainwright, 1975; Dominelli, 1978). These have included: problematising the family (Segal, 1983); identifying the lack of employment equity in the workplace (Adamson *et al.*, 1976; Barrett, 1981; Armstrong, 1984; Coyle, 1989); and demonstrating that simply putting women into positions that men occupy will not lead to the transformative changes necessary for liberating women (Donovan, 1985; Walby, 1990; Dominelli, 1997).

Marxist and socialist feminist analyses of the family also overlap with those of radical feminists. These have unmasked the sanctity of the family (Barrett and McIntosh, 1981), in issues related to physical violence (Mullender, 1997) and the sexual abuse of women and children (Dominelli, 1986, 1989; Kelly, 1988). These analyses differ from radical feminist ones in being open to working with men to change their behaviour (Dominelli, 1999). Also, socialist feminists have demonstrated that within capitalist social relations, men's waged labour contract compels women to lead hard lives when earnings fail to meet family needs (Dominelli, 1986). These difficulties are exacerbated if their men partners have been imprisoned (Newburn, 1995).

Women's involvement in waged work has reduced the number of families in poverty (Millar, 1996). Women's unpaid labour in the home contributes to poverty alleviation in that women's energies make good the gap between the 'family wage' and the income that a family requires to survive at a decent standard of living. Women do this by expending time rather than money to make consumables from scratch and shop for bargains (Dominelli, 1978). This unpaid domestic labour can be categorised as a compensatory mechanism that enables capital to extract more value from workers by paying low wages. The rise of the dual income family and the inadequacy of the welfare state's social security provisions can be interpreted in an exploitative light for both rely on women's unpaid work (Marshall, 1995). Women's domestic labour supports both public and private patriarchy and facilitates the privileging of men's waged work. Domestic labour acts as a medium of exchange through which women mediate financial dependency. Caring work is advanced for economic security through marriage (Rosenberg, 1995).

Jaggar (1983) criticises the false distinction between production and reproduction that is central to Marxist feminist analyses of domestic labour for reproducing the public–private divide in the economic sphere. Jaggar (1983) uses the involvement of men and women in both arenas to argue against this division. However, her stance highlights only part of the story. For although men and women are involved in both domains, they do so on different bases. Men, unlike women, are over-represented in the top echelons of the waged labour hierarchy and under-represented in the domestic realm (Walby, 1990). Black feminists (hooks, 1981; Bryant *et al.*, 1985; Bhavani, 1993) including Native American women (Shanley, 1984) and Chicano women (Moraga, 1994) have also critiqued white socialist feminists for ignoring the intersections of 'race', gender and class. These interact to give black women higher labour force participation rates but for less pay than white women. Moreover, a number of black women undertake domestic labour for white middle-class women for low wages (Daenzer, 1993). Marxist and socialist feminists have responded to these concerns with varying degrees of success (see Barrett and McIntosh, 1985).

In making sense of the relationships between men and women, socialist feminists have gone on to problematise masculinity. They have used feminist analyses to interrogate men's consciousness about their taken-for-granted privileging and revealed that this may not necessarily work to their advantage as *individuals* (Dominelli and McLeod, 1989; Dominelli, 1990, 1991; Cavanagh and Cree, 1996). A number of feminists' concerns about hegemonic masculinity have been taken up by men who have subsequently developed analytical frameworks for examining the implications of feminist critiques for themselves, e.g., Pease (1981); Bowl (1985); Hearn (1987); and Connell (1995). Some men, including those in the Working with Men Collective, have utilised pro-feminist analyses to create facilities for men (see Wild, 1999).

Problematising masculinity rather than men has strengthened the focus of feminist analyses on the social organisation of relationships between men and women. Instead of concentrating upon the biological basis of sexual differences in accounting for relations of dominance between them, they have underlined their socially constructed and interactive nature. Social workers have utilised radical and socialist feminist insights into masculinity in working with men, especially convicted violent offenders (Dominelli, 1991). Probation officers now aim to get men to take responsibility for their behaviour and develop rehabilitative strategies in the hopes of creating safer social environments.

Mainstream social workers have yet to incorporate socialist feminist analyses about the family into their endeavours. The absence of a feminist perspective is evident in family therapies that assume an unproblematic gendered division of labour and power within family relationships (see Minushin, 1974) and support services for children and elders which are founded on the assumption that women are responsible for doing the domestic work that is needed (see Stack, 1975; Finch and Groves, 1983). This is exemplified by social workers undertaking care assessments that ignore male members of the family. As Gladys, a forty-five year old woman I interviewed, claimed:

> The social worker wasn't interested in hearing about my brother who lives a few streets away from Mum and is always helping her. She kept on saying how much *I* could support her. Telling her *I* was never around counted not a jot.

Black Feminism

Black feminists have taken racism as the starting point of their analyses of the oppression of women (Jayawardna, 1986; Basu, 1997) and promoted more differentiated understandings of women's condition. Although a heterogeneous group, they aim to ensure that the story of the complexities of their position as women subjected to various forms of oppression is not neglected by white analysts. The racism evident within white feminist scholarship and action has created considerable difficulties for black women by devaluing their contributions to the evolution of feminist theories and strategies for eradicating sexism. Some black women have felt so offended by their exclusion from the feminist firmament by white colleagues that they have rejected the feminist appellation in favour of 'womanist', a term rooted in their own experiences of resistance (hooks, 1981; Phillipson, 1992; Hudson-Weems, 1993).

Black women of African origins in Britain, the United States and Canada have endorsed Africentric analyses (Thomas Bernard, 1995; John-Baptiste, 2001). These use experiences of those in the African diaspora to reclaim African contributions to human history, the development of human civilisations, African identity and black people's strengths in surviving racism and slavery (Asante, 1987; Thomas Bernard, 1995). More recently, Africentric analyses have been applied to social work practice (John-Baptiste, 2001). Additionally, black feminists have emphasised the importance of family and extended kinship relations for survival in a hostile white world (Stack, 1975). Instead of decrying their place in 'the family', these have stressed the strengths of mothering and its importance in ensuring the continuity of the 'race' (Bryant *et al.*, 1985). The focus on strengths has enabled black women to critique white women's characterisation of 'the family' as a site of oppression. The struggle against the sexism of black men is conducted within this context (Collins, 1991). Domestic violence (Mama, 1989) and sexual violence (Wilson, 1993) are acknowledged as problems that have to be addressed in ways that take account of racism.

Black feminists have also highlighted the centrality of theory and political activism in their approach to life and maintain that women can pursue political and economic goals alongside their mothering roles (Collins, 1991). Their theoretical frameworks have also sought to ensure that the experiences of women in the industrialising world are brought into the public arena in a powerful way (Mohanty, 1991). Through their theories and practice, black women have exposed the interdependencies between over-industrialisation in the North and under-industrialisation in the South (Mohanty *et al.*, 1991); the privileging of white women over black women (Higginbotham, 1992); and the exploitation of black women by white women (Davis, 1981), particularly in domestic services historically and in the present day (Daenzer, 1993); the enormous role that black women have played in the development of women's rights and liberation movement (hooks, 1981; Jayawardna, 1986; Basu, 1997); the extensive variety in women's experiences of oppression and their struggles for liberation (Wilcox, 1990); and the importance of seeing oppression as multidimensional and multifaceted (hooks, 1990; Collins, 1991). At the same time, black feminists have played crucial roles in black liberation struggles (Jayawardna, 1986) and in critiquing and challenging unacceptable behaviour amongst their own men (Basu, 1997).

Black women have concentrated on racist dynamics in white societies without ignoring the patriarchal nature of their own cultural systems and have taken black men to task for perpetuating the oppression of women in a range of arenas: physical violence (Mama, 1989; Bhatti-Sinclair, 1994); sexual violence (Wilson, 1993); female genital circumcision (Kassinjda, 1998); property rights and public roles for women (El Sadawai, 1979). Moreover, unlike some white women who have intervened in these arenas in a crude and inappropriate manner, black women have done so without speaking to their audiences from a position of presumed superiority. This enables them to validate their own cultures and identities whilst simultaneously challenging all forms of injustice perpetrated against women, regardless of racialised identities.

In exposing the complex nature of racial oppression and the constantly changing and adaptive nature of racism, black feminists have contributed to legitimating the diversity of voices amongst other marginalised women who have spoken out against racism from the specificity of their own oppression – immigrant women of non-Anglo-Saxon origins in Britain, Canada and the United States; Latino women; indigenous women; Irish women, Jewish women, Arab women, the list is endless. Some of their contributions are encompassed by the term 'global feminisms' (Basu, 1997). This refers to feminist activities across national borders without representing their national entities. This approach knowingly challenges the use of women's bodies as signifiers of ethnic boundaries (Basu, 1997) for this appropriates women's bodies to reinforce gender oppression. None the less, the symbolic imaging of women as 'the heart of the race' (Bryant *et al.*, 1985) can be used to affirm collective solidarities and contribute to their liberation along racial lines.

White social workers have been scrutinised for failing to acknowledge the significance of 'race' and racism in their work (Dominelli, 1998; Ahmed, 1990). As a result, there has been: the over-representation of black children in a child care system primarily geared towards meeting the needs of white children, albeit inadequately (Barn, 1993); the over-representation of black people, particularly black youths, in custody and detention (Dominelli, 1983; Cook and Hudson, 1993); and an under-representation of black elders in welfare provisions that reduce the impact of old age upon the quality of life enjoyed by older people (Patel, 1990). Black women's critiques of the failure of social workers to acknowledge the impact of racism in welfare matters (Devore and Schlesinger, 1983) has encouraged white social workers to examine the racism endemic within their own work with black 'clients' and look for ways of becoming anti-racist (Dominelli, 1988).

Racism has affected black people's career prospects and few are employed in social work. Of those who have succeeded, not many have reached the top ranks of management or academia (Dominelli, 1997). Progress in these areas has been slow (Dominelli *et al.*, 1995) despite the extensive range of initiatives that black people have applied to counter racism (Durrant, 1989; Ahmed, 1990). Black women's stay in top positions is usually short because they are made to feel unwelcome, undermined in countless subtle and unsubtle ways, and frustrated in their attempts to change organisational cultures (Durrant, 1989; Ahmed, 1992; Dominelli, 1997). I quote Josie Durrant (1989) when leaving her job as assistant director of social services because she became tired of expending her energies in constantly fighting an unresponsive system. She says:

> Local authorities don't encourage creativity ... You are expected to be a bureaucratic animal, worrying about budgets and the elected members' agenda (Durrant, 1989, pp. 24–5).

Postmodern Feminism

Postmodern feminists have deepened feminist analyses and sought to encourage more sophisticated understandings of women's position. To achieve this end, they have utilised the concepts of language, discourse, difference, deconstruction and positionality. Alongside earlier feminist work, e.g., Spender's (1980) *Man Made Language*, postmodern feminists highlight the significance of power relations conveyed through language (Flax, 1990). Language is important because objects are designated in particular ways through naming to embody forms of power (Flax, 1990). For postmodernists, language not only constructs meaning, it also organises cultural practices that expose their significance (Scott, 1990). Power is conceptualised as complex in that it comes from a number of different points, but is created through the complicated interplay of inegalitarian and fluid social relations. Resistance is an integral part of the fluidity of these interactions (Foucault, 1980).

Discourse is the structure of statements, terms, categories and beliefs that are expressed through organisations and institutions. Some discourses are more valued than others. Those that are considered less important are marginalised. Power and knowledge come together in discourses (Foucault, 1980). An analysis of these discourses can reveal the circumstances that shape the lives of particular individuals or groups. Difference is used to create meaning through a negation of its opposite. This relies on binary oppositions in which those who are subordinate or different are 'othered' (Wittig, 1988). In normalised discourses, the dominant group, just is. That is, it provides the standard whereby the others are measured. To understand this, their position, has to be deconstructed. Deconstruction refers to the exposure of a concept as ideologically or culturally construed rather than being a 'natural' reflection of reality (Collins, 1991). Postmodernism also reveals that seemingly dichotomous terms are interdependent (Flax, 1990). These insights facilitate an analysis of the links between the dominant group and subordinate ones along the specificity of their contexts. Positionality refers to the circumstances in which the speaker is located and from which discourse is made (Foucault, 1980).

Postmodernists deem identity a problematic and a fluid category (Modood *et al.*, 1994; Frankenburg, 1997). In more recent theory-building, postmodern feminists have formulated more sophisticated understandings of women's capacity to act as agents. This construes women as capable of making their own destinies whilst acknowledging that women also reproduce oppression amongst women (Gatens, 1996).

Key to postmodern feminists' critiques of other feminists has been their concern to constantly interrogate categories (Flax, 1990). Crucial to this is questioning the category, 'woman', and challenging essentialist homogeneous representations of women, especially those depicted in the early feminist slogan, 'sisterhood is universal' to signal that women are similarly oppressed by patriarchy throughout the world (Morgan, 1970). The postmodern individualistic representation of women has the potential to undermine the significance of systemic patterns of discrimination perpe-trated against women because they are women. This can be exploited by conservatives to: ignore the backbreaking nature of domestic work in industrialising countries (Basu, 1997); curtail women's sexuality (Kassinjda, 1998), reproductive rights (Steinberg, 1997); limit career promotion (Coyle, 1989); and enforce socialisation into domestic labour (Oakley, 1974).

The capacities of individuals to develop or act outside of society is implicit in postmodern thinking. In concentrating on the individual as the basic unit of analysis, Western postmodern feminists promote individual-ism with a very Anglocentric focus, but in many cultures, the individual only exists within the collective (Basu, 1997). I do not endorse the view that individual rights are lost within the collective, because individuals can grow as individuals within collective settings. In underplaying the significance of society, however one defines it, as a site in which social relations occur, post-modernists have decontextualised the individual and turned him or her into an apolitical being that exists in his or her own right and interacts only with similar individuals. This approach ignores the social construction of the individual who is created and constantly re-created through social interac-tions that take the presence of society for granted. Additionally, in being re-created as individuals within social relations, they also affect the creation and re-creation of a particular society within specific contexts.

A central difference between postmodern feminists and other feminists is their different analytical starting points. Postmodernists reject the metanar-rative of the patriarchal structure of society that is a key proposition in non-postmodernist feminist thought. Yet, in eschewing metanarratives, I argue that postmodernism perpetuates its own – that there is none. And it gets locked into stances that over-emphasise the individual at the expense of col-lective identities that people have created in their interactions with each other, and which form the basis of socially constructed metanarratives.

Consequently, postmodern feminists have an uneasy position within feminist lexiconographies (Nicholson, 1990). They have been critiqued for drawing upon theoretical frameworks that have been developed in part by other feminists who eschew the label 'postmodernist' and for relying heavily upon the works of postmodernist men theoreticians such as Derrida (1987), Lacan (1977) and Foucault (1980) whose writings have largely ignored women's experiences or need for liberation (Haber, 1994). Postmodern feminists have also been taken to task for potentially under-mining feminist notions of solidarity and collective action, forces without which many of the gains that women have achieved over the centuries would not have been possible, e.g., the right to vote, own property, exer-cise control over their children's education and hold custody. At the same time, postmodernist women are the beneficiaries of many of women's col-lective struggles for women's rights.

Social workers relate to postmodernist thinking insofar as they focus on individuals and their uniqueness as the basis of their interventions. However, this commitment has been honoured more in rhetoric than practice. For in traditional social work practice, all individuals have been assumed to belong to the homogeneous collective endorsed by their nation-state, thereby privileging the dominant group and its modernist views of the world (Lorenz, 1994). In constructing 'difference' as a deficit, social workers treat it as an absence that has to be made good, thereby reinforcing homogeneity and dominant norms.

Celebrating difference requires practitioners to draw on postmodern concepts. Language, discourse, difference, deconstruction, positionality, power and identity have considerable potential in assisting the development of anti-oppressive social work practice of which feminist social work is one example. Postmodern tenets are familiar to social workers for they echo points that have been made from other theoretical positions. And, they are relevant to developing empowering relationships which place 'clients' in the driver's seat.

Postmodern concepts enable practitioners to situate themselves as potential oppressors. These are important in the social work repertoire because they can be used to unpack assumptions underpinning working relations, policies and practice. Using these, practitioners can examine: the complexities of power in 'client'–worker relationships; reinforcement of white middle-class norms in assessment processes; and social workers' inability to create a non-dependent profession. Postmodernist thought can help social workers respond to the uniqueness of individuals without disempowering them. To create empowering relationships, practitioners have to deconstruct professional power which stems from their position as bearers of particular ideologies and implementers of a social mandate determined in the political arena. Within this, I worry that the danger of an individualism that disregards collective continuities inherent in postmodernism remains. This concern is shared by Leonard (1997), who suggests that postmodern welfare must draw on feminist solidarities and insights to create an emancipatory welfare.

In this section, I highlight the wide range of positions within feminism, its amorphous nature and lack of leadership hierarchy. These have made it difficult for some people to accept it as a movement. Yet, feminism's impact on academic thought, the politics of everyday life, and the expectations about social institutions and their functioning have been profound (Dominelli, 1992, 1997). The idea that women have complex and differentiated lives has given rise to new theoretical formulations that have become commonplace in feminist writings. These include: the challenges to dualistic thinking processes and their replacement with more holistic ones to place individuals more fully in their social contexts; recognition of interdependence between the different spheres of people's experiences, particularly the interconnectedness between private and public lives; and linkages between waged work and domestic labour in the home. Below, I consider how these insights contribute to weaving new patterns of feminist theoretical frameworks for practice by drawing on the strengths of various feminisms and the lessons to be learnt from analysing their problematic elements. At the end of this process, I establish guidelines for taking social work practice beyond the position of being an oppressive part of the modernist project.

Reconceptualising Feminist Social Work Theory and Practice

Social work occupies an interesting position within the nation-state as the collective expression of its desire to care for others in difficult circumstances, and as a professional activity whose practitioners work in the interstices between the national and local levels, and between the personal and political planes. Social workers as public officials who represent the public's wish to intervene in the private lives of fellow citizens, if necessary without their consent in cases of mental illness or child protection, engage with the contradictions encapsulated by this divide. Consequently, the division between the public and private sphere is crossed at a number of different points in practice.

Feminist insights about the nature of the public–private divide can contribute to reconceptualising it. Identity formation and the politics of everyday life (Smith, 1987) are other analytical concepts relevant in enriching and subsequently transforming social workers' understandings. In social workers' encounters with women, the division of women's lives into public and private domains is important. Here, the private sphere is articulated and regulated through public social policies that control access to welfare resources by defining eligibility, and impact on women's relationships with each other and the state. The public realm also affects women's private family life for it is also the object of social policies enacted by the state (Showstack Sassoon, 1987).

Many ugly secrets about the horrific abuse of women and children within the privacy of family settings become routinised knowledges within the social work domain. Ironically, this knowledge becomes privately appropriated by remaining 'confidential' information between practitioners and 'clients', rarely being shared beyond the realm of supervisory relationships and case files. However, by drawing on detailed knowledge of their lives and experiential telling, women have recounted their suffering to astonished audiences, and people have begun to listen. Feminist social workers and researchers have documented their stories. These accounts have converted women's private troubles to public issues through feminist social action that has gained the support of a wide range of women including social workers (Dominelli and McLeod, 1989). Feminists have pressed for government action in subverting the public–private divide by passing laws against domestic violence and child abuse in the home (Dworkin, 1981; MacKinnon, 1993); proposing laws against rape in marriage (Jaggar, 1983); building women's shelters (Dobash and Dobash, 1991); and providing resources to help men desist from abusive behaviours (Cavanagh and Cree, 1996). These efforts have also unpacked the historically specific nature of the citizenship the nation-state provides women (Lister, 1997). Linked to women's identity as subordinate beings, it is a marginalised status that feminists reject.

Though extremely contentious, the concepts of language, discourse, difference, positionality, and deconstruction are central to a social work practice that aims to rectify matters that impede the realisation of individual well-being and social justice. By helping individuals in their social situation, such practice addresses the essentials of an individual's psychological growth within a social context. Deconstructing the category 'woman' enables social workers to focus on women's complex and fluid identities within and across a range of social divisions and variations across time and space. The process of deconstruction involves interrogating taken-for-granted assumptions about women and facilitates identifying their strengths and weaknesses in many dimensions of their lives.

Valuing women's capacities across the entire spectrum of abilities encourages a reconceptualisation of difference. By emphasising difference as a strength within an egalitarian framework, feminist social workers celebrate rather than disparage women's diverse and multiple identities or use these to pathologise the caring work women do simply because these differ from white middle-class male norms for (paid) work. Rather than proceeding to validate preconceived misconceptions and stereotypes, a strengths-based perspective fosters a critical stance that allows practitioners to make judgments based on a careful and thorough assessment of the specific realities of a given situation.

Other feminist concepts relevant to social work practice are: interconnectedness, reciprocity, mutuality, ambiguity, power and citizenship. These can be found in every aspect of women's lives, but are particularly evident in caring work. Interconnectedness signals the interdependence that exists between people – the ties that bind them together in mutuality and reciprocity. The notion of interconnectedness is useful in facilitating growth within egalitarian relationships and can be realised in social work relationships with 'clients', employers, employees, family, friends or strangers. Mutuality and reciprocity are the building blocks of egalitarian relationships for they permit each person involved in an exchange to contribute from her/his specific strengths to the interaction. Acting together, interdependency, mutuality and reciprocity give birth to social solidarity.

Traditional social workers focus on interconnectedness as links expressed through a responsibility to care for others within the context of dependency, thereby differentiating it from a feminist social worker's version. In traditionalist guise, the individual being cared for only takes from the relationship whilst the carer only gives. This framing of their interaction endorses a one-sided view that ignores the dimensions of mutuality and reciprocity that draw on women's energies and have the capacity to move relationships away from constructions of dependency and onto those recognising interdependence.

Women's relationship to change is not straightforward. Ambiguity underpins many struggles that aim to become more sensitive to the needs of others, particularly when women are uncertain about what to do, but desire to move away from previous patterns of interaction because their inadequacies have become so apparent. Social workers' attempts to address issues of oppression are replete with instances of ambiguity. Ambiguity is illustrated in women's roles as carers when women feel the double bind of being responsible for others and wanting to help, but also wishing to be free of the responsibility and focus on themselves. Feminist principles of solidarity assist in negotiating through the uncertainties of ambiguity to create an inclusive citizenship that celebrates difference. Citizenship in this framework is about obligations within reciprocal relationships. In it, ambiguity is not obviated, but provides the basis for reciprocity.

Citizenship draws upon interconnectedness, mutuality and reciprocity to build social solidarities through which individuals accept responsibility for each other and commit themselves to a jointly defined common good to ensure that the well-being of one is a concern of all. Both give and take are involved in reciprocated social interactions. Taking action consistent with the empowerment of self in creating egalitarian relationships with others is the basis of a non-exclusionary citizenship not limited to implementation within specific national borders (Dominelli, 1997; Lister, 1997). Feminist social workers aim to promote the capacities of women workers and 'clients' to become full citizens capable of taking control of their lives within empowering social contexts.

Sadly, social workers' traditional view of citizenship is a one-way relationship where 'clients' take rather than give or do both. Showing gratitude for what is on offer regardless of suitability is a social work expectation that damages 'clients' wish to validate their own views and aspirations. It also undermines their self-esteem and rights as citizens. And, it permits the representation of welfare recipients as abusers rather than users of the system.

Empowerment relies on reconceptualising power as a 'transformative capacity' that is negotiated through social relations with others (Giddens, 1990). It sets the contours of a person's position in a specific social order (French, 1985). Understanding power relations – their creation and re-creation within social relationships, is essential to feminist theorising of oppression and developing alternative ways of organising daily life, and is crucial in identifying an individual's own 'standpoint' as socially constructed (Hartsock, 1987). Analysing the distribution of power and its impact on social relations assists in formulating plans of action that eliminate the privileging of one group over others.

Process issues are central to focusing on how to conduct empowering relationships (Humphries, 1996). Feminists' concern with process has been reflected in social work practice in the relationship between the worker and the 'client', between employees and their employers, and amongst employees. Feminist social workers engage in processual matters when establishing egalitarian relations between workers and 'clients', whether this is in a therapeutic relationship undertaken by a counsellor (Chaplin, 1988), a group involving a community worker (Jaggar, 1983), or a budgetary exercise executed by a case manager (Orme, 2000). Feminist social workers' have questioned simplistic divisions between 'clients' and workers in contrasting professional expertise to experiential wisdoms, to also validate the latter. Recognising and valuing what has conventionally been depicted as lesser knowledges – those held by the person being helped, fosters egalitarian relations between professionals and service users (Belenky *et al.*, 1997). This has led feminists to re-examine the relationship between women and the state and expose its centrality in mediating and reproducing patriarchal relations between women and men and paternalistic relationships between workers and 'clients' (Showstack Sassoon, 1987).

Following through on these analyses, feminist social workers have begun building new parameters for a profession that has oppressed 'clients'. They have redefined the profession's loyalties more towards the people that they are committed to serve – the women whose chances in life have been shaped by unequal opportunities and the carrying of inordinate amounts of domestic responsibilities. As woman-centered practitioners seeking to establish equality, feminist social workers have sought to empower women rather than oppress them by listening to their stories, validating their analyses of situations and engaging them in decisions about their lives (Hanmer and Statham, 1988; Dominelli and McLeod, 1989). They have supported women through traumatic moments and rejoiced in their triumphs over adversity. In feminist social work, women are the starting point of any analysis. However, supporting women in gaining control of their lives involves challenging patriarchal arrangements and evaluating state interventions and men's activities in light of their impact on the oppression of women.

Conclusions

Feminist theory and practice has much to offer feminist practitioners who can adapt its principles for professional practice. The existence of feminist social work is testimony to their capacities to do so. Feminist social work has encouraged the assumption of a gender-sensitive stance in working with women and insisted on valuing women's knowledge, talents and contributions to the profession. It has already had a substantial impact on social work theory and practice (Dominelli, 1992). Consequently, women have been acknowledged as beings with their own interests; specific aspirations for themselves, their families and close others; and their own ways of knowing; valuing and doing things (Belenky *et al.*, 1997). Despite feminist social work's failure to become the dominant paradigm in the discipline, its insights have been incorporated into a wide range of social work activities.

Feminist theories have the capacity to play a greater role in enabling social work practice to become more effectively anti-oppressive and inclusive. For this to occur, academics and practitioners have to validate women's lives by incorporating into their work the conceptual frameworks and experiential knowledges that feminists have highlighted. These include the differentiated concepts of interdependence, mutuality, reciprocity and citizenship. Additionally, they have to recognise women as agents with the ability to determine their own futures.

Note

1 I raised the issue in May 1996 with Professor Ron Amann, the then CEO of the ESRC, and received his reply. He asked that educators demonstrate the intellectual basis on which social work's claim to be an academic, research-led status rested through a workshop that could set the future research agenda for social work. I discussed this with colleagues, and at a meeting at Warwick University, Audrey Mullender (then Chair of the JUC-SWEC), Joan Orme and I decided to pursue the matter through JUC-SWEC, as the organisation most representative of social work educators at the October 1996 meeting. As a result of the ensuing discussions, a successful application to the ESRC Seminar Series followed. It produced the *Theorising Social Work Research Seminar Series* which explored this question at length and in time resulted in the ESRC accepting social work as entitled to a discipline specified place on its Training Board.

2

Contextualising Feminist Social Work Theory and Practice

Feminist social work is being developed in the same context as other forms of social work – that of a culturally specific nation-state subject to the pressures of globalisation, privatisation and internationalisation of locally expressed policies and practices. Social policy declarations establish the parameters of professional practice in a given locality. In Britain, the government's recent promotion of the mixed economy of care within state, voluntary, private and domestic sectors has profound implications for the roles ascribed to social work, the management of practice and social workers' relationships with 'clients' and the organisations catering for welfare needs (Khan and Dominelli, 2000). Social policies also transfer women's dependency on state funding to men in family settings and reflect a shift from public patriarchy to private patriarchy (see Walby, 1990).

Examining the significance of the globalised political cultural context in which feminist social workers operate forms the backbone of this chapter. In it, I consider the implications of globalisation within a gendered market-oriented welfare arena including its impact on feminist social workers' practice and aspirations for women 'clients'.

The reorganisation of social services within a globalised market has led to a (re)privatisation of the public welfare domain on the economic level, whilst the regulatory state is thrusting private activities into the public sphere through codes of conduct that affect most areas of life (Dominelli and Hoogvelt, 1996). These focus on the role and place of women in society, the family, and intimate personal relationships. The personal has been politicised, but not in the sense that feminists had anticipated. In the UK, the Blair government's emphasis on parenting classes to help working-class women become better parents is indicative of the new regulatory codes that control the private domain, especially for working-class parents. Addressing this issue in the USA, the Reagan, Bush and Clinton administrations have also demanded that mothers on welfare enter waged work rather than care for their children (Zucchino, 1997). These initiatives

41

privilege men at the expense of women, for parenting, like other forms of caring, remains women's responsibility and upholds state surveillance of their mothering capacities.

The regulation of daily life is fairly specific and revolves around woman's role as nurturer. Regulating the private sphere is contradictory. Policies protecting women's space, subvert women's credibility within it. The sanctity of the home – a hallmark of liberal society, is undermined by the twin demands for accountability in personal behaviour and the politicisation of culture. Many discourses on culture revolve around women, particularly their bodies as signifiers of specific ethnicities. This is linked to women as reproducers of that culture through their roles as mothers responsible for bearing, raising and socialising children into its precepts, and incorporating cultural considerations as routine dimensions of everyday life. Culture has become politicised and politics have become culturalised in gender specific ways. These developments reflect strategic reifications that portray culture as having immutable qualities that have existed as part of the 'natural' order since time immemorial. I have termed this the 'ossification of culture' (Dominelli, 1996).

Rightwing ideologues have depicted feminists' challenge of the ossification of culture and assumed male privileges as a 'cultural war' that pits men against women and vice-versa (Bloom, 1992). Alongside various fundamentalist groups, conservative media commentators and anti-feminist men's groups have attacked feminists' resistance to traditional definitions of womanhood and the social gains emanating from feminist struggles. In other words, culture is being played out as gender relations.

The new managerialism intensifies a politicised gendering of cultures in public sector working practices. In social work, this has affected not only interpersonal relations, but also the organisational culture of welfare agencies. Current professional developments occur within a new managerialism that reinforces men's power as managers and disempowers those working at the 'client' interface (Clarke and Newman, 1997). Social work is a 'women's profession', largely controlled by men who dominate resources and decision-making processes (Coyle, 1989; Grimwood and Popplestone, 1993; Dominelli, 1997). Consequently, women social workers may be implementing policies with which they strongly disagree (Dominelli, 1999). Conservatives who cling to managerialist orthodoxies label feminists who question new bureaucratic priorities difficult and threatening. Their stance re-asserts antagonistic relations between managers and workers relating to each other in a hierarchical, legalistic market-driven bureaucracy. Feminists' commitment to social justice for all people undermines this stance and places them in the firing line of polarised workplace relations. Workplace fragmentation allows individual dissidents to be picked off or become burnt-out. Endorsing collective action to transcend this tension exacerbates the marginality of feminist practitioners.

Dependency: A Key Element in Women's and Social Workers' Relationships with the State

Shifts in social policies contribute to a constantly changing, highly politicised contextual field within which social workers operate (Khan and Dominelli, 2000). At the institutional level, this contextualisation entails: legislation and prescriptive requirements for practice; practitioners' employment contracts and conditions of work; and the ideological expectations of individual workers whether employed directly by the state to undertake particular tasks in applying specified policies to welfare 'clients', or as private consultants relating indirectly to the state through grant funding or contractual arrangements for service provision (Dominelli, 1999). Even when working from private locations, social workers are expected to administer and realise state objectives and policies through the contracting process (Clarke and Newman, 1997). Social workers' attitudes towards these changes, although ambivalent for some, have provided new opportunities for practitioners to work with women (Lloyd, 1996) in less oppressive ways by allowing for a discretionary input to alleviate specific sufferings even though these have failed to advance the overall emancipation of women.

Globalisation sets the macrolevel context for social work policy and practice. It shapes the environment in which women's lives are embedded and is considered in further detail below. Globalising forces exacerbate women's dependency on men by influencing the conditions under which privatisation measures reinforce private patriarchy at the expense of public patriarchy. They do so by depriving women of public sector employment with its better equal opportunities policies, greater job security and fringe benefits, and by affirming family-based welfare provisions (Clarke and Newman, 1997).

Dependency involves a relationship of relying on others for the emotional and material support necessary for living. It becomes negative when expressed as a *power over* interaction in which the resource-holder seeks to establish control over or subjugate the recipient and denies that he or she is getting something out of the relationship (Memmi, 1984). Women's dependency on men or the state and the aggregation of resources within the family unit have been two pillars on which mesolevel social policy rests (Dale and Foster, 1986; Pascall, 1986; Dominelli, 1991). Within Western nation-states, these provide the foundations for a patriarchal view of the family, as a nuclear family unit with a breadwinning father, a financially dependent mother and two children, to the exclusion of other family forms (Eichler, 1983), a view that underpins social work practice at the microlevel. At the same time, employment as practitioners facilitates women's independence from individual men (private patriarchy) whilst making them dependent on the state (public patriarchy) for the opportunity to exercise this option (Dominelli, 1997). Although operating within limited parameters, public avenues to economic independence have enlarged women's choices. They have also created forms of institutionalised dependency that leave women within constrained circumstances, vulnerable to the vagaries of political uncertainty and challenge by unsympathetic individuals and groups (Zucchino, 1997). Women's entry into the public sector labour market to secure varying degrees of financial solvency through the sweat of their brow or to access entitlements through the welfare state via their role as mothers, has weakened women's direct reliance on men for economic support (Showstack Sassoon, 1987; Dominelli, 1991).

Social work's position as a dependent profession has traditionally relied on state and male patronage for its resources (Walton, 1975; Dominelli, 1997) and is an important feature of the context within which feminist social work has been developed. This forms an institutionalised dependency that women experience alongside an individual one as either 'clients' or workers. This dependency catapults professional activities into compromising and contested political terrains. Social work's role and purpose in society has constantly been argued over and cannot be assumed.

The 'founding mothers' views of social work as a people-centered, service-oriented activity (Dominelli, 1997) became marginalised when counter ideas espoused by men who became leading architects of modern social work were adopted as policy. A crucial one of these was the post-Seebohm reorganisation of social services undertaken by Elliott Jaques, Head of the Social Sciences Research Unit at Brunel University who favoured bureaucratic forms of social work practice (Jaques, 1975, 1977). Bureau-professionalism has become commonplace in British personal social services and paved the way for corporate management techniques to prevail following Roy Griffiths' review of social services (Griffiths, 1988). Jaques' vision also reduced social work to a minute part of a larger empire in which social workers' voices are rarely heard. Corporate management has entrenched social work as a business activity more interested in profit-making than in delivering needs-led services to excluded populations (Culpitt, 1992). Exacerbated by globalising forces, this trend subjects the domestic economy including social services provisions to international market discipline (Dominelli and Hoogvelt, 1996).

Ideologies of caring cast women as dependent on men and unable to manage others. Identifying women as carers rather than organisers or administrators has excluded then from management. Men have become the 'natural' heirs to managing large bureaucracies (Coyle, 1989). In Britain, men began to displace women managers when large bureaucratic empires replaced small local agencies in the 1970s (Walton, 1975). This shift has intensified social work's development as a 'women's profession' that is not controlled by women and laid the foundations for further reorganisations two decades later, this time under the thrust of corporate managerialism and globalisation. The advent of men into social work has not been entirely negative. Alongside women colleagues, men have contributed to the professionalisation of social work, raising its status in the professional hierarchy, and critiquing its social control dimensions, particularly along class lines (see Corrigan and Leonard, 1978; Ginsburg, 1979).

Today, the small number of professional social workers has become dwarfed by the other social professionals, particularly the health-based ones. Endorsed by policy developments, these seek to incorporate social work's remit into their own, as health professionals have actively replaced social workers in several arenas. A recent study by Borden (1996) indicates that medical practitioners commissioning services that can be undertaken by either social workers or health professionals, will choose the latter whose tasks they feel they understand better than the vague ones they ascribe to social work.

Employment in the welfare state has given women practitioners a degree of financial independence not otherwise available. This work simultaneously exploits them by being poorly paid and undervalued because it is deemed an extension of work that women do 'naturally' at home (Showstack Sassoon, 1987). This attitude locks social work in the 'women's work' sector of the economy, and endorses skimping on training as women are deemed to acquire the skills necessary as part of life experiences. On the 'client' front, social workers oppress women by reinforcing dependency on men, ensuring that women discharge their domestic roles whether they wish to or not, and fail to support women in maximising their options for growth and fulfilment (Brook and Davis, 1985; Marchant and Wearing, 1986). At the same time, women practitioners' understanding of women's oppression has enabled feminist social workers to alleviate women's burdens and create spaces for women to be self-determining beings (Chaplin, 1988), and thereby contribute to their struggles for liberation.

Globalisation Changes the Welfare State

Globalisation has provided the most recent socio-economic and political context within which social policy and social work practice are elaborated. Globalisation, as a macrolevel phenomenon with microlevel implications, has shifted the dependency relationship once more. Globalisation has three key dynamics: the imposition of market discipline on all aspects of social life; internationalisation of the state; and fragmentation of the labour processes. These are played out in the routines of everyday life as practice. Alongside contract government; these dynamics have had a profound impact on the welfare state including social work. Together, they have: turned qualitative professional relationships into commodities that can be measured and quantified; subjected service provision to market forces via privatisation, and deprofessionalised professional labour through an outcomes-based competence approach that converts professional work into a low paid proletarianised activity described as economically non-productive. This is Taylorisation impacting on professional or middle-class labour processes (Dominelli and Hoogvelt, 1996). In it, social workers have become highly regulated in a society that espouses deregulation. Managerially imposed procedures have repositioned professional social workers as technocrats whose capacity to exercise independent judgment is severely curtailed through bureaucratic procedures that commodify care (Dominelli, 2000). By reducing a professional's potential to respond to 'client'-identified needs, these exacerbate the controlling dimensions of social work practice and intensify existing gulfs between practitioners and 'clients'. Pre-empting the development of good working relationships between 'clients' and workers also ensures that the profession's lines of accountability rest with the state via the employers.

Becoming budget-holders has subjected social workers to increasing managerial control. Performance-based pay has been implemented in many areas and hangs like the sword of Damocles to threaten further instability in social workers' working environment. Meanwhile, computer technologies have been exploited by managers for closer surveillance of individual workers, including the amount of work practitioners handle, the types of 'clients' they attract and the resources they expend upon them. For professionals working within a market-oriented arena, tighter managerial controls have whittled away the discretionary dimensions of their jobs. Budgets and operating within strictly defined procedural norms have further restricted their options. Working within budgetary limits has further reduced professional discretion in matching needs with resourcing and exacerbated the limitations imposed upon them by procedural norms.

Discretionary powers are two-edged. They can be misused to create greater forms of injustice, e.g., to reinforce sexist and racist stereotypes (Whitehouse, 1986). Or, they can be tools whereby arbitrary rules are rectified to fit more closely the needs of a particular individual's situation and contribute to the realisation of more appropriate responses than is warranted by their straightforward application. A magistrate who uses discretion to mitigate the sentence of a man who has committed a minor traffic offence so that he will not lose his employment, illustrates this point.

Macrolevel changes inspired by globalisation have laid a firm foundation for spreading microlevel adaptions via a new managerialism (Clarke and

Newman, 1997) that exerts greater control over practitioners' work with 'clients'. Management's goal of imposing greater strategic direction over social work is linked to politicians' improved services, to reign in professional power, curtail public expenditures to avoid tax increases, and divert resources from public service provisions to the government's general revenue accounts. From there, money can be recirculated to provide the infrastructure for private provisions including roads and cash flow financing through subsidies, tax exemptions and other inducements that encourage private entrepreneurs to bid for contracts when public provisions are outsourced. Such transfers can be considerable. In the United States, business corporations collected $125 billion in this way in 1998 (Barlett and Steele, 1998). In Britain, privatisation sales have transferred substantial public resources to private entrepreneurs by selling state assets below their market value (Dominelli and Hoogvelt, 1996). The privatisation of older people's homes, children's homes and prisons provide social work sites through which such transfers occur.

As these transfers are paid for through government funding or the taxpayers' pockets, public expenditure cuts have not yielded significant reductions in overall public spending despite losses in direct services to people (Dominelli and Hoogvelt, 1996). Government financing of such movements of monies is likely to continue or even increase in future because many state facilities now being promoted for private purchase rely on large injections of public cash (Ralph *et al.*, 1997). Meanwhile, by setting the amounts that can be expended in funding welfare provisions and establishing the criteria for eligibility, the state as a purchaser of services through contractual agreements acts as an extremely powerful force in shaping the services that can be developed (Teeple, 1995; Dominelli and Hoogvelt, 1996). Thus, we have the simultaneous growth in managerial control over autonomous professionals alongside an explosion in private sector welfare provisions.

Privatisation within a Mixed Economy of Care

Social work has always operated within a mixed economy of care, i.e., one that has contained a combination of commercial for-profit agencies, voluntary non-profit organisations, state or publicly financed resources and domestic household provisions. This has allowed for considerable continuities over time, although the balance between these elements shifts. Until the 1980s, direct public sector provisions in Britain had been expanding to the detriment of commercial providers with large sectors of the public system having no private entrepreneurial involvement as in the criminal justice sector. The balance is now swinging the other way as private and voluntary sector facilities grow at the expense of public sector ones (Ralph *et al.*, 1997).

Alongside continuities in a mixed economy of care, discontinuities exist. The present round of continuities is marked by an increase in private sector provisions and a reliance on women's capacities and willingness to care for and about others. Discontinuities are evident in the restructuring of public services to resemble more closely private provisions in their mode of delivery, organisational culture and workplace relations. The growing *rapprochement* between public and private sector resources provides a revolving door that allows one to haemorrhage into the other and has enormous implications for both the professionals working within them and for the 'clients' seeking to use them, as entrepreneurial skills and business priorities set the care agenda. This turn of events can disenfranchise low income individuals and groups (Cochrane, 1993).

At the same time, community care legislation in Britain has emphasised de-institutionalisation and the closure of public facilities to impose a greater burden of care on families in the community (Ungerson, 1990). Women have been at the forefront in providing unpaid care (Finch and Groves, 1983). Or, as Hilary Graham (1983) calls it, 'a labour of love'. The unpaid domestic work women give to families and communities forms an unacknowledged subsidy to the state (Dominelli, 1978, 1986).

Deinstitutionalisation has also meant that people have been released into the community without adequate arrangements being made for their care. In certain instances, despite the best endeavours of social workers, appropriate follow-through has not been possible within existing resources. This has been particularly dire for people with mental ill health. Which 'community' do they belong to? Who will look after them? What happens if they have no family to return to? Women have had to plug the resource gaps between individual mental health needs and state provisions (Barnes and Maple, 1992). By assuming women's availability to care, policymakers ignore the current realities of women's lives, mixed as they are in complicated networks of caring and waged employment responsibilities that constrain their options in both public and private domains.

Policymakers' failure to address these questions work to the detriment of both the person with mental health problems and community-at-large as mentally ill people have been discharged from mental health facilities without the requisite support services (Gastrell and Edwards, 1996). A number have either forgotten or refused to take relevant medication and failed to maintain stable or functioning life patterns. Some have gone on to kill either innocent bystanders or themselves.

In Britain, Christopher Clunis, a discharged mentally ill black man abandoned by the care system in the community, murdered Jonathan Zito and raised the complexities of such policies in a particularly poignant way.

Issues of racism and sexism have been important in the trail of errors and mismanagement emanating from poorly thought out policies implemented with inadequate resourcing. These failures confirm arguments that the state opts for deinstitutionalisation when saving money (Scull, 1979). This configuration of circumstances ignores the price paid by those caught in a web of inter-related events, including loss of life and affirmation of racist stereotypes about the mental health of black people (Fernando, 1991). Community care policies also facilitate the realisation of capital assets tied up in property and lands held by large mental health institutions.

Professionals are being driven by market flexibility to redeploy themselves, continuously moving between and within sectors (Dominelli and Hoogvelt, 1996). Many practitioners work in the public sector one day and in the private sector the next as facilities are sold to entrepreneurs in various privatising bids. They may be made redundant as part of a restructuring exercise aimed at containing costs, asked to apply for their old job again in the public sector for less pay and with less secure conditions of employment attached, or forced into early retirement. Alternatively, they may submit a tender for a project through which they will secure employment as private entrepreneurs if successful. In short, a revolving door that blurs the boundaries between public sector and private sector employment has been created in the name of efficiency, effectiveness and economy. Such practices do little to enhance morale amongst service sector employees, the majority of whom are women. Nor do they necessarily increase consumer choice as policymakers claim (Twigg and Atkin, 1994).

Contractual openings, particularly part-time ones can be advantageous in enabling women to combine paid employment with other activities. Pursuing these options is easier for those who have other sources of income such as women taking early retirement. Lone mothers also apply for such posts to combine work with domestic responsibilities.

Revolving door opportunities provide other benefits. The contract culture within the mixed economy of care has created spaces for women to plan the delivery of services they might actually want and bid for them. Women who have submitted successful tenders can form resources that might not otherwise be available for 'clients'. Black feminists in white racist societies claim that the mixed economy of care works in their favour by providing opportunities for developing services more in keeping with their needs. It has also provided a base for networking with others in their communities to develop campaigns and voluntary activities useful in challenging poor provisions and creating their own. Working from home also enables them to spend substantial periods of time in the place that provides a haven from the daily onslaught of racism.

Exploitative dimensions to these possibilities are fostered through low pay for caring work and lack of income for unsuccessful bids. As successful tendering occurs in a small number of cases, the outcome confirms rather than challenges the inadequacy of a system that produces so few positive results. Competitive tendering is required for most contracts (Clarke and Newman, 1997), so there are many more losers than winners, i.e., people whose proposals do not get funded. This result represents an enormous waste of resources that could have been utilised to provide direct services. For someone has to pay for the time and money spent in pulling together detailed and often complicated bids.

The costs of producing unsuccessful proposals are borne by individuals and institutions. For energies expended for this purpose could have been used to deliver services and ease pressures on welfare facilities. And, a nagging question remains: How many failures can an organisation or individuals placing unsuccessful bids sustain? At what point do they go out of business, perhaps never having entered the commercial world in the first place? Who pays for the costs they have accrued in the meantime? These are all serious concerns for which the contractual process has no answers. Instead, it adds to the overall costs of welfare organisations, in a hidden capacity. Or, it exploits the unpaid labour of volunteers or those who can ill afford to have personal resources squandered in this way.

Women applying for contracted-out posts may have dependent children and be unable to work long enough to earn an income that meets their needs. They pursue part-time jobs not necessarily out of preference, but to care for their families and children (Oderkirk and Lochhead, 1995). For others, these developments provide an illusion of choice by enabling women to leave unsatisfactory public sector posts for anticipated more fulfilling employment in the private and voluntary sectors only to find their options circumscribed by contractual obligations. These possibilities can be illusory for the state as purchaser dictates the types of contracts and opportunities that materialise. In the context of uncertain job markets, women's choices are more take it or leave it than genuine options.

Handy for some, these patterns of employment lock women further into the secondary labour market where the gap between what they actually need for a decent standard of living and what they earn has to be made up through unpaid labour in shopping around for cheaper goods; doing without essential items; providing domestic labour for better-paid women and men; and working in the shadow economy. These hardships, bad enough when endured by professionals, are much worse for 'clients' who have even fewer options through which to extend inadequate incomes. They may experience periods of homelessness, living on the streets, begging and trashpicking over other peoples' castoffs to survive (Zucchino, 1997). Those who can do the odd day's work as domestic cleaners for those further up the income scale are amongst those who consider themselves more fortunate than those without such opportunities (Piercy, 1994).

Commodifying Empowerment

Privatisation has been promoted under the aegis of enhancing consumer choice. In Britain, the National Health and Community Care Act, 1990 (CCA) has facilitated an explosion in private provisions, especially for older people and has been a major vehicle for this development (Twigg and Atkin, 1994). 'Clients' have been sold the changes emanating from the CCA under the guise of choosing from an expanding range of facilities. They were to be empowered by an augmented spread of provisions that they could access and choose to use. Entry to the market is controlled by money and knowledge about what is available. Either the user or the social worker as budget-holder has to have the finances and information necessary to exercise the option that meets 'client' needs. Thus, a 'client's' potential to remain within the system is contingent upon either the state's willingness to pay for or their personal capacity to purchase services.

As many social work 'clients' are poor (Cochrane, 1993), their capacity to operate on these terms, and the choices open to them, are more fiction than fact. Social workers who have expended their budgets cannot act as purchasers on behalf of their 'clients'. Without funding, social workers can be placed in the invidious position of denying a need that they assess essential to a person's well-being. This creates a number of moral and ethical dilemmas that practitioners in a market-driven environment are unable to address satisfactorily. A social worker I interviewed told me of her anguish in telling an elderly man needing support services he had to wait until the next month's budget or someone on her current caseload died – whichever occurred first, for him to get these. The man died before either possibility happened. Responding adequately has been made more difficult as a result of a British court ruling that a person who has chosen a facility that their local authority cannot afford has to be satisfied with what is available because the state can only be compelled to provide services for which it can pay (Clarke and Newman, 1997).

Meanwhile, services have become commodities that are for sale; the user has been turned into an individual consumer who exercises choice under certain conditions. The commodification of service provision and the expansion of choice within the market framework has (re)constructed the 'client' as a consumer or customer. Empowerment has thereby become *re*defined as a commodity relation (Dominelli, 2000).

Official pronouncements on social care have clarified the framework within which the concept of empowerment is to be understood. Empowerment becomes a bureaucratic form that draws on technocratic procedures for complaints about the *receipt* of a poor or inadequate service. These relate to a particular professional's competence to deliver the service in question and individualise both the worker and the complainant. At no point is this approach to empowerment concerned with issues of who designs or determines the appropriateness of the facility or service that has been found wanting. Nor does it focus on the system and its inadequacies, including the lack of resourcing. Moreover, by concentrating on individual people, complaints procedures fail to focus on the numbers of 'clients' who have filed similar complaints, often against a number of different professionals. These could signal the possibility that there is more amiss than professional incompetence, i.e., the system may be at fault. Also, a possible 'class action' cannot be detected if the procedures are preoccupied solely with recording individual cases. Bureaucraticised complaints in social work and resource shortfalls in the mixed economy of care are used to scapegoat basic-grade, mainly women workers and deprive them of their voices, despite a rhetoric of empowerment. Thus, women may be working to policies they oppose, but for which they have to assume personal responsibility.

Deprofessionalising Social Work

The market context has devalued professional social work. It has become vulnerable to deprofessionalisation through a competence-based fragmentation of the labour process initiated by government cost-cutting measures and attempts at curbing professional power (Dominelli, 1996). The devaluing of social work is also reflected in changes of name for the profession. In Britain, successive governments since the 1980s have dropped the term social work in favour of social care to signal a greater emphasis on physical care and a disinterest in widespread university-based training for the entire profession.

Redefining social work is consistent with the government's willingness to deprofessionalise it. Social care, unlike professional social work, does not respond to the psychological, social and practical needs of vulnerable people and those experiencing hardship. Nor is it concerned with linking the individual 'client' agent to his or her social situation. These preoccupations are lacking in official definitions of social care which present the 'client' as a passive being. Upholding people's human rights and promoting their well-being in their social context requires more than the skills necessary to provide someone with physical care within the social setting implied by the term social care. This definition also renders invisible the private interactive relationship that characterises the bulk of the caring work that is undertaken primarily by women (Ungerson, 1990).

Social work education and training have thus been affected by the commodification and deprofessionalisation of social services. In Britain, social work training is set to increase through the national vocational training system. The bulk of it will occur through National Vocational Qualifications (NVQ) levels two and three (1). These are lower levels of qualification than the Diploma of Social Work (DipSW) and its holders are paid correspondingly less. Yet, people so qualified, the majority of whom will be women, are entitled to perform tasks formerly undertaken by those holding DipSWs. Qualified women social workers are losing ground to women at the lower levels of the profession.

Scaling down the qualification levels required for doing social work will exacerbate deprofessionalisation and lock women into an even lower-paid ghetto. In the new mixed economy of care, women remain poorly represented at the higher echelons where top managerial posts continue to be held by men (Foster, 1997), increasingly without social work qualification or knowledge. Women constitute the bulk of workers carrying out policies dictated by others who lack social work backgrounds. The gender dynamics of this situation have meant that in a profession characterised as 'women's work' (Walton, 1975), women have a limited say in defining either its boundaries or ways of working. These trends are unlikely to be altered by New Labour's latest proposals for reforming the personal social services and imposing a General Council of Social Care. Even the name social work does not appear in the title of the General Council – a fact consistent with British politicians' reluctance to promote what they consider a troublesome discipline. Relegating social work to a subset of social care is unlikely to alter this image. This (re)definition of the discipline has little bearing outside the United Kingdom. The profession of social work is recognised world-wide; that of social care is not.

Privatisation and the Individualising of Collective Welfare Concerns

Another challenge privatisation poses for feminists is its individualising impact. This is a serious obstacle for feminists deeply committed to the collective advancement of women. Feminists have used consciousness-raising techniques, small groups, networks and campaigns to promote their causes and show that gender oppression is rooted not in individual women's pathologies, but in the systematic appropriation of women's energies and contributions to society by those endorsing patriarchal arrangements. This realisation has enabled individual women to stop blaming themselves for their predicaments and recognise that the problems they encounter are not exclusively of their own making. Working together with women suffering similar difficulties, has been a favourite method of discovering their causes and finding appropriate solutions.

For women who have been isolated, collective work has provided lasting friendships and led to direct action. This point has been well illustrated by domestic violence campaigns (Mullender, 1997).

The processes whereby women interact with each other in these groups favour equality because feminists have attempted to develop egalitarian forms of behaviour within them. These have included valuing women's contribution to consciousness-raising, sharing group activities to enable each member to learn the skills associated with particular tasks or roles, and creating alternative resources for women (Frankfort, 1972). Developing collective approaches to problem-solving can be difficult in individualising environments where people in need of a service encounter providers in commodity relationships. By commodifying care, collective concerns have become individualised and fragmented.

The Backlash Against Women's Emancipation and Public Patriarchy

Globalisation, public expenditure cuts and conservative ideologies have prepared the ground for the political response of returning public welfare responsibilities to families. This represents a reversal of previous trends whereby private patriarchy became public patriarchy. Advocating the resurgence of private patriarchy has become some men's reaction to feminist sexual politics played out in the welfare arena. Blaming the welfare state for women's independence from men makes overturning gains in this sphere a significant dimension of their gender dynamics. Gilder (1981) declares that in supporting women, the welfare state has been 'cuckolding' men. So, men feel undermined in their role as providers when this function is usurped by the welfare state. Men's loss of power in family settings and workplaces has been an integral feature of the move from private to public patriarchy (Walby, 1990) and is crucial to their men contesting this switch through conservative men's movements. The return to private patriarchy is endorsed by men of diverse political orientations united by a wish to resume control over women's lives.

Articulated as policies strengthening family responsibilities, the virulent manifestation of rightwing ideology through welfare retrenchment signals a desire for the regrouping of men's powers in the private realm where they anticipate holding power anew. As a backlash, conservative men's 'cultural wars' entail an explicit rejection of any accommodation with women's needs for emancipation (Clark *et al.*, 1996). Redressing and protecting men's interests has become a major feature of the positions trumpeted by groups such as Families Need Fathers and rightwing theorists like Gilder (1981). In this unfavourable environment, the imperative to maintain feminist insights in social work cannot be stronger. Feminists have to rely on their own social action and the support of pro-feminist men and women to overcome these adversaries.

Does the return to private patriarchy necessarily cause a deepening of antagonisms between men and women? Can men and women pool their efforts to create less oppressive social relations for both? In so far as the state sheds its responsibility to provide welfare for people during difficult times, a common objective should make it possible to reply affirmatively to these queries. The issue of how this can be done without men gaining the upper hand and controlling developments as often happens in mixed groups (Spender, 1980) is one for feminists to address and strategise over. However, this task has to undertaken sensitively for there are women who would prefer to see men in control of their lives as dictated in the traditional heterosexual nuclear family. REAL women in Canada, the Pro-Life movements in Britain, Canada and the United States, illustrate the continued potency of a traditional approach to women (Schlaffy, 1977; Steuter, 1995).

The appeal of domestic life as a haven from the turmoil of the public arena is not confined to traditional or conservative women. Working women alienated by low paid jobs and exploited in the waged labour market have declared a preference for working in the home where the fruits of their labour are visible and enjoyed by those they care for and about (Knijn and Kremer, 1997). Feminists have to respond to this issue without presuming superior knowledge about their choices. The complexities of women's plight indicate the interconnected nature of public and private spheres and necessitate holistic responses to women. Eradicating women's oppression in the domestic realm requires its elimination in the public arena. Freeing women from the domestic burden of caring also requires changes in the organisation of both unpaid and paid work for men and women.

The Insider–Outsider Role

Heterosexual family relations shape the site in which women have intimate relations with men. They also foster unequal power encounters between men and women in the private domain and support the legitimation of these in the public one. In the publicly regulated world of private patriarchy, women often act in the role of insider–outsider to amass considerable insight into their position and develop strategies of resistance. Women are insiders because they live within the family, carrying out much of its work. Its boundaries provide the walls defining their domestic space. Within these, they have a certain degree of autonomy to act in accordance with their wishes. As insiders, women can gain knowledges of how oppression infiltrates their experiences. These they can share with other women within and beyond its cloisters. Their close encounters with men mean that they can also understand their experiences. Women are outsiders, for they are excluded from the public domain and do not belong to the domestic sphere in their own right, but as mothers, wives or carers of elder relatives. Women's position as outsiders is most clearly manifest in disputes with men where their privileging is evident. Here, unequal power dynamics between them define women as outsiders with a lesser voice or say in the family's affairs.

In Western countries, women's position of holding less formal power than men has until recently, been evident in a number of ways including prohibitions against women owning property if married, securing loans in their own right, acquiring custody of their children or controlling their own sexuality and reproductive capacities. Some of these dynamics continue to be played out to the detriment of men, women and children. Disputes over custody of and access to children are indicative of these situations. These can become extremely complicated if a number of different variables are involved. For example, in the break-up of transnational, interfaith unions, the woman is treated as an outsider if the man returns to his country of origin and lays claim to the children (Hegar and Greif, 1991). In these situations, cultural differences, racism and sexism can interact to lock women into the role of outsider and prevent any dialogue between the conflicting parties. Children's voices are also excluded when resolving such confrontations for they are rarely consulted on their preferred place of residence (Schofield and Thoburn, 1996).

Women's position as insider–outsider is also apparent in the public sphere, defined largely as men's domain. Here, women are outsiders, tolerated within it as long as they play the game according to men's rules. They can easily be removed, albeit not without protest, if they threaten the *status quo*. Once inside its ambit, women are also insiders who acquire specific knowledge about its dynamics. This they can use to destabilise its operations and challenge its unfair practices. When doing so, women's role as outsider is affirmed once more. Women's roles as insider–outsider, whether in the private or public arena provides a basis from which women can mobilise resistance against the restrictions imposed upon their liberation.

Postmodern Welfare

The individualising context of privatisation is conducive to the creation of postmodern welfare. As postmodern social work has yet to establish itself as a credible base for practice, discussions about it are primarily about its theoretical orientations. A major characteristic of postmodernism is to eschew metanarratives and group activities (Nicholson, 1990). Post-modern social work is likely to be more individualistic than a feminist one with its commitment to collective solutions and approaches to problems, even when delivering services to an individual. Postmodern and feminist approaches do not sit well together. In Britain, David Howe (1994) and Nigel Parton (1994, 1996) have written extensively about postmodernism in social work. Few feminists, e.g., Liz Lloyd (1998) and Fawcett *et al.* (2000), have advocated this approach. I (Dominelli, 1996) have criticised postmodernism on a number of grounds including its fragmentation of social life, its incapacity to explain change and inability to support group-based initiatives aimed at securing social justice.

Can postmodernism offer us the basis for formulating a social policy that meets the needs of people in the 21st century? I would argue that it cannot. This is not because postmodernism has nothing to offer the further development of social work theory and practice. Postmodernist injunctions to probe for those realities that lurk beneath surface appearances, become aware that discourses can convey meanings that are not obvious initially and validate differences rather than gloss over them, are of merit. But these are not the exclusive province of postmodernism. Any well-trained social worker without the benefit of postmodernist thought would learn about the importance of undertaking tasks in accordance with these principles early in their educational training programme. They are central to the problematic individualising discourses and practice methods that have characterised the development of traditional professional social work. For as Compton and Galloway (1975) have indicated, assessments probe beyond the presenting problem. Respecting the uniqueness of the individual and promoting his or her self-determination are amongst the basic tools of social work (Biesteck, 1961; Hollis, 1964).

Postmodernists mainly fear being labelled essentialist – a mantra they hurl at those who do not share their views (see Healy, 2001). For me, this stance is misguided because it misrepresents non-postmodernists' use of 'woman' as a socially constructed category, fails to acknowledge diversity within feminism and cannot explain *patterns* of discrimination. Postmodernists' neglect of the social sphere as a collective arena is problematic. To deny the existence of systemic inequalities that affect large numbers of individuals who have certain characteristics in common, as postmodernists would have us do, is flying in the face of the everyday realities that countless people on this planet have to address daily. It is a dimension that social work practice with its focus on the *person-in-their-situation* (Hollis, 1964; Younghusband, 1978) is, in theory, well-equipped to take up. Dealing with the individual in his or her social circumstances or context is an integral part of social work practice and should enable practitioners to begin tackling systemic inequalities as a normal part of their job

(Dominelli, 1997). Postmodern theories also lack a rationale for changing the *status quo* (Haber, 1994). And, they ignore the considerable degree of overlap between postmodernist insights and feminist ones. These constitute major reasons for my scepticism about its potential for a social work that ensures social justice.

Within its individualising framework, what would postmodernist social services look like? One in which every individual looked after him or herself? Can it cater for everyone or only for some? As there has not yet been an openly declared postmodern welfare state, it is difficult to tell. However, doubtful its viability as a collective response to meeting people's welfare needs is, the prospect of its becoming hegemonic is chilling. To begin with, poor women in low income countries would first like to experience the advantages of modernism, by having decent homes to live in, clean running water in their houses, inside toilets, electricity and other conveniences of life that postmodernist thinkers take for granted. Similarly, people on low incomes in the West would like to have the basic necessities of life assured (Zucchino, 1997). From a position committed to ensuring social justice at both individual and collective levels, it seems to me that postmodernism is a perspective that privileged people can espouse.

As to what a postmodernist state would look like, we have a few pointers that have been given to us by politicians who have argued that the individual is all. Margaret Thatcher, a former British Prime Minister who was elected by a collective entity, made the contemptuous claim that 'there is no society, only individuals'. And, as Baroness Thatcher on a tour of the United States, her response to the question of what to do with poverty stricken women with children on welfare was to send the mothers to work and put the children into orphanages – a collective institution, of course, although not one that would command the support of large numbers of women or their children.

Peter Leonard (1997) argues that a postmodern welfare can exist – provided that it benefits from feminist insights and takes on board a collective emancipatory project. I take the view that once this is done, what is left is no longer postmodernism. For its hallmarks are fragmentation and the rejection of unity. Thus, I maintain that it is possible to argue that the withdrawal of the state from publicly funded welfare provisions is the current forerunner of a postmodern welfare model. Given that the postmodern welfare state is one in which everyone looks after him or herself, I suggest that the latter part of the 20th century, like its precursor, have depicted postmodernist scenarios. So does the implementation of monetarist policies in the contemporary welfare arena.

What have arrangements and policies based on such assumptions produced? Rising levels of poverty, particularly for women and children

(UNDP, 1998), higher rates of crime and violence (Percy and Mayhew, 1997), and the sheer waste of human potential for developing individuals and their societies to levels that have yet to be attained. In the so-called civilised industrialised countries of the West, the withdrawal of publicly-funded welfare provisions has caused increasing immiserisation and widened the gap between rich and poor so that it is higher at the end of the 20th century than it was during the previous one (Morris, 1995; Teeple, 1995). There was only a small glitch during the 1960s and 1970s when the gap between rich and poor was closing – during the alleged 'golden age' of the publicly-funded welfare state (Ralph *et al.*, 1997).

Affecting the overwhelming majority of poor people, hardship has dominated women's and children's lives. Even working women cannot escape the clutches of poverty and are over-represented amongst the working poor as they are preponderantly located amongst a low paid, casualised work force (Walby, 1990). In addition, higher rates of crime, substance abuse and increased addictions are the direct result of fragmented social lives in which individuals lose links to the larger collective that validates their existence as individuals and provides the *raison d'être* for their continued reproduction and for whom it exists.

The wage contract has not alleviated women's poverty as women work in a segregated labour market in sectors inhabited primarily by women and replete with low wages and part-time working. Women's nurturing capacities have been appropriated to provide unpaid care and restrict them to employment opportunities that are not attractive to men (Armstrong, 1984). Women continue to act as a reserve army of labour that can respond to capital's needs for an easily exploitable workforce because they carry the primary responsibility for ensuring the reproduction of today's and subsequent generations (Beechey, 1980). Struggling to meet their responsibilities regarding the unpaid care they render to children, husbands and dependent elders alongside these jobs exacerbates women's condition. The advent of the dual career couple as an essential element in safeguarding current family incomes has meant that women who would have been at home to respond to the call for additional labour are not there. As long as they have to work, their immediately realisable potential as a reserve army of labour is lost.

One group of women – stay-at-home mothers on welfare, can be used as a reserve army of labour. With their capacity for flexibility, they can assume the low-paid jobs no one else wants. In characterising the lives of women on welfare as worthless for not contributing to hegemonic social relations, politicians who popularise workfare legitimate discourses that endorse their becoming a flexible workforce capable of filling the low-paid casual jobs required by globalising Western economies. By portraying them thus, they also fail to acknowledge the unpaid work these women undertake in the home, raising children and enabling their families to survive. This includes the work they do to negotiate their way through the maze of the welfare bureaucracy (Callahan, 2000).

Being of active working ages, workfare and the withdrawal of benefits, compel mothers on welfare into the labour market. Implementation of this varies according to country. In Britain, this led to the loss of the lone parents' supplement, a policy mooted by the Tories, but enacted by a Labour administration headed by Tony Blair. In the United States, coercive welfare was initiated through a series of measures proposed by the Republicans under Ronald Reagan, who coined the abusive epithet 'welfare queen' to disparage women whose daily struggle is to ensure survival of the obstacles they and their children face. Republican measures and approaches have been endorsed by subsequent administrations including the Democratic one headed by Bill Clinton (Zucchino, 1997).

At this historical conjuncture, welfare mothers are preferred sources of temporary labour to (im)migrants for they have been demonised as an undeserving group (Zucchino, 1997). Racist immigration policies and economic exigencies combine to limit (im)migrants' entry to adopt this role. Their labour is required in their countries of origins for jobs that capital relocates in the South where workers have fewerpublicly-funded welfare benefits, lower rates of pay, less unionisation and political elites who accept the logic of capitalist development and structural adjustment (Dominelli, 1998). In industrialising nation-states, these conditions enable capitalists to exploit their workers to a greater extent than in the West. This reality exposes another contradiction at the heart of postmodernism. It needs a nation-state as a collective entity that allow the fragmented, atomised individual to exist in circumstances that facilitate submission to the predations of capitalist entrepreneurs.

Workfare is gendered for the policy has affected predominantly poor women, black and white, whose opportunities in life are limited. Classist and racist dimensions are integral aspects of it. In the United States where the workfare policy was first promulgated, it has been applied primarily to black women who are over-represented on the welfare rolls (Murray, 1990) and provide the archetype of the 'welfare queen' who is alleged to reproduce a hard core 'underclass' of people that politicians define as a menace to society (Morris, 1995; Zucchino, 1997).

The media and politicians have constructed the myth of the 'welfare queen' to suit their purposes. Although the empirical facts belie the stories being promoted by them, American media pundits, rightwing ideologues and politicians have insisted these are young teenage women seeking housing and living a life of ease on welfare by becoming pregnant to access social security benefits such as Aid for Dependent Children (AFDC). AFDC was terminated in 1996 with the passage of the Personal

Responsibility and Work Opportunity Reconciliation Act (Reconciliation Act) to prevent such alleged abuses of the system. Poor families' access to medical care in the form of Medicaid, and food stamps was severely restricted at the same time (Zucchino, 1997).

The passage of the 1996 Reconciliation Act has meant that the federal government guarantees initiated under Frank Delano Roosvelt's New Deal through the Social Security Act of 1935 to help maintain children have been withdrawn. This has had a monumental impact on the lives of poor people. Its passage has resulted in 8 million children on AFDC and related benefits being struck off the welfare rolls along with 5 million others, mainly their mothers (Zucchino, 1997). These people have been left to survive as best they can with minimal support from the local state in which they reside.

Women receive welfare benefits for their children rather than themselves. Hence, the biggest losers are children who have not yet entered the workforce and whose chances of not being penalised by poverty have been seriously curtailed. A subterranean message in workfare approaches to welfare is that poor children cease being a collective responsibility. Yet, they will be expected to contribute to the broader community when they become adults ready for either exploitation as low paid workers, carers of older people or a group that ruling groups use to discipline other employees by threatening their jobs. Or, they may opt out of the social contract that encompasses the wider society and endanger the social order. This latter possibility is utilised by ruling groups to legitimate more authoritarian regulation of private lives and intervention via the state, as has occurred in both Britain and the United States in the enactment of stricter forms of police control over ordinary citizens to maintain 'law and order' (Young, 1999).

In Britain, the different demographic makeup of those on welfare has not prevented American pundits like Murray (1990, 1994) from pressing similar claims here. Although the gendered and class dimensions of those on welfare (mainly poor women and children) apply, 'race' does not. Unlike the United States, only a few British welfare recipients are black. None the less, the dynamics of humiliating poor people are similar. So are their mythical characteristics as perpetrated by politicians typified by Peter Lilley and John Redwood who, despite research to the contrary (Morris, 1995), accuse young unmarried mothers of jumping housing queues and relying on social security (*The Independent*, 14 August 1995) instead of getting married to acquire husbands that support them or securing employment to pay their own way. Such attitudes deny the value of the work these women do in caring for children; ignore the reality that the job opportunities available would not provide a living wage let alone raise them out of poverty (Oderkirk and Lochhead, 1995); and reject the interdependent nature of social existence.

These developments indicate that poor women do not have the right to family life, despite the dominant ideology portraying women as mothers. Nor do their children. For in punishing their mothers, the state inflicts severe penalties on children, thereby flouting their human rights in the process even those theoretically protected by international covenants such the Universal Declaration of Human Rights that grants individuals social rights and the Declaration of the Rights of the Child that accords children the right to 'full development'. The latter agreement has been signed by all Western countries bar the United States. Signatories such as Britain and Canada have been indicted by the United Nations for not fulfilling their obligations to children. Social workers can play an important role in connecting gender to the realisation of social rights and facilitating access to welfare provisions by advocating against the hardship and inequalities being established through the current restructuring of the welfare state.

Conclusions

A postmodern welfare state that relies on individuals purchasing their own welfare instead of pooling social resources for the benefit of all individuals living within a given geographical boundary or community is one that only privileged people can afford. Buying welfare resources regardless of the country in which they live, is a happy state of affairs enjoyed by those who have money. But it is not an option open to either poor people in the West or those who live in low income countries elsewhere.

Comparing health care costs between countries with publicly-funded national schemes those with privately-funded ones favour the former. The American 'pay as you go' approach has higher costs borne by individuals and more money expended in administrative services than in the national plans previously favoured by Britain, Sweden and Canada (Dominelli, 1991). In calling for a publicly-funded welfare state, I am not endorsing bureaucratic welfare provisions. Critiques of the bureaucratic welfare state's failure to serve the needs of poor people are extensive and well-documented across a range of social divisions including gender (see Marchant and Wearing, 1986; Dominelli and McLeod, 1989), 'race' (Dominelli, 1988, 1997; Ahmed, 1990), disability (Morris, 1991) and class (Corrigan and Leonard 1978).

I am arguing for a publicly-funded welfare state that is created by users, workers and taxpayers, but accessible to all at the point of need because this is the most cost-efficient and dignified way of providing unstigmatised welfare services to all. Such a welfare state needs to be rooted in actualising every individual's human rights at both the personal and collective levels. Achieving this requires a collective commitment to and on the part of every individual. It also has to acknowledge interdependence between peoples and a reciprocity that includes users and workers in the creation and delivery of these services. Social workers can advocate the formation of a collectively endorsed publicly-funded welfare state because they know in detail the hardships individuals and communities endure if they lack access to it. The lives of poor people on the margins of society can lead to an array of social problems that are experienced by individuals as depression, alienation and exclusion. If society excludes people in systematic ways, it is not surprising that individuals seek their survival in whatever ways they can, regardless of their legality. Increasing rates of crime, violence and substance abuse become responses to the exclusion of people from a social contract that leaves them out.

Interdependence, mutuality and reciprocity enable us to conceptualise a society that owes individuals a living just as much as requiring each person to contribute to its furtherance as a collective entity. These ideas form the basis of a social compact that social workers can and should argue for in the interests of promoting social cohesion rooted in principles of social justice. It is what I call 'The I exist, therefore I have rights' principle' (Dominelli, 1991). Its corollary is that because I have rights, I have an obligation to promote the social well-being of myself and others. A publicly-funded welfare state becomes a structured way of delivering on this commitment. It also promotes the realisation of citizenship in accordance with feminist principles (Lister, 1997). In a globalisating world where the individual's right to welfare is precarious and women, drawn into the workforce as a reserve army of labour, still carry responsibility for providing familial care, public welfare resources are a necessity. Social workers can contribute to their development using feminist principles of practice.

Note

1   The Scottish equivalent of National Vocational Qualifications (NVQs) are Scottish Vocational Qualifications.

3

Redefining Professionalism

Responding to an agenda of creating a welfare state that meets the needs of all peoples for a dignified existence in the 21st century calls for a redefinition of professionalism for the current dominant one has been found wanting, particularly by those involved in the 'new' social movements, including women, black activists and disabled people (Dominelli, 1992; Ahmed, 1990; Oliver, 1990). These critics give primacy to the 'client' as a key partner in the decision-making process and pursue the objectives of social justice. Their concerns should be taken seriously by social workers who are well placed to do so.

Traditional understandings of professionalism have been defined by men (see Flexner, 1915). These have relied on the use of expert knowledges to control the interaction between workers and 'clients'. The expert's knowledge is privileged as objective and lying in the public domain of paid employment, but access to it is restricted to those who undergo a specified socialisation process that concludes with the certification of the professional as fit to practice using that knowledge in specified ways (Heraud, 1979). Privileging the expert, shifts the balance of power towards professional knowledge because the 'client' is deemed to have a lesser or inferior knowledge. In the process of expertise acquisition, the knowing that comes from experience becomes devalued and consigned to the private realm (Belenky *et al.*, 1997).

Professionals in medicine and law have endorsed the private appropriation of knowledge in the public domain by limiting access to their expertise through training and socialisation systems that have been tightly defined and circumscribed by their professional bodies. Only those who have undergone the requisite training in approved educational establishments can lay claim to the label that entitles them to hold a licence and exercise a right to practise. Moreover, doctors and lawyers have maintained that each has specific sets of knowledge particular to their respective profession (Heraud, 1979).

The medical profession's assertions are being challenged by alternative medicines which claim knowledge covering similar terrain. Unlike scientific medicine, these knowledges can be privately acquired by individuals through the public domain without regulated training. Thus, they have more permeable boundaries regarding their accessibility to the 'patient', as the boom in health store sales of alternative, so-called natural products, is demonstrating. Stricter controls may be imposed upon alternative knowledges and restrict both its accessibility and claims, as the Canadian government is threatening to do with homeopath medicines (*The Globe and Mail*, 24 March 1999). The imposition of such controls may be successfully resisted. But, these knowledges may continue to be devalued as a result of being in the domain of everyday knowledges held by private citizens rather than paid experts. These developments may bring the public–private divide in medical professional knowledge sets closer to that of social workers. The struggle over knowledge claims is not one-way, i.e., towards its democratisation. In Britain, counter movements aimed at restricting or professionalising knowledges are also occurring. For example, as social work struggles to maintain its professional identity and position as a university-based social science, nursing has successfully placed its training in academe to enhance its professional status through Project 2000.

Social workers have not followed male models of professionalism, although they have sought to professionalise. Contemporary social work has seldom laid claim to an exclusive expertise. Rather, it has aimed to engage 'clients' in a partnership with professional workers by seeing its goal as enabling the individual to achieve self-determination or empowerment. The failure of social work to argue its corner against restrictive knowledges and practices including the licensing of practitioners has resulted in social work being denied categorisation as a profession during Flexner's allocation of professional status to various occupational groupings in 1915. That the tasks were also undertaken by women without specialist training fueled Flexner's (1915) belief in the correctness of his approach. Unremarked at the time, the gendered nature of his decision is strikingly evident to us now (Dominelli, 1997c).

Whether social work is a profession and how it should be defined remains contentious. I (Dominelli, 1997c) have argued that the founding mothers tried to create an alternative definition of professionalism to that offered by men in establishing social work as we know it. This has had a number of features aimed at ensuring that high quality care could be accessed by all those needing it (Walton, 1975). This care was to be professionalised by: having a body of knowledge and skills that practitioners would acquire through training, i.e., not every 'streetwise granny' could be a social worker; rooting its knowledge bases and skills in both experiential and empirically researched realities; involving 'clients' as active agents capable of making choices about what to do in determining the nature of the problems to be addressed; and realising social justice and individual well-being. Another objective was to foster an open profession in which training was accessible to those who wanted to join (Walton, 1975). Having active rather than passive 'clients', valuing experiential knowledges; accomplishing political ends by opposing inequalities in practice and allowing anyone to obtain appropriate training, characterise the key differences between social work as a profession and the male model offered by Flexner (1915). That social work has failed to actualise its goals is another story. But it can be summed up as a consequence of the compromises a dependent profession made to survive reactions to its questioning the *status quo* (Dominelli, 1997c).

In this chapter, I examine contradictions that social workers encounter in implementing their visions of the profession, consider the challenges which feminists have mounted against traditional views of it and argue for its redefinition using feminist insights.

Professional Social Work

In becoming professionalised, social work has moved welfare issues from the private arena into the public one, a trend that has intensified since it became incorporated into the welfare state after the Second World War (Walby, 1990). However, social work's professional development is problematic for it conducts its public remit within the privacy of the hearth. A key contradiction within which social workers operate, is being part of public patriarchy, but condemned to practise within the private domain. Practitioners are required to ensure that the domestic arena functions effectively so that activities occurring within public patriarchy can remain unperturbed by the waves of change shaking microlevel arrangements in the private sphere. That social work has not written its script according to the injunctions of private patriarchy has been a failure which rightwing ideologues have been unwilling to forgive. They castigate the welfare state and social work 'do-gooders' for failing to: keep marriages together regardless of the plight of women within them; prevent young men from embarking on a life of drugs and crime; and stop young women from having babies when they are little more than children themselves (see Gilder, 1981; Murray, 1990, 1994).

Women social workers who launched the profession had to accept some tenets of traditional professionalism with its empirically-based knowledge claims and restricted access to its ranks to ensure the survival of social work. Pressures to conform to dominant definitions of professionalism have included: defining the profession's limits and boundaries; identifying a set of knowledges and skills to be taught to practitioners through specified training; operating in a way consistent with a professional ethos, i.e., in a detached and objective manner; upholding standards appropriate to the profession; controlling access to the profession; and promoting new developments (Heraud, 1979). In social work, this has required practice to assume a value-free and apolitical perspective. Individual casework and later psychodynamic casework became preferred avenues for achieving the goal of professional recognition. Except in a few countries where legislation protects the title of social worker, exalted professional status has not been forthcoming. Social work has been variously called a semi-profession, a vocational calling, or voluntary work anyone can do with little or no training (Younghusband, 1978).

Practising social workers have not pronounced upon social work's current professional status to any significant degree as they have been sidelined in public discourses by media pundits and politicians. In Britain, the media orchestrated backlash against anti-racist social work during the summer of 1993 is a powerful illustration of the dynamics through which powerful others exclude practitioners from debates about their own work (see Appleyard, 1993; Pinker, 1993; Phillips, 1993, 1994). Social work's position as a dependent profession, i.e., one that relies on convincing either men politicians who hold the pursestrings of the welfare state or men running facilities in the private sector, has hindered practitioners' ability to set up a profession in their own terms (Walton, 1975; Dominelli, 1997c) by having to compromise ideals for funding. Being accountable to the 'clients' they serve and the greater public exacerbates these pressures. Partnerships that hold professionals responsible for their actions become fora for establishing accountability. These provide avenues that people without other resources or access to appropriate mechanisms can use to influence developments. Building effective partnerships requires professionals to respond to the concerns of those using their services and adapt their organisational structures to facilitate their involvement (Panet-Raymond, 1991). Without these alterations, partnership becomes a paternalistic way of disempowering 'clients' (Panet-Raymond, 1991; Richards *et al.*, 2000).

I argue that there are valid reasons why social work has continued to reject the course of the more established professions and still lay claim to professionalism. But, I suggest that it is now time to reconsider where the profession is going, and how it can become attuned to 'client' demands when professionals respond to their agendas. Feminist insights linked to the creation of egalitarian relations can be useful in (re)formulating its future vision. So are those emanating from black activists and disabled people.

Part of my rationale for advocating this view is internal to the profession. Other elements are external to it. An internal reason has been social work's difficulty in establishing its unique professional credentials for refusing to follow the footprints of medicine and law. Eschewing elitism has threaded its way from the Settlement Houses to present day community action as the theme resonates amongst substantial numbers of practitioners

(Trainor, 1996). Contemporary community workers and organisers are vocal in their desire to validate the skills of ordinary people in articulating their needs and finding solutions to social dilemmas (Cannan and Warren, 1997). Countering professional powers of naming is affirmed by practitioners promoting less oppressive ways of working with 'clients'. This principle remains crucial to realising the profession's values of 'client' self-determination and empowerment. Fears that in becoming elitist, social workers will fail to stand against the injustices that block the realisation of the rights of downtrodden peoples are genuine. Following traditional professional preoccupations will intensify the control dimensions of social work practice at the expense of its more empowering ones. The methods whereby social workers secure professional status remain elusive, whilst retaining anti-oppressive goals continues to be controversial. Even the different professional associations guarding its remit do not agree on the direction the profession should adopt.

An external reason is the impact that 'clients' have had in contesting the boundaries and remit of the profession, particularly since the late 1960s. Service users have critiqued the profession's failure to meet their needs as they define them and are unwilling to perpetuate the imposition of elitist professionalism upon them. Their arguments are that for much of its history, practitioners have failed to uphold the rights of oppressed groups and contributed to their oppression rather than endorsing their emancipation. So, women, black people, older people, disabled people amongst other oppressed peoples have demanded that social workers take their agendas for action within their professional stride if they wish to continue claiming that they support them (Shakespeare, 1999).

Social work's oppressive capacities have been generated largely through the reproduction of everyday relations of domination, as when confining women to domesticity against their will. However, it can be more overtly fascistic, as exemplified by its support of the racialised oppression practised by Aryan supremacists in Nazi Germany (Lorenz, 1994) or the cultural genocide of aboriginal peoples in Canada, the United States, New Zealand and Australia (Haig-Brown, 1988; Furniss, 1995; Armitage, 1996; Bruyere, 2001; Tait-Rolleston and Pehi-Barlow, 2001). Another oppressive relation is produced when practitioners hold people individually responsible for their position and urge them to change their behaviour without protesting the inequities in the social system in which they reside. This approach retains considerable sway on the forms of social work practice tolerated by ruling groups in a given society (see Phillips, 1994).

Traditional understandings of professionalism rely on 'expert' knowledge to control the interaction between workers and their 'clients'. Additionally, they are used to impose expert knowledge upon service users, individualise social problems and restrict these to the private domain so that their 'treatment' can be individualised. Equally important, individualisation enables professionals to deem the problems people encounter as those of their own making and pathologise them for their weaknesses and failures. These, professionals allege, are rooted in inadequate personalities or poor moral character (McKnight, 1995). Social work, following these precepts serves as a smokescreen perpetuating social injustice without comment from practitioners who know about the hardships of life at the grassroots level through their daily interactions with people.

For women, this has meant hiding domestic violence and sexual assaults; accepting the burden of caring for others whether or not this is reasonable; emphasising the joy not the despair that women experience, particularly when unable to meet domestic obligations or rise to their roles in unfavourable circumstances. Having official interventions respond to their requirements not as women with needs of their own, but as mothers, wives or carers responsible for the well-being of those dependent on their unpaid care (Marchant and Wearing, 1986), amplifies women's isolation. Some women have little desire to change their lot, preferring instead, material resources to comply better with domestic demands (Dominelli, 1983). Sadly, substantial financial assistance has rarely been forthcoming from the so-called caring services (Seebohm, 1968; Perlmutter, 1997).

Regardless of the problem to be addressed – discordant marital relationships, inadequate communications between parents and children, sexual and physical violence that men perpetrate against women and children, or family poverty, social workers have not traditionally explored power relationships within family settings. Instead, interventions into these situations have drawn on psychological concepts that locate problems within the individual, often within the context of family dynamics that are deemed dysfunctional if the people involved do not adhere to the sex role stereotypes propounded by their theories (see Minushin, 1974). These are handed on as 'practice wisdoms' and seldom interrogated for their hidden assumptions (Rojek *et al.*, 1988).

Consequently, women seeking to change their situations receive little support from practitioners charged with promoting their growth. Women's failure to counteract conventional socialisation processes has reinforced high levels of mental illness, particularly in the form of depression, as women have felt unable to bolster their capacities to either cope with or alter their situations on their own (Brown and Harris, 1978; Rowe, 1983). Social workers' traditional emphasis on women as carers has meant that they have not engaged men in these issues (O'Hagen and Dillenburger, 1995), tending to bypass them wherever possible. Was this an early informal form of radical non-intervention (Mathieson, 1974)?

Social workers have tended to ignore the specific needs of working-class, black, disabled and older women by negating difference in practice. Given the commonality of gender between them, why have women social workers typically served other women so poorly? Part of the answer lies in a practice ideology that tends not to treat individuals as gendered beings living in racially stratified communities or subjected to other social divisions that maintain hierarchies of oppression. Responding to woman as an undifferentiated category also lurks in the background and ensures that the specificities of individual women's experiences are bypassed (see Mohanty, 1991; Jayawardna, 1986). This means that feminist commitments to improving living conditions for all women is lost in dynamics that neglect the realities that privilege one group of women over another, a point that requires an analysis of the specific contexts in which a woman lives.

Having an oppression-blind stance emanates from social work's commitment to universalism. In the West, this is a liberal tradition deeply embedded in treating everyone the same – an outlook that presumes a level playing field and equality of access to social resources. This tradition formally disregards 'differences' and the lived realities that indicate that people do not have the same starting points in life. Inequalities of wealth, power and other factors stand in the way of their doing so. These condition women's positionality which becomes structured around intersecting inequalities based on gender, 'race' and other social divisions that provide barriers to self-actualisation (Collins, 1991).

Lorenz (1994) claims that social work has endorsed the ideology of universalism because it has become enmeshed in building the nation-state in which social workers' legal mandate is rooted. Its borders define the boundaries of their authority, although occasionally, they have to operate in the international arena as in the case of cross-border child abductions, transnational adoptions or the sex trade in children. A national focus requires practitioners to deem their clientele a homogeneous group for the purposes of obtaining a stable national arrangement that draws lines around who is included and who is excluded from the state's ambit with some certainty (Lorenz, 1994). Although the populations encompassed by the nation-state have been assumed homogeneous, we know they are not. At a basic level, homogeneity presupposes a nation-state peopled by men as real citizens able to express their status in the public arena, while women as their subordinates operate within the domestic one (Pascall, 1986). Expressed in locality and culturally specific ways, this presupposition seems to hold whether the nation-state in question is in the West, the East or the South (Basu, 1997).

Social workers' responses to the nation-state as a homogeneous entity has been ambiguous despite the presumption of a value-base espousing equality. In the case of racism, this has been achieved by ignoring the specifics of 'race' but acting as if these exist. 'Race' has been constructed as a key definer of exclusion from a homogeneous national mix. For instance, by Lorenz'

(1994) own admission, social workers in Nazi Germany contributed to the identification of Jewish people who subsequently became victims of the Holocaust. Social workers in Canada, the United States, Australia and New Zealand have been an integral part of welfare systems that have deprived aboriginal children of their families and cultures, contributing to the policies of cultural genocide endorsed by their relevant nation-state (Haig-Brown, 1988; Furniss, 1995; Churchill, 1998; Hill, 2000; Bruyere, 2001; Tait-Rolleston and Pehi-Barlow, 2001). These are unlikely to be the only examples on the world stage of the racialised abuse of professional power, although a study that examines the details of such events has yet to emerge.

In these situations, I argue that 'difference' has only been overtly omitted. It implicitly provides grounds for treating people differently, i.e., as inferior, and neglects their right to retain a self-defined identity and be valued for whom they are within the heterogeneous population of the place in which they reside. Nowadays, by racialising difference and treating it as a deficit, professionals perpetuate the over-representation of 'black' people in care settings and prisons and their under-representation in the higher echelons of the workforce (Barn, 1993; Bruyere, 2001). Systematic patterns of discrimination indicate that equal opportunities policies notwithstanding, even when social workers explicitly set out to honour 'difference', they are more likely to violate it (see Dutt, 1999).

Feminist Challenges to Traditional Professionalism

Feminist social action began in the broader political arena as a questioning of women's social position in general. Feminists later focused their attention on particular groups of professionals, including social workers. Black and white feminists have criticised traditional social work practice for failing to meet their needs as women fulfilling particular roles within specific contexts. Feminists have challenged professional social workers by insisting that they acknowledge private troubles as social problems, redefine professionalism to validate user knowledges and encompass anti-oppressive stances to practice (Dominelli and McLeod, 1989).

Feminists' challenges are interesting because several of their precepts are consistent with the espoused values and tenets of social work. These include: recognising the uniqueness of individuals in their social context, a variation of the feminist theme that a woman's personal plight reflects her social position; being committed to 'client' self-determination which can be used to meet feminist demands for empowering women; and involving 'clients' in the assessment processes and action plans as a way of promoting 'client'-led practice. These principles facilitate activities that can respond to feminist concerns for addressing power differentials within social relations.

Feminists have problematised elitist *power over* relations that endorse inegalitarianism in helping relationships because these accord higher weighting to 'expert' knowledges and devalue 'client' knowledges (Belenky *et al.*, 1997). As a result, 'client' experiences of their problems are not affirmed as valid sources of information and their wishes are not taken as paramount in determining the focus of the work. The help provided may, therefore, violate 'client' definitions of need (Foucault, 1980). And, practitioners may fail to address identity issues relevant to the individual or group receiving assistance.

The control that professionals exercise in their interactions with 'clients' promote exclusion and elitism, contribute to feminist scepticism about the application of expert knowledges (Frankfort, 1972) and encourage the development of egalitarian alternative services. But, in countering elitism, feminists should not devalue useful professional skills that social workers bring to their job. Otherwise, in a hostile climate in which women's skills are not appreciated, feminist stances can be misused to uphold common-sense logic that disparages women's work. Cost-cutting governments not committed to ensuring the well-being of all citizens can draw upon feminist critiques of practitioners' failure to practice appropriately to undermine service provision and professional social work. Emphasising a need to balance its books, government can shed facilities and employees. This enables the state to escape its obligations to meet human needs in accordance with the international conventions that it has ratified.

Besides challenging professional arrogance as symbolised by devalued 'client' knowledges, feminists question social workers' strict adherence to the public–private divide. Querying the sanctity of dividing women's lives into these two spheres has been particularly evident in work involving physical and sexual violence against women and children (Gamarnikov *et al.*, 1983). Feminists have redefined these as public rather than private problems and their doing so has impacted on social work. Suddenly, issues that social workers had been accustomed to addressing as private woes hit the public stage, in dramatic ways as women spoke out against their abuse (Armstrong, 1976). Although the full ramifications of this insight remain unclear, feminist agitation against domestic violence has ensured that the police, courts, probation officers and social workers handle the issue differently now than they did a few years ago (Mullender, 1997). Though limited, feminist gains on this matter have been significant, e.g., feminists have challenged the low status that police have accorded 'domestics', as assaults against women by their partners has been called, and brought these into more mainstream crime fighting (Horley, 1990). Their endeavours have been more successful in some countries than others. In Canada the police, not abused women, lay charges against violent men.

The danger that white feminist discourses used to challenge traditional professionalism exclude other women has been identified in black women's accounts of domestic violence. In these situations, already marginalised groups of women have to work harder to include their voices and resist exclusion. As black feminists have reminded white feminists, racism has to be addressed when dealing with domestic violence or any other issue. Amina Mama (1989) has pointed out the differences in black women's experience of domestic violence, highlighting the specific difficulties black women encounter when they are assaulted because racism impacts upon men and women in black communities. These have ranged from having their experiences belittled when depicted as accepting domestic violence as a cultural norm to jeopardising their right to remain in countries like Britain when they have entered as sponsored dependents of husbands or fiancés. Also, black women seeking professional assistance have had to cope with workers' racist stereotypes of black male violence. And, racism has shaped black women's experience of sexual violence and deterred them from accessing social work support (Wilson, 1993).

White social workers who operate on the basis of stereotypes are less able to respond to the specific needs of black people on a range of other issues. A white social worker who believes that black people 'look after their own' will not conduct a thorough assessment of a situation and may refuse black elders support services on the assumed grounds that they are likely to receive these from their extended family, especially its women members (Dominelli, 1988; Patel, 1990).

In highlighting 'difference', feminists have challenged professional social workers' tendency to oppress 'clients' by treating them as homogeneous entities. Besides being especially critical of social workers' failure to address issues of racism and sexism (Bryant *et al.*, 1985; Ahmed, 1990), black women have incorporated disablism (Begum, 1993), ageism (Patel, 1990) and homophobia (Lorde, 1984; Parmar, 1982). And, they have questioned white practitioners' failure to work with men adequately (Collins, 1991).

The critiques through which one group of feminists interrogates another have led to new developments in feminist social work theory and practice (Dominelli, 1992) and validated the varied experiences of women (Dominelli, 1997). Feminists' constant dialogues with each other have acknowledged 'woman' as a highly diverse and complex category, before postmodernism emerged in social work (Banks, 1981), e.g., white feminists have responded in varying degrees to the points black women have raised in their critiques, including their failure to work with men (Cavanagh and Cree, 1996). In feminist theory building, these interactions reflect feminists' aspirations to be non-dogmatic. Being inclusive of difference means accepting, responding to and validating women's right to speak about their own lives in their own terms. Legitimating the right to self-expression of women whose voices have been silenced gives feminist reflexivity a deeper meaning (Belenky *et al.*, 1997). Additionally, feminist social work has validated experiential knowledge by stressing the inadequacies of responses that neglect women's needs.

Despite the espousal of equality as a value, social workers' handling of 'difference' or diversity has been contradictory on both individual and collective levels. Social workers committed to recognising 'difference' often do not know what to do with it, especially if public policies and discourses pull them in opposite directions. This difficulty is illustrated in an Australian women's refuge aimed at including black women. Wilson (1996) documents their story and suggests that white women workers are ambivalent about their commitment to equality and are reluctant to set aside their privileged knowledges. Their hesitancy or 'ambivalence', Wilson (1996) argues, creates conditions that exclude black women from decision-making arrangements except in a token capacity. To this interpretation of events, I would add that white feminists' failure to appreciate diversity as a strength and a fear of becoming excluded themselves exacerbates their dilemmas. The resulting position is that the white women are unable to value the knowledges and experiences of black women as equal to theirs.

White women's fear of the unknown underpins and undermines their interaction with black women. Difficult questions they have to face include: What will happen if we constantly have to interrogate our taken-for-granted world-view? What will replace our privileged status? Will real equality materialise or will patterns of dominance be reversed so that we become the losers? Without answers, they are frightened to engage in meaningful dialogue with the black women. The case below illustrates that aiming for a win–win situation without knowing how to achieve it can block the creation of egalitarian relations. Amy, a white woman practitioner I interviewed, articulates this view as:

> Working with black women as real equals has been scary for me at times. It has required a leap of faith, a trust that they would do the right thing by me. But how could I ask for such a thing given the history of oppression and colonisation that exists between us? Could I, in their shoes, forgive and forget the appalling legacy they will carry forever?

Amy has been frank in her revelations. Seeing herself as an oppressor with hope for a better future and having trust in others are central to her capacity to move forward. There is guilt to be overcome, vulnerability to consider and a healing process to be embarked upon before mutual acceptance can become a reality (Bishop, 1994), an insight crucial for professionals to note. White people have to work on and know themselves – their fears and aspirations, before they can engage effectively with those they have 'othered'. Put in different words, they have to address their emotions as well as acquire the intellectual understandings and practical skills for working in anti-oppressive ways across racialised differences, or any other kind of division that is deemed 'inferior' whether this is gender, disability, class, age or sexual orientation.

Training that assists the process of crossing the oppressor divide often focuses solely on intellectual understanding, thus shortchanging those engaged in transformational processes. Moreover, Amy's comments reveal a dichotomous way of organising her feelings and responses that pit her interests against those of black women, thereby locking her into a conceptualisation of the situation from which it is difficult to extricate herself. Believing in her capacity to see things from different perspectives and acting upon these understandings is crucial to overcoming this problem.

Feminist analyses have problematised discourses of difference as 'deficit' and highlighted 'the family' as a key concept for social workers to unpack in practice (Brook and Davis, 1985). At the same time, black women have found white feminist critiques of the family (see Barrett and McIntosh, 1981) irrelevant (Bhavani, 1993). Black families are sources of strength that provide support networks and skills to enable black people to survive in racist societies (Bryant *et al.*, 1985; Collins, 1991). White feminists have sought to make good the shortcomings that black feminists have pointed out (see Barrett and McIntosh, 1985). These responses follow from their capacity to be self-reflexive, critical of their own work and willing to transcend racist divides. Sadly, this places the burden of identifying the need for corrective action upon black women.

Black feminists have also identified and challenged the differentiated relationships that the state has with black and white families for these reinforce inequalities. For example, black women have had their reproductive capacities restrained through measures including forced sterilisations (Bryant *et al.*, 1985; Sidel, 1986), while white middle-class women have been berated for not utilising theirs to capacity. In Britain, immigration rules have fragmented black families by placing restrictions upon black women that do not exist for white women, e.g., being denied Child Benefit for dependent children living overseas (Gordon and Newnham, 1985). Black mothers live in constant fear that their sons will be apprehended simply for being on the streets. Generally speaking, white women, especially middle-class women, do not have the same worry. The list could go on. The main point is that family life means different things to different groups of women for the opportunities they have to raise families as they wish is often constrained by powerholders who do not share their views, and women's experiences of family life can vary dramatically from each other.

To respond to egalitarian aspirations regarding daily living, feminist social workers have to value and work with 'difference'.

Social workers who disregard the positive significance of 'difference' are more likely to evaluate it as pathological and respond inappropriately to people in need. For example, problematising black families in general (Dominelli, 1988) and being suspicious about black people's ways of raising children or thinking these are not equal to those utilised by white people will result in social workers unnecessarily taking more black children into care than white children (Barn, 1993). White practitioners who view black families as deviant and their child-rearing practices as inadequate will find it easier to sever the ties between black children and their parents and perceive their welfare needs as being better met by white families. Part of the solution to this difficulty is not to cast white ways of doing things as better. This requires transcending the normalisation of white middle-class values (see Foucault, 1980; Frankenburg, 1997). So, in traditional constructions of reality, dominant discourses express professionalism as simultaneously racialised and gendered.

Redefining Professional Social Work from a Feminist Perspective

Feminist social work aims to deliver the best services possible to women in the here and now by addressing oppression in both paid and unpaid work. This goal subjects every aspect of human social relations to scrutiny and changes within an egalitarian framework. Feminists' demands for widespread social transformation has resulted in its lack of appeal as a major method of intervention in statutory social work. Yet, many of its critiques of the *status quo* have been influential in its theory development, practice and training (Dominelli, 1992).

Redefining social work from a feminist perspective has at times placed it in conflict with its state mandate. This happens because feminists have endeavoured to subvert both public and private patriarchy when supporting women 'clients' who have challenged their oppression and considered additional ways of empowering women 'clients' and workers. Feminist social workers have argued for a woman-centered practice (Hanmer and Statham, 1988), although their responses to women also carry repercussions for children and men (Dominelli and McLeod, 1989). Feminist social work is more than woman-centered because it is part of the broader feminist movement and this shapes its ultimate goal of ending the oppression of all women whether this occurs through public patriarchy, private patriarchy or other oppressive structuring of social relations.

In redefining professionalism from a feminist perspective, every aspect of professional ideology and practice is examined as part of feminists' commitment to a holistic transformation of social relations whether in relationships with 'clients', colleagues, employers or the state. Feminist practitioners seek change at the 'client'– worker interface within the workplace to secure egalitarian relationships in both personal and professional life. Feminist social workers respond to a woman's needs for services to enhance her well-being as a whole person by understanding socially structured gender oppression and its interconnections with other forms of oppression. Feminist social workers consider the impact of gender oppression upon a woman's specific situation while acknowledging her capacities as an active agent who can make her own decisions. They also seek to end women's subordination to men without oppressing others, women, men and children.

There is no question of a feminist social worker imposing her ideological views upon either 'clients' or colleagues, although they may engage in critical dialogue about particular issues. Feminist social workers' commitment to an individual woman deciding for herself the specific contribution she makes to feminism's agenda for social change (Cook and Kirk, 1983) means that the 'client', not the social worker decides the extent, if any, of her involvement in its broader goals. Feminism's broader political objective is achieved through alliances with others and involvement in their activities, many of which lie outside the scope of social work practice itself. Significant in their relationships with women 'clients' is the impact of feminist values in shaping the *processes* through which workers interact with 'clients' and bring insights of women's complex, multi-layered personalities and different social situations into their dialogues with one another.

Feminism is a worldview with a political philosophy about women, the world they live in and their relationships with others. It is an actively chosen outlook rooted in women's life experiences not in their biology. Being a feminist social worker impacts on a woman's professional and personal relations – in what is deemed important and how they relate to others. But, feminist social workers are the product of the societies in which they live and may fall short of their ideals when implementing these in practice (Dominelli and McLeod, 1989). For feminists, like other women, have been socialised to endorse social relations characterised by the imposition of one person's or group's power over others. Transcending this socialisation is an ongoing struggle. Despite subscribing to a theory and practice that endorses egalitarianism, feminist social workers can inadvertently support oppressive social relations as unintended consequences of poorly thought out actions. It can also occur when they fail to recognise privileges accruing to them as a result of interactions between gender and other dimensions of oppression. Playing down a privileged status may feature in the treatment of women different from them across a range of social divisions. This happens when they do not deconstruct the category woman; or erroneously believe that gender oppression means that women have more in common with each other than differences between them (Morgan, 1970).

False Equality Traps

Women create 'false equality traps' (Barker, 1986) when they assume that other women have similar experiences of patriarchal oppression and access to the same opportunities, ways of knowing and states of being. They occur within social work and without, and can be perpetrated by any woman inadvertently. False equality traps reflect seldomly acknowledged power differentials between women and a presumed equality. Postmodern feminists reframe this as treating women as an essentialist category (Rojek *et al.*, 1988).

Being aware of various conditions that create false equality traps is essential to feminist social workers. False equality traps are particularly important in social work because they can be created through a range of interactions. These include identity-based relationships, between workers and their 'clients', co-workers and employers. Some are formed through interpersonal interactions or personal relationships between women. Others are systemic. A number of dynamics reveal their presence. Two key ones are: minimising women's experiences of oppression; and denying women's experiences of oppression.

Minimisation is enacted when the specificity of women's experience of oppression is undervalued and women are assumed capable of coping with whatever is thrown at them. This action seeks to reduce differences between women. The 'we are all sisters together' motto (Morgan, 1970) which ignores the differentiated bases of women's oppression is indicative of this dynamic. One minimising false equality trap manifest in social work practice is to assume parity of access to resources. Although buttressed by policy imperatives and resource constraints, this occurs when a middle-class social worker asks a poor working-class woman 'client' to come to her office for an interview without offering financial assistance or transportation knowing that the woman cares for young children and has no money for transportation. If the woman fails to keep her appointment, the worker takes this as evidence of the woman's unwillingness to be helped rather than a result of the constraints of poverty and a bureaucratic approach to her difficulties. The *work* involved in reaching the office has been deprecated through a presumed equality in accessing resources and the desire to hold the woman *personally* responsible for her situation without considering all the factors at play in it. In this, I am not arguing that the 'client's' responsibility for her behaviour becomes diminished, only that what *she* can do is only one part of the equation.

Social workers who deny women's experience of oppression argue that women now have equality. This stance rejects structural bases to oppression. But as is illustrated below, the boundary between structural and personal forms of oppression is blurred. Moreover, structural dynamics that create false equality traps can easily become personal ones because these intersect and interact with each other.

In social work, practitioners also deny women's experience of oppression by presuming that what a woman says about her specific experience of it is of little consequence if she is coping. Denial dynamics are similar to minimising ones in disparaging the particularity of women's experiences of oppression at the interpersonal level. But it is different in that denial ignores the systemic nature of the specificities of women's oppression. The following case of domestic violence exemplifies this process. In it, a white middle-class social worker hears a white working-class woman claim that she is unable to leave her violent partner because he is all she has. Instead of hearing this as a reason for further probing, checking out its meaning in practical as well as emotional terms and doing so in a manner that makes the woman feel that she is being listened to, the social worker dismisses her by saying, 'Oh, OK. Here's the refuge number if you need it in future'.

The social worker does not welcome the woman's comments as an opportunity to explore her difficult life situations with her. Nor does she assist her in making her own informed decisions by helping her acquire information about the risks she is taking and support and resources that she can count on. Interrupting the dialogue, the practitioner interprets the woman as meaning that despite the difficulties and desire to leave, she can cope with staying. In this instance, the middle-class social worker by-passes the systemic nature of domestic violence and presumes that the working-class woman can take action without further assistance. She assumes that all women experience oppression as women similarly to herself and ignores the more privileged knowledge of and access to available resources that she has by virtue of her class and professional position.

The example below highlights a denial of the systemic oppression of working women. It indicates how women are required to address the lack of social support services for dual career women (as waged and unwaged workers) through interpersonal relationships that may become exploitative. A middle-class woman social worker employs a working-class woman to do domestic chores so that she can buy quality time with her children. Her actions perpetuate false equality trap dynamics by minimising how poverty oppresses working-class women and denies them the opportunity to spend time with their own children. As employer, the middle-class social worker does not connect her plight – the lack of quality time with her children with that of her working-class counterpart. Additionally, the middle-class woman fails to recognise her personal contribution to the systematic oppression of the working-class woman by privileging her needs and engaging in a wage relationship in which she cannot pay a decent wage because it has to come out of her own low salary. Her relative privileged status is minimised when she claims that she provides employment for a woman who needs it, possibly to feed and clothe children. Processed through interpersonal relationships, the middle-class woman may assuage the guilt she feels by being kind to the working-class woman and not 'taking advantage of her'. She may even rationalise her choice on the grounds that all working women are underpaid and spend little enough leisure time with their children. In this scenario, the middle-class woman exercises *power over* the working-class woman. Both are united in being oppressed by society's failure to: ensure women's access to low-cost, high quality child care facilities; pay living wages to working women; and get men to share household chores equally with women. Institutionalised inequalities between men and women and politicians' ideological refusal to socially support domestic work are played out between women as interpersonal exploitative relationships that deny systemic discrimination.

Both women are placed in this position because housework is considered private work, where problems must be resolved individually. But, their interaction is rooted in the systemic oppression of all women. In settling for private responses to the problem of inadequate or non-existent socially supported services for working women, the questions of reorganising paid work and involving men in domestic labour do not get raised. As an individualised wage relationship, the interaction between these two women reinforces private patriarchy and lets public patriarchy off the hook.

A further illustration of the denial of women's specific experiences of oppression concerns old age. Social workers are prompted to oppose ageism, work in gender-neutral terms and ensure that all people are treated with dignity. In sticking solely to this analysis, they neglect the empirical reality that old age is largely synonymous with older women who are disproportionately represented amongst the ranks of the poor (Status of Women, 2001). Responding to their needs only as older people reproduces false equality trap dynamics which fail to address women's specific needs as women holistically.

Avoiding false equality traps requires feminists to reconceptualise power on a number of different levels and consider the variety of power relations that can exist amongst and between women. This includes recognising power as a non-zero-sum entity stemming from a number of sources that (re)create it through social interactions. Appearing in many guises, its most common forms involve *power over*, *power of*, and *power to* (French, 1985) relations. *Power over* dynamics can emanate from a range of different points – status, role or position in a hierarchy, and charisma (Weber, 1978). The power social workers hold over 'clients' is indicative of this. It is authorised by their position as employees within a particular bureaucracy as well as from their legal mandate. It can serve as the basis from which women can oppress other women by silencing their voices. Women 'clients' fear of social workers' power to take their children away from them is a clear example of the *power* that social workers hold *over* them (Strega *et al.*, 2000).

Power to forms of power indicate the capacity to do things or take action. Its realisation relies on social workers working collaboratively with others to achieve a specific purpose or goal held in common. Recognising 'clients' capacity to act is necessary for feminist social workers intending to work jointly with 'clients' to develop, agree and implement plans of action that meet their needs, or collaborate with colleagues. Working together is not a tokenistic or bureaucratic action in which 'clients' are asked to 'sign contracts' to indicate willingness to do what social workers think adheres to agency requirements.

Power to relations enable women to share power with other women for specific reasons, but requires both parties to the relationship to agree to do so. In their interactions, neither party is considered completely powerless (Dominelli, 1986) because each has the capacity to exercise agency and can exert some control or choice over what each is prepared to do or not do. *Power to* can become *power over* if one party seeks to dominate the other. Resisting subordination involves the *power to* challenge existing social relations in various ways (French, 1985).

Power of emanates from identity-based collective action, e.g., women who form a gender based group to achieve a common goal exercise *power of* relations. A group of sexually abused women working collectively to survive and challenge male violence against them are displaying power as women who are not prepared to suffer silently. These woman are exhibiting power that is linked to membership in the group and utilising it to reverse an unjust situation. In the process of taking action, women empower themselves and grow in confidence to become survivors. From there, they can move on to become thrivers or women who set their own agendas in their lives.

In the course of achieving their goals, the *power of* can become the *power to* resist oppression (French, 1985). And from there, without a commitment to egalitarianism and due attention to process issues, *power to* can become *power over*. Values rooted in the acceptance of other people as agents who are equals are important in ensuring that one form of oppression is not supplanted by another. Achieving egalitarian objectives requires feminist social workers to re-conceptualise their understanding of power relations and move from thinking about power as a zero-sum entity to one that is negotiated and re-negotiated through social interactions (Dominelli and Gollins, 1997). It involves what Giddens (1990) calls the transformative capacity of power to be enacted in professional interactions between practitioners and 'clients', amongst social workers themselves, and between social workers and their employers.

The workplace is also a site for feminist social action. In it, feminist social workers demand that working relations amongst colleagues are egalitarian and that employers and employees recognise and value the contributions that women make to organisational endeavours. Their vision for the workplace includes: eliminating sexual harassment; working within a non-sexist environment; having leave provisions which enable women and men to take care of children, whether in the mundane to-ing and fro-ing from school, when they are sick, or need to visit the doctor or dentist; and having flexibility within their working schedule to attend these and other domestic tasks including elder care. If these responsibilities are substantial, jobshare or part-time working arrangements without loss of health care, pensions, promotion or other rights, are necessary.

Managers can treat women's promotion prospects seriously by providing women with access to training, career advice and guidance, mentoring schemes, and promotional opportunities (Grimewood and Popplestone, 1993). Men should also be entitled to care leave if they are to assume their share of domestic responsibilities (Segal, 1983). Men's rights to engage in family activities should not be secured at the expense of women as has happened in Nordic countries where men and women share one basic leave entitlement (Dominelli, 1991). In these locales, a gendered division of labour in which women earn less than men means that despite formal shared parental care of children, women continue to bear a disproportionate share of those tasks. This outcome indicates the interdependency between public and private domains; necessity of overhauling the organisation of work; and need to replace arrangements that prioritise men's needs over women's. Depriviliging men of workplace benefits accrued at the expense of women whose roles as workers intersect with those as mothers and carers is also required.

Feminist managers have challenged the new managerialism for failing to support people's welfare needs and having economic exigencies take precedence over social ones. Thus, feminists are interested in inverting the primacy of economic matters over social considerations to put people's well-being at the centre of policymaking (Dominelli, 1991, 1997). Feminist social workers argue for the creation of an economic system that responds to people's social needs rather than greed for ceaselessly increasing profits.

Conclusions

Professional social work from a feminist perspective has women as its starting point, but carries implications for social work with children and men. Feminists have played a central role in placing gender relations on the social work map, challenging existing definitions of professional social work, and redefining it in more egalitarian, power-sharing directions. Given the gendered nature of the profession, it is surprising that feminist social work has not been adopted more broadly in practice.

False equality traps present a key danger besetting practising feminist social workers. Feminist practitioners are aware of hurdles in forming egalitarian relations, understanding power as a complex and multi-faceted phenomenon and engaging with other women as active agents. Despite the problematics of practising feminist social work, working with service users in more egalitarian ways is a promising avenue to walk down because it offers the opportunity to: explore power-sharing; learn how to dismantle the barriers to egalitarian social relations; build the bridges necessary for surmounting these obstacles; transcend the false-equality traps that fail to resolve a myriad of problems; value difference; and create alternative ways of working and being. Changing workplace relations to accommodate men's full involvement in domestic activities is also important in redefining professionalism in egalitarian dimensions.

4

Working with Men

For too long, men have been absent partners within social work relationships. Although men have formed the major 'client' group in some areas of practice such as working with offenders, social workers engaging with men in family-based interventions have been the exception rather than the rule (O'Hagan and Dillenburger, 1995). As Wilson (1977) has pointed out, women usually act as intermediaries between officialdom and their families. Practitioners' reluctance to involve men in their family-focused work has been evident on both sides of the gender divide. Social workers, the majority of whom have been women, have worried about their ability to deal with the men inhabiting the lives of women 'clients', particularly if they have been violent or abusive. Others have believed that men have little interest in dealing with the problems that women and children endure, so that there is little point in wasting time and resources working with them. The absent father or husband was just that, the absent father or husband. Men who have felt their authority challenged through statutory interventions have not been averse to being ignored by professionals who hold formal power over them.

This chapter problematises masculinities as these impinge on social work practice with men. I draw upon, though am critical of, Connell's (1995) work to get into the link between masculinity and men's identity as men within social work whether as 'clients', workers or partners of the women and children involved in social work. Introducing men into the feminist social work equation raises a number of contentious issues for which there are no easy or agreed answers (Orme et al., 2000). In this chapter I consider whether feminist social workers should work with men, under what conditions and how. I also question whether men have a role as practitioners in professional social work.

The Complexities of Sexual Politics

During the early days of the women's movement, 'sexual politics' became the term feminists used to epitomise unequal power relations between men and women (Millet, 1969). Although the language for describing these has changed over the years, the essential feminist message remains. Social relations continue to privilege men simply because they are men. Social divisions are organised on the basis of oppositional dichotomies that privilege the part of a dyadic pair that is deemed dominant (men for gender dyads) over the other (women). This makes personal relationships between men and women political ones. That is, they are indicative of power relations that operate to disadvantage women whether the arena is the home or in public spaces (Smith, 1990).

This unequal power dynamic is straightforward as long as only gender relations are considered. It becomes more complex when other social divisions are examined because each intersects with and is affected by the others, e.g., 'race' is gendered and gender is racialised. So, as long as the social attributes shared by men and women are the same, men will continue to be constructed as the privileged gender, e.g., a black disabled older man will be privileged over a black disabled older woman. Oppositional power dynamics promoting inequality are evident amongst social divisions other than gender. So, the privileging of whiteness over blackness as a social construction (Dyer, 1993) results in a white disabled woman being privileged over a black disabled one. Privileging is interactive and context specific and has to be analysed as such.

Men in Social Work

Social work provides a site in which sexual politics are played out so that dynamics endorsing male supremacy operate within social work as well as outside it. In social work, their study had been neglected until feminists questioned the role that social workers played in maintaining women's oppression. Early feminist writings on the (white) family and social work (Brook and Davis, 1985) and in a broader range of activities (Marchant and Wearing, 1986; Burden and Gottlieb, 1987) began to unpack social workers' collusion with patriarchal relations unless they were explicitly committed to challenging them, which most social workers at the time were not.

Social work is defined as a 'women's profession' (Dominelli, 1992; Grimwood and Popplestone, 1993). Although numerically dominant, women do not control it. Decision-making processes and policy formulation remain firmly under men's control (Hallet, 1991; Grimwood and Popplestone, 1993; Dominelli, 1997). Gendered dynamics complicate women's relations with male colleagues. Women practitioners are likely to be managed by men and take this as the norm. Women occupying these positions appear as aberrations because managerial skills are associated with men (Coyle, 1989) and their unusualness is remarked upon (Dominelli, 1997c).

Men are abandoning direct work with 'clients'. Men have become even more reluctant to join the practitioners' ranks during the past decade. Unlike women, they use practice as a steppingstone to a management career (Howe, 1986). Their withdrawal from the 'client' interface has coincided with declining job opportunities and wage-cuts in public sector jobs compared to private sector ones and a questioning of men's suitability to work in sensitive areas such as child care (Pringle, 1992). The downward trend in men's employment as practitioners has been reflected in fewer men seeking social work training, thus affecting the number of qualified men practitioners available in future. According to CCETSW statistics on student recruitment, men's enrolment in British social work courses dropped from constituting 35 per cent of the student body in the early 1980s to about 25 per cent in the early 1990s.

On the 'client' front, feminist social workers have generally ignored the needs of men as 'clients' and seldom questioned the appropriateness of not working with men. Those who have followed through by engaging men in practice have faced a number of obstacles including the opprobrium of other women (Dominelli, 1981, 1999). Women debating this issue have yielded a number of responses, not one of which is straightforwardly simple. Some women support working with men because no one would do this work otherwise. Others reason that women need to model alternative ways of working with men for both men and women. A third rationale centres around feminists' demands that men examine their oppressive behaviour and change their roles to non-oppressive ones (Wild, 1999). Ultimately, they argue, men have more to gain than lose in becoming pro-feminist (Dominelli and McLeod, 1989; Wild, 1999).

Those countering this position argue that women have more important things to do than work with men. They insist that women's resourcefulness should be devoted to improving women's lives and responding to their substantial unmet needs (Dominelli, 1999). For radical feminists, the question of working with men does not arise. Their ideological perspectives dictate that women should not because it drains women's energies (Firestone, 1970). These can be better used to meet the needs of women with more limited access to resources than men. Radical feminists also maintain that women working with men perpetuate women's roles as carers of men (Eisenstein, 1983).

The tensions between these two positions remain (Orme *et al.*, 2000). Although radical feminists have been central actors in developing facilities dedicated to women at the local level, institutional sexism has hardly been dented by a focus on working with and for women. The complexities of patriarchal relations as they are manifest at the personal, institutional and cultural levels and men's capacity to work against the interests of women who are not onside, lends credence to Scully's (1990, p. 3) message that, 'the debunking of patriarchy is not accomplished by focusing exclusively on the lives and experiences of women'. Women and men have to engage in the formulation of anti-sexist theories and practices with both genders if the oppression of women is to end. Additionally, the arrival of a strong anti-feminist 'men's rights' movement (Drakich, 1995) has made the view that feminist should not work with men less tenable than it ever has been.

In the meantime, men have been drawn into the debate about their role and place in social work (Pringle, 1992; O'Hagan and Dillenburger, 1995) and society (Connell, 1995). They too have arranged themselves on both sides of the divide. Some men have argued against feminist encroachments on *their* terrain and resisted attempts to create equality between men and women on the grounds that the current patriarchal arrangements make the best use of the different talents held by men and women (Lyndon, 1992). Other men have argued that women's attempts to gain access to *their* public domain, particularly in the field of employment, constitutes unfair competition (Brooks, 1996). They set themselves the task of reversing any gains that women have made including legislative ones aimed at realising equal opportunities (Brooks, 1996). These men feel that they have more to lose than to gain from women's demands for liberation.

Men who support women have adopted pro-feminist stances and drawn on feminist insights to address a number of questions that feminists have raised. These have problematised masculinity, men's violence against women and children, and the role of men in child welfare work (Bowl, 1985; Hearn, 1987; Pringle, 1992, 1995; Wild, 1999). In exploring these issues and attempting to work out solutions, these men have worked collectively with other men and encouraged them to: develop a full range of emotions, thereby giving expression to their nurturing capacities; participate fully in child care by redefining fatherhood as more than an economic relationship; undertake a fair share of domestic and caring duties; support women in their claims for equality in the workplace; and establish violence-free zones in which interpersonal relationships can flourish (Snodgrass, 1977). These issues have been taken up by a range of men's organisations that consider themselves pro-feminist, e.g., the Achilles Heel Collective and the Working with Men Collective in the United Kingdom, the National Organisation for Men Against Sexism in the United States, Men Against Sexual Assault in Australia. Their activities have been endorsed by a range of pro-feminist men theorists and scholars like Zaretsky (1976); Tolson (1977); Pease (1981); Bowl (1985); Hearn (1987); Rutherford (1992); Jackson (1995) and Connell (1995).

A number of authors writing on masculinity – Connell (1995), Hearn (1987) and Zaretsky (1976) amongst others have spoken positively of the impact that feminist theory and practice have had on their work and thinking about men. In the field, groups such as the Working with Men Collective in London have already initiated practice that seeks to work with men in ways that establish egalitarian relations with others, particularly women. Their work has included promoting men's ability to understand and conceptualise their experiences as men by drawing on feminist concepts and insights to develop guidelines for practice that endorse feminist approaches and ways of working. Men practitioners adopting feminist principles have extended these to include a concern with process, outcomes and relationship-building as a way out of men's instrumentality and objectification of other people (Pringle, 1992, 1995; Dominelli and Gollins, 1997). Objectifying people is an essential component of the 'othering' processes that facilitate the creation of relations of domination (Memmi, 1965). Social relationships organised in binary pairs in which one part opposes the other, establishes an oppositional othering that constitutes one element as privileged at the expense of the other (Memmi, 1965). 'Othering' processes create an individual or group in a subordinate position and others in subordinate ones by defining them as inferior compared to the dominant one by focusing on 'differences' and categorising these as deficits or less desirable. Treating people as objects dehumanises them, denies their dignity as human beings and makes it easy for people wishing to exercise *power over* them to bypass their rights. Objectifying people also enables violence to be perpetrated upon them (Memmi, 1965). 'Othering' processes occur in the everyday routines of life, often as subtle processes of exclusion that make the person being 'othered' feel unimportant, worthless or as of no social standing (Essed, 1991). These also facilitate the unobtrusive reproduction of inequalities in ordinary encounters between people. 'Othering' processes constitute part of the normality of life, perpetrate injustice and deny people's feelings of belonging.

The Men's Movement

The pro-feminist and anti-feminist positions constitute the polar ends of an amorphous collection of men's responses to feminism in what has been loosely termed the 'men's movement'. The men's movement has developed in the context of and at times largely in reaction to second wave feminism. Early groups began during the late 1960s and early 1970s in North America, Europe, Australia and New Zealand. The men's movement, like the women's movement is not monolithic and a number of different strands have developed within it. These can be characterised as follows: pro-feminist; mythopoetic; spiritual; father's rights; and anti-feminist. The boundaries between them are sometimes blurred. For example, some mythopoetic groups support some feminist initiatives; some father's rights groups are not simply defending men through painful episodes in their lives, but are virulently anti-feminist.

Pro-feminist men's groups like Men Against Sexual Assault in Australia, the Working with Men Collective in England, the National Organisation for Men Against Sexism and Black Men Against Sexism in the United States share feminist aspirations of ending male violence against women and giving men more freedom to develop the nurturing sides of their personalities, including the realisation of their expressive traits by looking after children. They are also interested in the *process* elements within relationships between men and men and women and men.

The mythopoetic men's groups are concerned with finding the 'original' man – the 'wildman' featured in Robert Bly's (1985), *Iron John*. These men use myths and rituals to reconnect men to mythological father figures who have abandoned them for a very long time. In exploring their feelings, they are committed to giving men permission to express the full range of emotions, particularly those indicating their sadness and loss in interpersonal relations with other men, women and children. Grief and loss are addressed in men's interactions with each other. Taking their emotional development seriously and changing men's relationships with children by encouraging a greater involvement with them are characteristics that they have in common with pro-feminist men. However, the end points of their journeys are very different. Mythopoetic men seek 'strong' men who can exist independently and be assertively male. This may or may not involve living in egalitarian relationships with women. Their arguments around the complementarity between men's and women's roles can be used to oppress women as well as free men from unsatisfactory elements in today's dominant forms of masculinity. Mythopoetic groups share with spiritual groups, the sacred rituals of manhood whose continuity is assured by being passed down through the generations by the fathers (Bly, 1985).

The spiritual men's groups are concerned with re-establishing the historical traditions that have nurtured men as a masculine force and whose remit has stemmed from beyond the mortal world. Their activities include searching for ways of linking man with his environment in a respectful manner. Some of the aboriginal men's groups have sought this kind of connection with their ancestors and previous deities as a way of renewing men and their societies after the ravages of colonialism and racism (Bruyere, 2001). Whilst these may not explicitly label themselves pro-feminist, some claim that contempt for women is a European invention and seek to establish less oppressive traditional relationships with women in their own ethnic group, as do, for example, Ashinaabe peoples in Canada (Bruyere, 2001), the Maori in New Zealand (Ruhui, 1998).

More recently in the United States, white men have sought to draw parallels with their aspirations for male renewal through the use of religious based groups, e.g., the Promise Keepers. This is a group of Christian men whose main commitment, expressed through a pledge to honour their responsibilities as men, is one of ensuring that men live up to the best ideals of patriarchy, thus bypassing the feminist agenda and its demands for change in the social relations governing interactions between men and women. Similar comments have been espoused in Louis Farrakhan's 'Million Men March' which attempted to renew African–American men without addressing their relations with African–American women.

The Father's Rights groups include, Families Need Fathers in Britain, and the Coalition for the Preservation of Fatherhood in the United States. These began by being concerned about men as an oppressed group, but looked only at the personal relationships they formed with women and children. Many joining these groups are troubled men with failed marriages or who have lost custody of children through the courts. Some Father's Rights groups are anti-feminist in their orientation. Claiming men are a victimised group because feminist gains have undermined their position, especially in child custody cases and disputes over the splitting of marital assets following divorce, they blame women for social ills currently besetting men (Drakich, 1995; Brooks, 1996). Many of the problems men encounter in the public arena, particularly uncertainty over the employment prospects on which hegemonic masculinity is largely predicated, are a result of economic change. These have altered men's lifestyles including their capacity to act as breadwinners and are not the product of gains by women (Young, 1999). Women are an easily identifiable scapegoat. The elusive capitalist who took his job, and with it a large part of his identity as a man, to another part of the world where workers are more easily exploited and cheaper to hire, is a more difficult target to capture.

Anti-feminist men's groups like the National Coalition of Free Men in the United States, share a woman-blaming agenda with many in the Father's Rights groups, but claim to address a broader range of concerns. They are reluctant to identify themselves too closely with those in Father's Rights groups, although they support individual men in custody and other disputes with their former women partners. These groups divide women into 'bad' women – the feminists and 'good' women, the non-feminists. And, despite their names, these groups welcome as members women who are committed to subverting feminist demands for social change, particularly those aimed at getting rid of unjustifiable gender-based privileges for men.

Exaggerating feminist gains has been a central feature of the anti-feminist men's backlash. Its main objective has been to undermine the few gains that women's struggles for equality have achieved. Especially important in this regard have been: controlling the upbringing of children following divorce; retaining contact with children when child sexual abuse has been disclosed; pursuing women and children when contact has been restricted following physical assaults on them; and controlling women's fertility and reproductive powers. Thus, young women's rights to contraceptive devices, women's unfettered access to abortions, lesbian women's right to access sperm banks and unmarried mother's willingness to raise children without men in the household, have been prime targets of their change agenda (Brooks, 1996).

Other demands raised by men attempting to rollback feminist advances have aimed to regain men's privileged access to well-paid employment opportunities and reassert male power over women and children (Murray, 1990, 1994). In the United States, the country that has promoted affirmative action more than others, these issues, including accessing tertiary level education, are overlain with a racist backlash. White men seek to exclude both white women and black people from two arenas that a racialised public patriarchy had formerly defined as their preserves (Gilder, 1981; Murray, 1990, 1994).

In addition to women-blaming agendas, anti-feminist men's groups are particularly worrying because they are also against governments that implement progressive social policies. They blame governments for supporting women and passing laws aiming to rectify historical injustices including gender and racial oppressions (Drakich, 1995). Social policies and legislation enacting affirmative action have been targeted as objects for reversal. These men oppose equal opportunities programmes on the grounds that these discriminate against white men (Clark *et al.*, 1996).

Complaining that white men can no longer presume the privileged position of not having to compete on an equal basis with white women or black people, they demand a return to private patriarchy by ending public patriarchy. That some white women, e.g., REAL women in Canada, support white men in these claims is not surprising (Steuter, 1995). Some women enjoy holding power within their domestic world and do not wish to see this challenged by feminists who want both men and women working equally in this domain as well as the public one (Schlaffy, 1977). Also, given the awful choices for women in the paid labour market, working at home to care for children and dependent relatives can seem a greater attraction by comparison (Oderkirk and Lochhead, 1995).

Social workers need to be aware of the wide range of positions men hold about feminism and its impact on society as well as understand the complexities of human interactions between men and women. This is because they are often statutorily required to become involved in dispute resolution between men and women or deal with the resultant traumas and aftermath of situations in which men act aggressively. Social workers may find that women seek to escape violent men just at the point that these men try to re-assert control over them. The risks to themselves and the women and children they are helping can range from verbal abuse to physical assaults including murder. Consequently, their interventions have to be handled sensitively, with care and the support of their supervisors and colleagues back in the office (Dominelli, 1991, 1999).

Problematising Masculinity

Feminists have problematised men's identity as men because they exercise *power over* those who have been cast in subordinate positions to them, primarily women and children (Dworkin, 1981). In Western societies, this ordering of social relations enables men to act from privileged positions in which their 'superiority' over women is taken for granted. Although experienced in specific ways by each group of women, this division becomes important in relegating women to the domestic sphere where the nurturing of other people is primarily undertaken whether or not they are waged labourers (Walby, 1990). Meanwhile, men inhabit the public sphere where the allegedly important paid work of the world is done. The goal of equitably sharing the world's work remains to be achieved. Feminists have consistently challenged this division of labour and sought to encourage women into posts in paid employment and holding public office on par with men (Coyle, 1989). They have rejected a division of labour that locks women in the home and insisted that men undertake their fair share of domestic work (Benston, 1969).

Classifying men as the 'gender of oppression' (Hearn, 1987) does not mean that men are not oppressed along other dimensions, particularly those of class and 'race'. Nor does it imply that men do not suffer under a patriarchal system that exploits them too. I (Dominelli, 1986a) document the capacities of Algerian men and women to form loving relationships despite their exploitation by a global capitalist patriarchal system that keeps men working for low wages that are incapable of meeting their families' needs whilst women's energies are absorbed by the unpaid work necessary to cover the gap between the wages men bring home and the resources families need to survive.

If it is inadequate to focus on women as an undifferentiated category; the same holds true for men (Connell, 1995). Some groups of men hold more power than others and this gives them differentiated access to society's power and resources. The most privileged men are white upper-class men who own and control the bulk of the world's resources. According to a United Nations Development Report (UNDP, 1996) a mere 387 men own 45 per cent of the world's wealth. Set within a framework of the dominant discourses of what he terms 'hegemonic masculinity', Connell (1995) terms the diversity amongst men 'masculinities'. Socially created divisions amongst men operate as binary dyads of domination and subordination that set up hierarchies of privilege amongst them, e.g., working-class men are subordinated to middle-class men and black men to white men. (Staples, 1988) Hegemonic masculinity forms the context within which men define themselves as men and focuses on economic man with control over women and children as its particular expression of manhood, establishes man as provider and protector and sets up ideals that are impossible for men to realise because these are predicated on men exercising power over others to maintain control in their own lives (Whitehead, 2000).

However, masculinity is more complex than a framework based on binary opposites suggests. Class and 'race' intersect with each other and other social divisions not in additive but in complex and complicated ways. The category, working-class men, encompasses both black and white men; heterosexual and homosexual men; old and young men; disabled and non-disabled men. The list of intersecting possibilities is endless. An individual man may be black, gay, disabled and young or old. Oppression from all of these attributes would impact upon him simultaneously as he goes about his everyday routines. Forged in the crucible of social interactions, a fluidity in these identities is created by and through their interplay (Modood, 1988; Modood *et al.*, 1994; Dominelli, 1998). Moreover, identity is constantly changing for it is enacted and re-enacted, sometimes in different ways, through social relationships. It is easier to think of the male gender, like the female one, as stratified on a multiplicity of dimensions that complicate interactions amongst men, between men and women, and between men and children. To respond to a given man's needs, a social worker has to conceptualise his situation as one of a whole person with multiple dimensions to his identity and living in a particular social context.

Working with Men

Gender as a socially constructed set of relations between men and women, (Gilmore, 1990) avoids the biologising of these interactions (Walby, 1997). Polarising relationships between men and women in biological terms is unhelpful in an analysis that deems oppression a socially constructed phenomenon that operates in and through social encounters. If the interactive nature of these encounters is not recognised, it becomes easy for individuals to be stereotyped and pathologised on the basis of their biology. This becomes a form of essentialism that becomes a pessimistic way of saying that it is not possible to change people's behaviour in more desirable directions (Eagleton, 1996). For if being a man is *ipso facto* a source of oppression, what can any man do to change his destiny in life, or, why would he be motivated even to think about wanting to change (Pringle, 1995)?

Men have been defined as the 'gender of oppression' (Hearn, 1987) and feminists would accede that men's actions have caused women woe at both personal and institutional levels. For this reason, radical feminists refuse to work with men and argue that men's violent natures make them unfit to act as practitioners working with women and children (Echols, 1989). Socialist feminists have taken issue with this view, claiming that whilst patriarchy is a cause of gender oppression, particularly as it applies to women, men do not escape its enslavement. Patriarchal relations damage both men and women – stunting men's emotional growth and oppressing women (Dominelli and McLeod, 1989). In addition, socialist feminists maintain that men, like women, suffer from the exploitation of their waged labour under the capitalist system. Men's privileges come with a price-tag attached, but in their role as practitioners in social work, men have to take account of the privileges and disadvantages that come with their gender (Pringle, 1992, 1995).

Feminists and men who are feminist sympathisers have seldom spoken in detail about how and under what conditions women should work with men. Leonard and McLeod (1980) reveal that social workers ignore men in cases of domestic violence, but argue that men need therapeutic intervention if their behaviour is to alter. In one of the early feminist writings on the subject, I (Dominelli, 1981) describe a men's group that I organised in the hopes of getting men to stop beating women partners. Bowl (1985) maintains that men should use feminist insights to improve their social work skills and play a greater role in developing the profession's progressive interventions. Dominelli and McLeod (1989) suggest that men have more to gain than lose in eliminating patriarchal relations and ending their oppression of women. I (Dominelli, 1991) consider the complexities of women working with men sex offenders and highlight difficulties that can arise. Later, Cavanagh and Cree (1995) edited a collection of articles that focus on using a feminist perspective to work with a range of men 'clients'. Their accounts include violent men, but also men who experience loss and marital problems of a non-violent nature. Jim Wild (1999) has followed a similar tack in providing examples of how to work with men according to feminist principles.

Problematising masculinity from a social work intervention perspective is undertaken by Glaser and Frosh (1988); Box (1987); Pringle (1992, 1995) and O'Hagan and Dillenburger (1995). Writing from related disciplines – criminology and social policy, they ask whether men as the group primarily responsible for abusing women and children, should as a category, be entrusted to do social work. Glaser and Frosh (1988) and Box (1987) are especially concerned that men should not automatically assume that they are fit to undertake work with victim–survivors of men's assaults. The extensive uncovering of male paedophile rings in residential establishments for children has raised questions about children's safety in the care of men. Pringle (1992, 1995) explores this issue at length and concludes that under certain circumstances, men should be allowed to practise social work with vulnerable groups. He suggests that there should be built-in safeguards for the women and children with whom they work. Joint working involving both men and women colleagues is posited as one way of addressing this issue.

I (Dominelli, 1989, 1991, 1999) am somewhat more circumspect. Although I do not think that men should be barred from social work practice just because they are men, I suggest that 'fitness to practice' tests should be passed by all those wishing to enter the profession, particularly if they wish to work with vulnerable people. All practitioners, including women, should pass the 'fitness for the profession test' as part of a life-long education and training experience. I (Dominelli, 1989) am fairly specific in my recommendations for realising this in practice in work with male sex offenders. I argue that in cases of child sexual abuse with a man the alleged perpetrator, it is *in*appropriate for a male worker to interview a child immediately after disclosure. I suggest that this is conducted by a woman although a man social worker might become involved later when the child's confidence in men has been built up again.

Whilst I endorse custodial sentences for such offenders (Dominelli, 1989), unlike Nelson (1982), I question the use of traditional imprisonment as the way forward. Instead, I recommend the building of special establishments for the incarceration of sex offenders because traditional prisons simply replicate power relations of dominance that they have to unlearn. In these alternative institutions, men would focus on rehabilitation and altering their behaviour so that it sustains egalitarian relations rather than exploiting those who hold less power than they. I suggest that their period of containment lasts until victim–survivors of men's assaults acting as adjudicators have the men demonstrate the capacity to interact appropriately with women. For women, an adjudicator would be a woman victim–survivor who has dealt with the trauma of her own assault. Sitting on the management committee of such establishments, she would pass judgment on convicted offenders, but not the one who has attacked her. Her role would be to assess whether a given offender's behaviour had reached acceptable norms of conduct (Dominelli, 1989). And, she would incorporate a victim's perspectives into her deliberations.

I am also sceptical about gender-based joint working teams as practised in probation settings (Dominelli, 1991, 1999). Women probation officers co-working in groups with sex offenders can occupy tokenistic positions that collude with sexism. In these teams, men offenders often challenge women officers and look to men officers to validate whatever the woman probation officer says. Additionally, women probation officers are penalised for not working with such offenders (Dominelli, 1991, 1999). Although this contravenes equal opportunities policies, a number of women I interviewed claimed they were unable to decline such work because if they did, they would be condemned as ineffective probation officers and jeopardise their chances of promotion. Yet, the reasons women had for not undertaking this work had little to do with their abilities to carry out a probation officer's duties. Some simply did not wish to relive the traumas of their own previous or current sexual abuse or domestic assault every time they dealt with a violent offender. But such information is extremely sensitive and they did not wish everyone in the office to be privy to it, even under conditions of confidentiality.

The Relevance of Feminist Social Work Theory to Working with Men

Dominelli and McLeod (1989) suggest that feminist social work began not in statutory settings, but in communities through social action and moved from there into academic and statutory social work when women involved in such activities changed employment and sought to transform policy and practice in their new workplaces. Since then, the numbers of men and women involved in theorising gender relations in statutory settings, developing feminist oriented forms of practice, and teaching feminist social work have expanded. Now, there are feminist principles and guidelines that can assist practitioners to theorise and practice in accordance with anti-sexist pro-feminist principles relevant to men (see Hearn, 1987; Pringle, 1992, 1995; Wild, 1999).

Social work as a profession is well placed to work with men in anti-sexist or pro-feminist ways. To begin with, social workers are obliged to work with whomever asks for their services. Its value orientation endorses self-determination, respect for the person, and non-judgmentalness (Biesteck, 1961). These values are useful when working with men. Finally, social work's goal of changing individual behaviour equips practitioners to tackle a theme that feminists have identified as necessary in achieving it: redefining masculinity. To initiate behavioural changes that support the well-being of women and children, social work's values and goals have to be linked to feminist principles of practice. Improving the well-being of women and children will also enhance men's.

Anti-sexist approaches and feminism have both overlaps and crucial differences between them. Feminism has traditionally been an activity in which women engage as a result of their experiences as women and desire to challenge inegalitarian relations that privilege men in the hopes of introducing a new world order in which women have a full place in the sun. Anti-sexism is something that both men and women can engage in. It usually means questioning women's subordinate role in society, but the focus of change is men's interactions with either women or other men rather than transforming society for women. Less ambitious in scope than feminism, it is more concerned with introducing micro-level changes through interpersonal interactions without worrying about macro-level ones.

A key issue in working in anti-sexist ways is the commitment not to impose gender stereotypes on either men or women and thereby limit their scope to experience the entire range of emotional experiences and work opportunities (Phillips, 1993). Social workers committed to anti-sexist practice seek solutions that enable women to transcend the limitations imposed by simply being deemed mothers who look after their children, and men as fathers who provide economic support for their offspring. Practitioners working with men and women to resolve 'family' problems no longer consider women solely in their nurturing roles nor men primarily as breadwinners.

Anti-sexist approaches enable social workers to engage men in caring tasks and suggest that women consider avenues of fulfilment other than 24-hour child or elder care. Social workers can support women who wish to leave their partners, if they are violent or find resources and networks that will meet their needs as independent women whether or not they retain links with their families and children. A major danger in undertaking anti-sexist work is the ease with which men and women social workers can collude with the dominant relations endorsing patriarchy without being aware of doing so because taken-for-granted assumptions about appropriate roles for men and women run deep.

Feminism is not against men's well-being, but it is firmly against sexism and privileging men's welfare over women's. This includes privileges emanating from practices that: endorse the preferential treatment of men over women on sexist grounds in any arena; give preference to boy children over girls; require women to subordinate their needs to those of the men in their lives; and exert unilateral forms of control over women's sexual and reproductive capacities. Social workers cannot support a sexist *status quo* be anti-sexist, feminist, pro-feminist or woman-centered. Feminist social workers would address questions of which interventions best ensure the well-being of women, men and children. Instead of conceptualising women's welfare as being gained at the expense of men or children or vice versa, they think of how to end gender oppression and affirm the well-being of all as an outcome of the process of empowering women.

Achieving this goal requires new forms of interaction across gender divides. These are rooted in egalitarian principles so that the liberation of one group of people is not gained at the expense of another. Cognizance has to be taken of other social divisions interacting and intersecting with gender at any one time. The multiple dimensions of a person's identity, including those in the social worker's own personality have to be examined, for these interact with the 'client's'. Taking account of the complex dynamics involved in therapeutic relationships is an essential element of a practice that engages with diversity.

Gendered Social Relations in Social Work

Gender dynamics impact upon three key social work relationships. These occur between: workers and 'clients'; working colleagues; and employees and their employers. Gender relations are significant in all these relationships and not only when involving members of the opposite gender. As shown below, in worker–'client' relationships, gender dynamics are relevant when men practitioners work with women, women practitioners work with men, men practitioners work with men, and women practitioners work with women.

In social work, women and men often work in the same teams, making it imperative to explore and understand gendered dynamics. For a team to successfully meet anti-sexist aspirations consistent with feminism, each individual member has to be committed to working in egalitarian directions. Each person has to be aware that team members cannot work effectively together unless there is mutual respect and shared goals operating amongst them. Teams can be an important source of affirmation when they work well (Payne, 2000). If they do not, women will become isolated and find that their team is little more than a collection of individuals occupying the same building space.

Until recently, gender relations have featured less openly in statutory social services settings. A numerical preponderance of women coupled with the assumption that women cannot engage in gendered power dynamics with each other have induced a laissez-faire attitude of gender indifference to the subject (Dominelli, 1991a). In it, sexism is not deemed an issue because women dominate at practitioner and user levels (Dominelli, 1992). By focusing only on personal relationships, this construction of the problem ignores the roles that internalised sexism, institutionalised sexism and systematised patriarchal relations play in contextualising practice and shaping the experiences and expectations of men and women, whether as workers or clientele (Dominelli, 1991a). It also fails to acknowledge how women contribute to the subsequent reproduction of sexist relations through their work. For example, women socialise children into gendered views of the world that endorse the superiority of boys over girls from childhood to adulthood (Belotti, 1975). Ignoring gendered relations hinders anti-sexist development by relegating sexism to the back burner. Feminist social workers' insistence that sexism is not restricted to personal interactions between men and women, or even women and women, but has institutional and cultural contexts has shifted some resistance emanating from a gender blind approach.

Women interacting with other women may generate unhelpful dynamics by assuming that being an oppressed group precludes their acting oppressively towards others. Whilst women share experiences of oppression as women with other women, this does not mean that these are similar. Although being oppressed along gender lines may provide a basis for empathetic understandings with one another, this reaction does not follow automatically. Women can still oppress other women along a range of social divisions, including 'race' and class. This occurs, for example, when a white middle-class woman practitioner first meets a black middle-class women social worker in their agency and assumes that she is a cleaner. This reaction reveals the racist assumption that black women are *in*capable of performing high status work.

The internalisation of the sexism implicit in hegemonic social relations between men and women may result in women practitioners colluding with sexist assumptions held by male 'clients'. A woman social worker may relate to a man on a stereotypical basis if she is not aware of gendered power. Moreover, in their relationships with men 'clients', women practitioners should not think of power as existing only along gender lines. Social workers can impose *power over* relations on men 'clients' along other social divisions such as 'race' and class. Additionally, there are the statutory powers with which social workers are endowed. The multifacted dimensions from which power emanates precludes easy solutions to gendered problems. For instance, a social worker doing an assessment of a disabled male elder by talking over his head to his carer or acting as if he were absent by referring to his wife when making a community care assessment, exemplifies *power over* relations embodied in disablism, reinforced by statutory powers associated with the job.

Gender dynamics can work against women social workers despite the status attached to their position because bureaucratic forms of power have been developed with men in mind. These can be used to extract women's compliance with organisational policies and goals that they find objectionable. Gendered relations are evident when women managers hold managerial powers over men employees. Although formal authority remains with women managers, their position can be tenuous, particularly when they are dealing with men colleagues who make a presumption of incapacity regarding their skills to manage (Grimwood and Poppleston, 1993; Dominelli, 1997). Women managers may also be outmanoeuvred in their relationships with male managerial colleagues and have to form specific support networks, e.g., Women in Management Groups, to facilitate encounters with those who are unsupportive of their plans. Yet, women managers have access to power and resources not available to main grade workers whether men or women.

In 'client'–worker relationships involving men only, the worker's commitment to anti-sexist and non-sexist relations is crucial in avoiding collusiveness with men who disparage women (Dominelli, 1999). The question of collusion is likely to arise in work with offenders where men form the majority amongst both worker and 'client' groups. Feminist pressure for action against such dynamics in the areas of physical and sexual violence has encouraged men probation officers to acquire experience in anti-sexist work with violent offenders (Cavanagh and Cree, 1995). Moreover, feminist demands for equality in the workplace and the identification of gender as an issue in working with women offenders have resulted in equal opportunities policies becoming commonplace in the probation system (Gelsthorpe, 1989). Their effectiveness in improving working relations for black and white women and black men is another question (Cook and Hudson, 1993). However, as this topic is explored in Chapter seven, I will only highlight it here. Holistic approaches endorsed by feminist social workers can improve situations for women living with violent men as the scenario below indicates:

Case Study

Harold, a 34 year-old white miner, was married to Sue, aged 30. They had 3 children – James aged 8, Alice aged 6, and Timothy aged 4. Harold and Sue had been childhood sweethearts and both had wanted Sue to stay home with the children.

Their relationship had flourished until two years ago when Harold was made redundant and became unable to find alternative employment. After the first year, Harold's meagre redundancy pay and unemployment insurance payments ran out and the family applied for income support. Harold became extremely depressed and began to have violent mood swings. Sue hated having him around the house. They began to have endless rows about the most trivial things.

Harold desperately wanted a job, but ads in the local paper and Job Centre were mainly for part-time work which did not interest him – clerical work, cleaning and so on. Sue, who read the adverts with him decided these were jobs she could do. Against Harold's wishes, she successfully applied for and obtained a full-time secretarial job in a local factory.

Harold was furious with this outcome and refused to help her manage what he considered her other more important responsibilities so that she could take up the offer. Undeterred, Sue asked her mother who lived nearby to help look after the children while she worked. As the 3 children attended either classes or nursery school during the day, Sue took them to school in the mornings; her mother picked them up and took them home at the end of the day. The children did not object to the arrangement as they enjoyed going to Grandma's and already saw it as their second home.

For things to run smoothly, Sue had to ensure that Harold's lunch was prepared before she went to work. When she returned in the evening, she had to make dinner for all of them, help James with his homework, and do some housekeeping including the laundry and ironing. Her weekends were full of catching up on sundry domestic chores.

After six months, Sue was exhausted. She decided to talk to Harold with the aim of getting him to share the load. Harold reacted by shouting at her, overturned a table and slammed the door on his way out of the house. Sue who was shaken but determined, felt that although she would do what needed to be done with the children, she would leave Harold to fend for himself. No more lunches prepared for him, no more laundry, no more cleaning up after him. Harold responded by becoming verbaly abusive.

A few weeks later, Sue started working overtime. The children stayed with her mother during her late shifts. On one of these occasions, when she got home, the house was a tip and there was nothing to eat in the fridge. Sue blew her top. In the argument that followed, Harold grabbed her by the hair and began to punch her. Sue was hospitalised for two weeks by this attack. Although she would not press charges against him, she demanded a divorce. Harold refused and begged her to take him back. Sue would not change her mind.

Meanwhile, James started acting out at school. He was caught fighting with a younger boy. Apparently, James had been bullying him for several months. As a result of these incidents, a social worker was assigned to work with the family.

The social worker, a white woman called Sal came to visit Sue. Sue told her about the ongoing divorce proceedings that she was reluctantly going through not because she no longer loved Harold, but because she was afraid that he would become more violent over time and would make life unbearable for her and the children. Sal listened to Sue's story and sympathised over the difficulties she was having.

Given the range of problems the family was experiencing, she regretted that she would have time only to work with James, hoping to teach him how to resolve conflict in a non-aggressive manner. However, she gave Sue a list of women's groups that she could join. 'They may be able to help', Sal added as she got up to go, satisfied that as Harold was no longer in the house, none of the 3 children were 'at risk' of being abused by him.

As soon as Sal left, Sue crumpled up the list and threw it in the bin. Tears began to stream down her face as her despair and frustration welled up through them.

The social worker's intervention in this case was driven by: economic considerations expressed in terms of the time that Sal could spend with this 'family'; child protection issues; and the fragmentation of Sue's situation into discrete and separately manageable parts. Except to sympathise with the range of issues to be addressed, there was no attempt to respond to Sue's needs in a holistic way. Nor were gender issues considered.

The outcome reached in this case was not that of a heartless or incompetent social worker. Rather, it was the result of a particular construction of social work intervention – one that was guided by agency exigencies rather than 'client' needs. So, Sue received a minimalist, bureaucratic response aimed at discharging the agency's statutory obligations with little regard for her well-being. Agency exigencies constitute what Bourdieu and Wacquant (1992) consider professional constructions influencing practitioners' practice.

A feminist social worker would have taken a holistic view of Sue's position and attempted to support her on a number of different levels, although she may have drawn on others, or worked in alliance with various groups to do so. She would also ensure that the needs of all members of the family were identified and addressed, even if by other caring professionals. Clearly, Sue had a number of unresolved issues concerning her relationship with Harold. Both hegemonic masculinity and femininity are problematic in this case. Harold has rigid views of his role in the household and needs assistance in coming to terms with the loss of a self-concept that had been effective for him as long as he was the family breadwinner and Sue went along with him.

Even if Sue persists with the divorce proceedings, Harold will have to change as a person to take account of the new economic realities confronting him as a white working-class man whose job skills are no longer in demand. And, he will have to change his behaviour and attitudes if his encounters with Sue over the care of the children are not to become another battleground, an eventuality that could complicate the children's relationships with both parents following a divorce settlement. He would also have to change if he is to form new relationships with other women and not replicate the same unacceptable patterns of behaviour that he has demonstrated with Sue. Finding a way of talking to Harold and getting him to accept the need to re-evaluate his role and position in life would be an important part of the work that is done with Sue. Helping Harold access resources such as those made available through the *Working with Men Collective* or assigning a pro-feminist male practitioner to work with him could be a way forward.

Without external intervention and support in admitting that his behaviour is unacceptable, Harold is unlikely to refer himself to men's self-help groups, even if he were to know of their existence. But, as we have seen, social services has a remit that centres primarily around addressing the children's direct interests. Thus, they are unlikely to respond to Harold's need to reassess his life and re-orient it in more appropriate directions. His current course scarcely meets his requirements let alone those of others important to him.

Harold's situation highlights the gaps in the services available to either help men or support women living with violent men. The probation service is not involved as Sue has decided not to press charges, so Harold cannot access the services developed for violent men who have been sentenced. Neither would the lawyer processing the divorce get involved in this dimension of the work. Referral to mediation, if this were to happen, would focus on his interactions with Sue in relation to the welfare of the children. But it would not engage him in having a fundamental rethink about his role as a man. Developing the necessary facilities requires institutional including legislative changes and a redefinition of masculinity – a step that also requires attitudinal and cultural changes in society at large. As part of their work, feminist social workers could advocate for such changes in alliances with others rather than undertake these activities directly themselves.

The expectation that women will pick up the pieces to provide financially for the family and undertake domestic labour to meet family requirements are evident in the demands made of Sue and her mother. Advocating changes in the cultural expectations in which these are embedded is also something to which feminist social workers can contribute. Additionally, a feminist social worker would respond to Sue's immediate needs as she defines them. Likely to be included amongst these are feelings of emotional loss and abandonment by her former partner following the loss of a relationship she had once enjoyed and neglect by a system unconcerned about her lack of resources and needs as a woman as it relates to her only in her capacity as a 'fit' mother.

Central in responding to these would be helping Sue receive individual counselling, join women's groups and engage with a range of support networks. Addressing the issue of inadequate material support to meet the physical needs of the family including those of getting child care and household tasks accomplished whilst Sue works is also crucial. Providing Sue with the space to take a break, have a rest and plan for the future would be part of this. So is talking to Sue's mother to check that she is being given some choice about Sue's expectation that she contributes to hers and the children's well-being and copes with the demands being made of her.

The needs of each child would have to be considered and addressed in their own right. James' socialisation as a little boy drawing on the tools of hegemonic masculinity to deal with the problems he encounters would have be tackled, but not in the instrumentalist way that the social worker intervening in this case is doing. A deeper and more nurturing vision of manhood and role models for achieving this in practice are also important (Wild, 1999). This necessitates changes in hegemonic cultural expectations about men and have to be dealt with at that level. The school has to be involved in propagating this vision amongst school children more generally. The children's emotional needs also have to be addressed. These include the separation of their parents and the hostile atmosphere that pervades their home (Hester *et al.*, 2000). Furthermore, the care of children has to be reconceptualised as a community concern so that alternative support services can be made available to parents and children who want them (Dominelli, 1999).

Finally, a feminist social worker would work to develop unstigmatised, universally available services accessible by those requiring them at the point of need. Early stage intervention or preventative services could have been used to support Sue before crisis point was reached. The purpose of doing so would be to bring resources to the attention of people who need them or identify those that might have to be developed. For example, had

Harold been able to use counselling facilities immediately after losing his job, he could have been helped to deal with his new position more effectively and with less damaging consequences to Sue, the children and himself. In working with women within family settings, feminist social workers have to act in holistic ways at the personal, institutional and cultural levels to ensure that the supports capable of sustaining the well-being of men, women and children are there to be drawn upon when required.

Conclusions

The family, as a contested patriarchal site cannot be assumed safe for children, women and men. Social workers focusing on men as breadwinners and women as mothers use a range of interventions that enforce patriarchal views. In working in this way, the father's role is ignored except in its economic ramifications. Women and men have created more complex relationships that social workers need to understand.

The principles of solidarity and social worker's legal remit suggest that feminist theoretical formulations and principles of practice ought to include men, albeit on a different, though not unequal basis, to women. Whilst allowing for this opportunity, the space for women to work with women must remain protected. This is to facilitate women's growth as women and enable them to establish their own agendas for change.

Working with men requires a reconceptualisation of masculinity in accordance with feminist insights and a holistic approach to men and the relationships in which they engage. Men's emotional needs, have to be brought centrally into the equation. Moreover, the social positions of both men and women as they are currently defined have to change. Problematising masculinity has been an important feminist contribution that has prompted a reconsideration of men's roles in society and redefinition of their relationships with women and children. Progress in this arena also requires a reformulation of men's relationships with other men (Whitehead, 2000). Securing changes in all these directions means that women and men have to work to support each other's emancipatory endeavours. To facilitate this, feminist social workers have to dialogue with men social workers to identify areas in which women can work with men and those that men are solely responsible for addressing. Men social workers will also have to reconsider the nature of the relationships to be established between men social workers and men 'clients' if feminist principles are to be upheld (Pringle, 1993, 1995).

5

Working with Children and Families

The bulk of social work practice occurs within family settings where interventions proceed as if the relationships that occur within them are unproblematic. But the family has re-emerged as a highly contested political institution and a key instrument of social policy. 'The family' is central to struggles over redefining families and women's roles within them as feminists argue for diversity and forms that meet women's aspirations whilst moralists and religious fundamentalists across the globe demand a return to patriarchal arrangements. The vociferous voices of patriarchal moralists have regendered women in neo-traditional ways to reassert their responsibility for ensuring that family life proceeds in accordance with patriarchal injunctions and retains its status as a safe haven. Alongside these developments is a conservative men's critique that castigates feminists for exposing the family as a source of oppression for women and children (Clark *et al.*, 1996; Brooks, 1996). The orthodoxies they proclaim fly in the face of evidence that indicates women endure gender-based hardships across cultural domains (Basu, 1997).

Conservative men have taken the initiative in dismantling feminist gains in women's reproductive rights, sexuality and determination to assume educational opportunities and paid employment on par with men. Issues around reproductive control particularly the accessibility of contraceptive devices and abortions, have been catapulted into the limelight with devastating consequences. Their attack has: undermined the ideological acceptability of women's reproductive choices in the former Eastern Europe with its previous relative ease of access in these areas providing that the necessary resourcing was available; led to clawbacks in publicly funded services in the industrialised West with an overabundance of material resources inadequately distributed; and subjugated women's needs to national priorities in industrialising countries where women's right to choose family size, receive health care during pregnancy and its aftermath are restricted by poverty and saving national resources to pay foreign debt (Basu, 1997).

105

Popular discourses about 'the family' portray it as essentially unproblematic. But, the prevalence of physical and sexual violence in the family indicates that the safety of its members cannot be presumed. Feminists have exposed the family's failure to care adequately for substantial numbers of children, particularly those that have been physically and sexually abused. These revelations have become a basis for rightwing attacks on their integrity. The myth that the family is automatically the best place for children has been hard to challenge effectively. For although feminists have succeeded in making physical and sexual violence issues of public concern, the solutions that have been accepted by the public have been conventional private ones.

An examination of the realities of women's and children's lives reveals complexities and burdensome tensions for women to manage in order to find time and resources for themselves and children. The narrow focus of Western social policy on nuclear family relations have denied different family forms public support and devalued women's skills in accessing a richness of social relationships that are based on friendship, community and extended kinship networks by assuming that these are self-sufficient sources of assistance. Some social policy directives, e.g., those pertaining to single parent women on welfare have trivialised this family form, and the stringent criteria applied for family reunions for recently arrived 'immigrant' women, suggest that the right to engage in family relationships does not apply to them (Dominelli, 1991).

Child welfare work has to be reconceptualised to emphasise the positive promotion of well-being through preventative strategies rather than focus as it does primarily on issues of child protection with their surveillance of women's mothering skills (Swift, 1995). This would mean moving away from concerns about the ability of the 'client' to mother the child(ren) according to dominant definitions of the task, and social workers to mother the mother, whilst neglecting the lack of social resources available to help them fulfill an important social role – motherhood, to situating women and children within their social context and seeing social problems as involving individual responses to constraints and opportunities. Women's potential to promote individual well-being has to be supported as part of an interaction between personal responsibility and life-sustaining social conditions. Also necessary in advancing this project is rethinking fatherhood to affirm men's parenting capacities. Developing this aspect of men's lives requires positive interventions in both workplace relations and public policies. Care is also required to ensure that men's rights are not upheld at the expense of women and children.

To progress child welfare in a substantive manner, communities need to take responsibility for children so that they are not considered the private property of their parents and are accorded rights in their own name. In this, from the day they are born, children's self-realisation becomes a priority and their dependency on adults should be construed as a responsibility for their physical, intellectual and emotional care throughout their development. Children's rights in this framework are not something that are *given* to them at specifically defined arbitrary points as they grow into adults. Rather, they have inalienable rights whose successful realisation is the responsibility of all adults within their communities, not just their parents. Lee Maracle, a First Nations woman, defines this responsibility as follows:

> Look around you ... See these children ... Pay attention to them. Life is precious – short. You are all visitors. These children are your guests. You own nothing but your kindness to them (Maracle, 1993, p. 20).

This chapter examines how social workers intervene in family settings to facilitate behaviour that affirms dominant ideologies about families whether or not they apply in specific cases. This approach has not always favoured women and so I also consider how feminist insights can be used to counter their deleterious effects on women's well-being. I suggest that feminist scholarship and practice have much to offer social work practice. None the less, a feminist approach to working with women, children and their wider families has yet to become firmly embedded in the profession.

Patriarchal Families

Patriarchal relations between men and women figure largely in family settings in most countries today, although they are differently expressed depending on local cultural traditions, ethnicities and other factors. 'The family' in the West has traditionally been defined as the white heterosexual nuclear family with an economically dependent wife and breadwinner husband (Eichler, 1983). This view has been challenged by feminists seeking egalitarian relations between men and women (Segal, 1983) and recognition of diverse family forms because traditional approaches have ignored the existence of a range of familial relationships. These have included: extended families endorsed by 'black' people (Bryant *et al.*, 1985; Collins, 1991), white working-class people (hooks, 2000); single parent families headed by either women or men (Glendinning and Millar, 1992; Basu, 1997); families with parents of the same gender (Arnup, 1995); and lone parent families at the younger and older end of the age spectrum (Browne, 1995).

Recent incorporations of religious discourses into debates about families have further complicated the arguments. This phenomenon is fairly widespread as fundamentalists in the world's major religions use cultural and traditional teachings to uphold male supremacy in their attack upon feminists questioning the rule of men within what was formerly considered the private arena and their domain to govern. The attempts of Fathers' Rights Groups in Canada, England and the United States to clawback paternal control over women and children have to be probed in this context (Drakich, 1995).

The undermining of feminist points of view has to be understood as part of the struggle to prevent women who have not begun to question the allegedly 'natural' patriarchal order of things from doing so. Hence, it represents a desire to limit the spread of feminism as much as one seeking to destroy the convictions of those who have already accepted its precepts. Despite an acknowledgment of the considerable variety and the cultural specificities of family forms, the arguments over an acceptable definition of the family during the United Nations Social Development Summit in Copenhagen in 1995, indicates that the struggle over the concept is about both an ideology as ideas and practices that govern relationships between men and women in intimate interactions with each other. Discourses over the governance of social relations between men and women, particularly through heterosexual encounters, have prompted the expression of homophobic views that subject lesbian women and gay men to attacks that exclude their opinions about their rights to family life from influencing public discussions (Arnup, 1995).

Conservative retrenchment in this area has not gone unchallenged. The organisation of rightwing proponents of stereotypical family forms has encouraged feminist organisations to advocate alternatives, e.g., Women Against Fundamentalism. Black people have demanded recognition of the legitimacy of extended family forms (Bryant *et al.*, 1985). Leftwingers like the Pro-Family Left in the United States have supported a diversity of family arrangements in the social policy arena. The endorsement of state support for families advocated by leftwing groups represents a version of public patriarchy that does not sit well with rightwing groups determined to re-establish the family as a private patriarchal domain. Gay and lesbian couples in the United States and Canada have gained some recognition for their family forms. However, state recognition of their challenge to hegemonic familialism has been tempered by their being governed by heterosexual norms including that of avoiding financial responsibility for individuals' welfare. Thus, gay and lesbian families like other family forms, have financial dependency foisted upon them through social policies.

Additionally, the attempts of pro-feminist men to engage more fully in child care arrangements and sharing in housework cannot go unremarked. Although more men are undertaking domestic tasks, women continue to bear the bulk of these responsibilities (Walby, 1990). Women spend more time doing them and are more fully involved in undertaking the more mundane day-to-day aspects of domestic work whilst men take over the 'fun' parts (La Rossa, 1995). Retaining some scepticism over the extent to which the 'new' man is a figment of cultural images rather than a reality reflected in the daily conduct of men is advisable (La Rossa, 1995). To engage men fully with the tasks of reproducing themselves and their families on a daily (never mind a generational basis) requires major transformations in the organisation of paid and unpaid work, the family and gender relations between men and women. And, there will have to be widespread attitudinal changes with regards to the place of children in society. Western nations are currently a long way from setting these objectives as goals.

The family in its various guises has provided a remarkably stable way of organising intimate social relationships to ensure the care of children and dependent relatives. Cries lamenting its breakdown or dethronement have existed alongside this continuity. Demands for the reinstatement of 'the family' as the basic unit of society have attracted state support for 'the family' in a number of Western countries that lack formal family policies. This support is often classist and racist (Dominelli, 1991). Poor white and black women may find their rights to family life observed more in their denial than realisation (Sidel, 1986). Poor women on welfare, especially lone mothers, have been subjected to increased surveillance of their mothering skills and compelled to leave their children to enter the paid workforce at low rates of pay. This has usually meant leaving children in the hands of lowly paid or unpaid childminders who may or may not be able to stimulate children's overall development, given that child care often has to be fitted in between a number of other caring commitments and domestic chores. Poor women's options have rarely extended to costly high quality care that middle-class women with a greater command of financial resources can purchase (Glendinning and Millar, 1992).

Additionally, women from low income countries have been drawn into this equation, particularly in Canada and the United States where they provide the bulk of domestic workers, often as live-in help. Domestic workers are usually black women who receive an appalling deal for they are subjected to controls regarding their workplace, immigration status and citizenship that tend to deprive them of employment rights, settlement rights, access to welfare services, entitlement to welfare benefits and family life (Daenzer, 1993). Their experiences are classist, racialised and gendered. They are expected to undertake housework and child care duties on a regular basis and may be exploited sexually by male employers and financially through the payment of low wages. The state plays a key role in enforcing conditions of oppression in their situations by blurring the boundary between the private sphere of the home and the public realm of work. This is achieved by treating domestic workers as non-workers with regards to employment rights and as housekeepers when it comes to having leisure time (Daenzer, 1993).

White women employers can oppress black women domestic workers by demanding they are on call 24 hours a day when they rarely pay them for such services. They are likely to engage in surveillance of their private affairs and leave them with little spare time, privacy or family rights of their own (see Silvera, 1983; Arat-Koc, 1995; Daenzer, 1993). A contradiction lies at the heart of these caring relationships when women in waged work employ them. One group of women is using another to provide the space for undertaking paid employment. Their relationship is structurally exploitative as women whose own financial resources are limited and often insufficient for her own family's needs, cannot afford to pay other women high wages. Dual income families are increasingly required to sustain decent standards of living and to keep families out of poverty (Young, 1999).

These women are also interdependent. Poor working-class women need the money accrued by working for middle-class women to raise their families on (usually) a subsistence basis. Middle-class women need jobs to provide for their children. The lack of social policies that either socialise or subsidise domestic caring labour, particularly elder care and child care, add to the burden that individual women have to bear in squaring the endless circle of demands made of them. Inadequate provisions compel women to solve social problems through personal relationships, pit women against women, and affirm domestic labour as 'women's work'.

Middle-class women can achieve some modicum of independent existence and individual fulfilment because they can employ other women, usually white or black working-class women (Daenzer, 1993) to do chores that are traditionally considered theirs. Women are not responsible for the structural contradictions within which they shape their lives. The social construction of these situations, virtual exclusion of men from the domestic arena, and individualising of the problem of women's access to social resources including child care, alongside the expectation that women personally resolve the deleterious repercussions of their position, are key issues to be resolved. The framework in which women lead their lives and constrains their options within untenable arrangements unless women organise collectively to challenge it, also needs changing.

Contested Families

Families occupy contested terrains in which there are many competing and conflicting interests over structure and function. The implicit gendering of the domestic division of labour results in women being expected to take whatever the state and public throw at them. Women's interests as women in family settings receive short shrift. Despite their varied and disputed nature, the media portrays families in the West in fairly stereotypical ways.

Feminist thoughts on the subject have become controversial for questioning and redefining it in non-traditional ways. Objections to rethinking families and women's roles in them have permeated academic discourses and contributed to the backlash against challenges to the merits and demerits of traditional families for women.

In child welfare work, the framing of problems to prioritise children's interests over and against women's pose difficulties for feminist social workers committed to the liberation of women and non-oppression of children. For some feminists, working with families epitomises the intractability of these dilemmas. Sue Wise (1985), for instance, claims that statutory work with women and children from a feminist perspective is practically impossible because the rights and interests of women can be easily pitted against children's. Eileen McLeod and I (Dominelli and McLeod, 1989) argue that this need not be so. Yet, working according to feminist principles in this arena is complicated by the contexts in which social work is located. These include state policies around the family and broader debates about the role and place of women in society (Dominelli, 1988).

Social policies have often been formulated to further the classical paradigm of the traditional white nuclear family, regulate women and treat those not conforming with it as deviant (Eichler, 1983). Women who do not comply with its familialist norms have been pathologised and personally blamed for society's failure to take seriously its obligations to children. Policymakers and practitioners have responded to such women by castigating them for operating outside this framework and required that they be taught to comply with familialist expectations or be punished severely for their transgressions. Social workers have played key roles in reinforcing this ideology, enacted in practice through pathologising individual women. Moralising and ostracising have been twin strategies for attacking deviant women.

Recently, Western social policy directives pertaining to single parent women on welfare, have imposed caring responsibilities upon them, offered training to make poor working-class women better mothers by improving their parenting skills or providing education to inculcate moral virtues in unmarried mothers (Sidel, 1986; Kelsey, 1997; Zucchino, 1997; Blair, 1999). Similar approaches have marked state responses to mothers in prison (Faith, 1993). Social workers have been instrumental in reproducing patterns of censure inherent in these discourses, particularly regarding women's roles as mothers and carers.

Workfare, or the policy of compelling mothers on welfare into waged work (Blair, 1999) has altered the relationship between the state and women as mothers and carers. Women are now expected to accord primacy to becoming self-sufficient whilst fulfilling caring responsibilities by personally making arrangements, presumably with other women, to have children adequately looked after. Thus, women's demands for equality in the labour market have intersected with social expectations about women's caring roles as not being publicly supported. This definition of women's lives is likely to have its most deleterious impact on poor women and children who lack finances to buy social resources that ease the contradictory demands this framing of their social roles imposes upon them.

The expectation that poor women will go out to work also characterises responses to recently arrived 'immigrant' women domestic workers in Western, Middle-Eastern or Asian countries who are required to live without families, extended or nuclear (Williams, 1998). Social policies and immigration rules promulgated to govern their presence suggest that the right to engage in traditional family relationships does not apply to them. National preoccupations and the narrow focus of social policies on the nuclear family, deny various groupings of women the right to define family relationships in ways that either meet their changing situations or support them in developing new alternatives. Such policies also confirm women's roles as isolated carers unable to access a richness of social relationships from friends, community and kinship networks.

An examination of women's and children's lives reveals the diversity of formations in which they actually reside and the wide range of burdens that they are expected to carry. Women and children in poor families may be coerced into accepting appalling and inhumane working conditions, having their sexuality strictly controlled whether within or outside marriage and being denied access to education to the limit of their talents (Basu, 1997). Women do not necessarily accept constraining definitions of their roles. Historically, they have resisted in ways consistent with the opportunities available to them within particular situations. Women's resistance has ranged from covert non-compliance within the routines of everyday life, e.g., being late preparing food to take time out for themselves but not admitting to such reasons, to organising collectively with like-minded women (Collins, 1991; Dominelli, 1991; Basu, 1997).

Children's Rights as Inalienable Human Rights

Social workers' remit within families centres on operating in accordance with the 'best interests of the child'. But the interpretation of this phrase is controversial. This concept is embedded within dichotomous thinking in which there is a winner and a loser and the interests of one party are pitted against those of the other. It is also a means through which woman and mother-blaming occurs. Casting women as evildoers gets men off the hook, particularly when men, not women, have initially caused the child(ren's) problems as in cases of child sexual abuse. This approach fails to ensure the well-being of children who are usually excluded from making decisions about themselves by paternalistic adults who assume this power on their behalf. Childhood is framed in ways that disempower children. They are perceived as dependent on adults who provide care and financial support. This I have called the exercise of adultism or the imposition of adult power over children (Dominelli, 1989). Children are also conceptualised as 'innocent' beings who are to be 'protected' within the private sphere of the family.

Children's rights are poorly endorsed in practice despite social workers' endeavours to ensure the 'best interests of the child'. For it is always the adults who define what this phrase means. And when they don't agree, the courts decide. This formulation of childhood has meant that the family with little or no support from the community has been responsible for providing a safe and nurturing haven for children. At the same time, catering solely to the 'best interests of the child' fails mothers, who once labelled inadequate by practitioners, find it difficult to regain a position as valued carers. This is one reason why mothers fear social workers entering their lives (Strega *et al.*, 2000). In faulting women's child care practices, social workers castigate their mothering work, label them as incompetent, and threaten them with losing their children. The latter is extremely potent for women whose children are what they care most about, whether or not they are initially responsible for causing the problems that prompt social workers to intervene. The intertwining of women's roles as mothers with their identity as women, means that being labelled a bad mother undermines an individual woman's sense of self as a valued being and she feels she is a 'bad' woman as well as mother. Social workers expend enormous sums in investigative initiatives that often do not confirm child abuse and neglect (DoH, 1995). This squanders public resources that could be used to support children and families or address the structural inequalities that impact on their lives.

Women's Mothering Skills are the Main Focus of Social Work Intervention

Child welfare work is the mainstay of social work with children and families. Mothers are at its centre. Practitioners have problematised the mothering skills of particular women. However, only feminists have critiqued hegemonic views of motherhood (Daly, 1978; Chodorow, 1978; Richardson, 1993). Feminists have questioned definitions of motherhood that fail to take account of women's needs in carrying out their mothering roles and result in a poorer deal for children (Lyons, 2000). Whilst feminists have latterly acknowledged the joys that women derive from motherhood, they have also sought to expand the range of choices open to them.

Social work interventions have focused on women's capacities as mothers. However, mothering in practice has been defined in fairly stereotypical and idealistic ways despite Winnicott's (1964) attempts to couch parenting skills in more realistic 'good enough' terms. Sex role stereotyping has been accompanied by white middle-class values being taken as the normative yardstick. Lifestyles that have extended beyond the narrow range of normality sanctioned through attachment theories (Bowlby, 1953) have been deemed deviant. In the West, women have been pathologised for failing to meet white middle-class standards of care and childrearing practices. And, as indicated in the previous chapter, fathering has been cast in restrictive ways – primarily as an economic relation. Although the concept of 'good enough mothering' has been created to ensure that caring professionals do not formulate impossible standards for women to emulate, it remains a highly potent ideological mechanism of practice.

Child welfare work in family settings tends to be crisis interventionist and linked to child protection issues (Dominelli, 1999) within the overall framework of child care being women's responsibility. This has downplayed the responsibility of communities in caring for children; the importance of support networks for primarily women carers; the use of preventative approaches to working with families; and men's involvement in such work (Dominelli, 1999). More often than not, social workers focus on policing women's mothering skills (Swift, 1995) whilst ignoring the absence of social resources to help them in this task. Current formulations of child welfare work pre-empt its ability to address poverty and other structural inequalities while asserting women's individual responsibilities for coping with adverse social conditions. Angela, a white single parent whom I interviewed expressed her frustrations at being so treated as follows:

Case Study

I got really pissed off with this young (white) social worker who came to see me when one of my neighbours (falsely) reported me to social services for abusing my children. (She) said I'd hit Johnny (aged 4) over the head with a plank and left him and his sister (aged 3) in the house on their own when I went out partying.

She (the social worker) came in all high and mighty, took one look at my place (a large bedsit) – no carpets, just a tatty sofa bed, 2 cots, a table and chairs and sat perched at the edge of her seat, looking like she couldn't wait to get away from me fast enough. Then she said, 'This is no place to raise a child'. I was scared stiff of losing Johnny and Diane. I couldn't sleep for days. I kept seeing the two of them crying for me and me not being able to get to them. All she (the social worker) seemed interested in was taking them away from me.

Fortunately, the investigation into my case did not reveal child abuse or neglect. I never leave them on their own. My mother is always here with 'em if I go out. But they (social workers) act as if I have no life of my own to lead. My world revolves around my children. But sometimes, I need a break. I just have to get away from it all. But when I asked her if they (social services) could provide us with money for a family holiday, for me to take Johnny and Diane to the seaside, she said she couldn't help with that. I'd have to find the money myself or earn it. How could I do that? I tried to get some help from the local church. They could give me £50. But that wouldn't pay for a week at Butlin's (a holiday camp for families) for the 3 of us. And I can't go out to work 'cause I can't pay a child-minder. Why can't she help me by providing something so simple? She (the social worker) won't have to think twice about taking her holiday this year, I'll bet. I could climb a mountain with my two tied to my back more easily than finding money to go on holiday.

Angela does not express the problem she needs to tackle in this way, but poverty lies at the heart of her troubles. Poverty alleviation is not seen as a social worker's responsibility, so she thinks its impact as a source of stress and constraints is irrelevant. Focusing on child protection issues in a bureaucratic and individualised manner stultifies the social worker's capacity to empathise with Angela and bars her from seeing her collusion with institutional classism and sexism, i.e., the lack of high quality accessible child care facilities. In casting Angela as a consumer of agency services, the practitioner does not valorise Angela's resourcefulness in coping with adversity. And, in their interaction, both women consider the problem as one Angela has to solve personally. Angela does not define her interests as conflicting with those of her children, although she does want and need some space for herself – an insight a feminist practitioner would utilise in supporting both Angela and the children. She would also address the need to enhance Angela's income and resources.

Women's economic dependence on men is not usually explicitly considered by social workers who assist women to live without male partners. Meeting women's material needs in the aftermath of a breakdown in their relationships with men whether as partners or fathers has been a major barrier to women's autonomy in re-establishing themselves after divorce or escaping from domestic violence (Horley, 1990). Social workers in Britain are poorly placed to provide material resources and other forms of support. Although 80 per cent of practitioners' caseloads during the past two decades have consistently required substantial injections of cash to address the problems of poverty, financing of this nature or even access to well-paid jobs to which they can refer their 'clients' are not within their purview. Social workers are constrained to tinkering with women's psychological needs and instead of critiquing the failures of social organisation, focus on women's interpersonal relations with men and children, and mothering skills.

Poor mothering has served as a label for blaming women for many of the problems experienced in families. These have included holding women responsible for child sexual abuse committed by men partners for having failed to protect the children (Armstrong, 1978; Krane, 1994). Additionally, social workers working with the non-abusing parent, usually the mother, do not address her needs as both a mother and as a woman (Dominelli, 1986; Hooper, 1992). Instead, they concentrate their efforts on enabling the woman to support the child after disclosure and take extremely difficult decisions such as getting rid of a partner upon whom she might have relied for economic and emotional support without compensating for this loss by providing material resources and involving her in other networks of care.

This approach has been guided by the principle of working 'in the best interests of the child' that is enshrined in childcare legislation throughout the Western world. Presented as child-centred, it is more accurately described as child-focused because it does little to involve the child in deciding what these are. Also, its framing pits the interests of the mother and child in opposition to each other by giving the child's concerns precedence over those of the mother instead of considering ways in which the needs of both can be reconciled through a more creative approach to childhood, motherhood and fatherhood.

Traditional familialist ideologies and practices have been reinforced by the conservative men's movement and New Right politicians. Children's welfare has been co-opted to this end. Fathers' Rights Groups have begun to use the slogan, 'the best interests of the child' to re-assert the old English common-law tradition of a man's rights over women and children in demanding the *presumption* of joint custody over who should be looking after the children in disputes with their former wives. Arguing equity between the sexes, they offer joint custody as a form of co-parenting that does not leave fathers out in the cold. They insist that joint custody arrangements will make fathers more responsible. They promise to: pay maintenance as required; be there for their children on a day-to-day basis; and retain contact with them. However, research into this subject reveals a less appealing picture for the award of joint custody has not worked out except in cases where the men and women involved have voluntarily agreed to co-parent, established good communications and a high degree of trust between them (Drakich, 1988).

Additionally, formulating child welfare work in 'the best interests of the child' creates antagonistic relations between parents including their extended kinship system and the state by according one or the other 'rights' *over* children. This disempowers children from having a say in their upbringing. It also prevents the formation of egalitarian partnership relations between parents and the state, thereby excluding the possibility that the latter can help parents and children meet their responsibilities as part of a broader based collective responsibility of caring for one another. Moreover, within the individualistic framing of social relationships advocated in Western societies, hegemonic definitions of the family enable social workers to ration resources by separating women into 'good' mothers who can receive support and 'bad' mothers who cannot.

An example of this division is social workers' response to lesbian mothers. Lesbian women's claims to motherhood on the same basis as heterosexual women have been routinely denied in the courts and in the documents that social workers file (Forster and Hanscombe, 1982; Arnup, 1995). A number of women who have been awarded custody of children in disputes with former spouses have had the ruling contested when their sexual orientation became public. Although lesbian and gay movements have worked hard to endorse the principle of parenthood for lesbian women and gay men, their gains remain precarious (Polikoff, 1992). For example, a male sperm donor in California took a lesbian mother to court to demand joint custody of the child. The principle of the 'best interests of the child' has been redefined by anti-feminist men's groups in American contexts as a question of 'fit motherhood' to exclude lesbian mothers from being able to parent children whether they are biologically theirs or not.

Against this backdrop, one has to place the increasing acceptability of lesbian and gay couples as foster parents in British social services (*The Guardian*, 3 January 2000), and feminists' realisation that both heterosexual women and lesbian women are fighting to retain their roles as valued women who are also mothers. In this sense, the struggle is for recognition of the diversity of women in a variety of social roles. Important messages for feminists to advocate include that: women are more than mothers; mothering is socially valuable; and mothers can be found amongst the entire range of women.

Social workers can reduce women's options if they unthinkingly follow dominant discourses about the family. For example, social workers who approve foster and adoptive parents can easily propagate traditional views of the family and apply criteria of selection for these positions that are discriminatory in their outcome (Small, 1984) if not intent, against single parents, white working-class families, black families and same gender couples. As Darlene, a black middle-class woman who applied with her husband to be a foster carer before their relationship ended said, 'The minute I told her Daryl and I had split up, the social worker told me I couldn't proceed with the application.'

Current social work responses have sought to redress their traditional emphases on nuclear families by including extended family networks, as say with the family group conference system that has been adapted from a model developed by Maori peoples in New Zealand (see Jackson and

Nixon, 1999; Taylor, 1999). However, I would argue that in countries like Britain, this approach continues the tradition of being child-focused rather than being child-centered, for children have little scope, even in their teenage years, to steer the proceedings in directions that they wish while adults play a facilitative and enabling role (Dominelli, 1999). Moreover, these interventions are espoused within a context that is concerned more with reducing state inputs into sustaining children and their families than with their welfare. Neither has it involved the wider community in meeting its responsibilities to children and families in any significant manner.

Fathering as an Economic Relation

Fathers as breadwinners is a concept that emphasises the male role as economic provider and has traditionally been used to frame men's relationships to women and children in family arrangements. Although divorce offers an opportunity for a 'clean break' from these obligations, the state has intervened to re-assert them.

Welfare states in Britain, the United States and other countries have imposed a requirement for divorced men to pay maintenance for their children regardless of its impact on the economic viability of a subsequent family that they have created or the wish of women to have clean breaks from former partners. As in Britain through the Child Support Agency, these states have expended considerable public monies chasing up recalcitrant payers. Many men are unable to contribute to the levels demanded of them.

Success in getting men to pay directly for their children has been virtually impossible to achieve, especially if they have formed other relationships and cannot afford to maintain two families on one salary. Even if court-determined sums could be collected from individual men, they are substantially less than each family needs to rise above poverty. The state's approach endorses a private solution to the public issue of providing children with a secure income. The invocation of private patriarchy to support a failing public one has meant that communities are no longer considered part of the child care equation. Rising public demands for 'dead-beat dads' to pay for children regardless of the wishes of the children or mothers concerned, although children are not generally consulted on this matter, signal that collective support for children is receding further into the distance.

Conservative men have defined child support a 'men's issue' to draw women and children into their ambit. Their attempt to gain control of the child care agenda is geared towards resuming male power within family settings (Drakich, 1995). Women who have been ordered to make support payments when they do not have custody, are more likely to do so, even though they earn less than men in similar circumstances and encounter difficulties gaining access from custodial fathers. However, more women are currently likely to contest and be awarded custody of children than men, many of whom walk out without intending to seek it (Gregory and Foster, 1990).

The State as Parent

Public patriarchy has only partially replaced the paterfamilias in the domestic realm. Although challenged by feminists who argue that violence and the domination of women and children is an integral part of masculinity and familial relations, the view that the men who perpetrate violence against women and children are an abnormal few – 'rotten apples' who do not reflect the majority of men, persists in the public domain. Thus, private patriarchal familial relations continue to be publicly endorsed. Part of the public's unwillingness to accept feminist definitions of women's realities has been feminists' reluctance to endorse either public patriarchy or private patriarchy. For patriarchal relations fail to guarantee the well-being of women and children, regardless of whether it comes in public institutional or domestic familial form. And, as we saw in the previous chapter, patriarchy also serves poorly the needs of many men.

The state seems particularly inept at successful parenting (Strega *et al.*, 2000). The inadequacy of public patriarchy in this task becomes evident when the state assumes the role of parent when children are taken away from their families and placed in the care of local authorities. Children who have been in care are more likely to be over-represented amongst the homeless population; they are disproportionately evident amongst the ranks of the unemployed and young offenders. Young women in care are more likely to become pregnant (Coll *et al.*, 1998). Unlike birth parents who relate to their offspring throughout their lives, the state tends to cut off assistance and fails to demonstrate further interest in the futures of its former wards once they attain the arbitrary age of 18 (or 19 depending on the jurisdiction). In an ironical twist, state incompetence replaces parental incompetence. State parenting fails through a short-termism that excludes long-term planning. Yet, in unproblematic families, relationships between children and their parents last throughout life as their roles evolve into grandparents and beyond. Moreover, at the point of finally discharging its duties, the state expects the resources that the young person has not had until then to magically appear without effort on its part.

The question asked by Lynne Segal (1983), 'What is to be done about the family?' remains a troubling one for feminists, whether it is in relation to supporting private family arrangements or those involving the state as parent. It needs further theorisation, research and practice developments. Meanwhile, public funding of child care facilities – a strong goal in the feminist agenda for social action for some time, seems more beyond than ever. Child poverty in Western countries has increased substantially over the past two decades as retrenchment-oriented political regimes assume political control to attack welfare provisions (Mishra, 1990; Teeple, 1995; Ralph *et al.*, 1997; Lyons, 2000) and reduce family support services, most of which have been provided for children, not their mothers.

Patriarchal Control of Women's Reproductive Capacities Through 'New' Technologies

The development of the reproductive technologies including artificial impregnation by donor, *in vitro* fertilisation, fertility drugs and surrogate motherhood, raise enormous moral and ethical dilemmas for social workers. Reproductive technologies aim to enhance women's choices in bearing offspring. Whilst not wishing to deny women the chance to have and raise children, feminists highlight legitimate concerns about this construction of motherhood and women's identity primarily in relation to children. This approach identifies women in terms of their biology, commodifies their bodies and construes their main role as breeding machines. Casting children in these debates as parental possessions does little to enhance children's rights or well-being in their own terms. And it turns children into commodities brought to market.

The expansion of women's choices through reproductive technologies is not an unalloyed benefit (Stanworth, 1988), especially when linked to familialist ideologies and women's role as custodians of the next generation. Reproductive technologies can diminish women's control of their reproductive capacities by increasing men's powers over them, especially those ensconced in the medical profession (Stanworth, 1988; Steinberg, 1997). The new reproductive technologies (see Stanworth, 1988; Steinberg, 1997, for details of these) are impacting on interpersonal relationships, leading to other configurations of 'family' relations. Some of these challenge traditional notions of 'the family' and create alternative family forms as another dynamic arising from their use.

The new technologies can intensify state authority over women's reproductive rights and deny them control over their own bodies, particularly if they are poor or have problems with substance misuse, including drugs, alcohol or tobacco. Poor women who are pregnant have been compelled to undergo medical treatment for substance misuse because the state has deemed their behaviour to carry a high risk of harming the foetus (Callahan *et al.*, 1999). Similar issues have arisen with regards to women who have contracted HIV/AIDS and become pregnant. Baby K in Canada stands as a precedent whereby a separation was made between the rights of the mother and those of the foetus. The young woman involved had to undergo treatment for drug addiction to promote conditions for its healthy growth (Callahan *et al.*, 1999). In reaching this decision, the court judged the woman an incompetent mother whilst the foetus was developing in her womb. Dealing with the woman solely in her capacity as a mother, the judgment affirms the polarisation of women's and children's needs. It also indicates a willingness of the courts and medical profession to assume control of a woman's right to make decisions about her own body (Steinberg, 1997), giving the rationale for doing so as 'the best interests of the child'.

Pathologising the individual woman concerned, the court did not ask how a social worker could reconcile the mother's needs with those of her developing foetus. The court could have endorsed feminist oriented interventions aimed at assisting the woman to determine why she misused substances, i.e., the problems she was running away from or trying to solve through this type of behaviour, and ordered the allocation of resources to help her address these. Working in a partnership with the woman, a feminist social worker would work to answer these questions and find alternative ways of addressing her difficulties. Doing so would have established a relationship in which to build a road to the woman's recovery as an independent being capable of making her own decisions about her life while at the same time safeguarding the foetus' chances of developing normally to term had the woman decided that she wanted to give birth. Such an approach would have bypassed the polarisation of the woman's interests as a woman with those of her as a mother reinforced in the judge's framing of the problem and the decision reached.

The rise of the new reproductive technologies at a point in time when there is a shortage of cute healthy white babies for adoption, and the eugenicist implications of people who choose the perfect mother for their perfect baby, cannot be overlooked (see Achilles, 1992). The convergence of these forces place the imperative of addressing racism and disablism at the forefront of these developments. Sexism is also relevant, for a number of women have aborted female foetuses because they or their (extended) family prefer sons to daughters. The public outcry against post menopausal woman giving birth demands that ageism as expressed in the stigmatising of older mothers is also countered.

Reproductive technologies have increased women's options for becoming mothers whilst denying them control over the directions being pursued by reaffirming the control of men and the medical profession over women's reproductive capacities. These have raised a number of issues that practitioners working with children and families have failed to consider adequately. Social workers, in an inferior status to medics, are poorly placed to respond to the difficulties that the medicalisation of women's reproductive capacities raises.

For example, what should a social worker do when a child conceived through donor insemination wants to find out the identity of its biological father in societies that argue that this knowledge should not be divulged? Would they want to continue with this position when the child might need to be matched with someone who is related to them because it needs a bone marrow transplant? Who should they consider the 'parent' responsible for the child when it may have as many as three mothers and three fathers depending on the mode of conception and contractual arrangement for its delivery? Who is (are) the 'client(s)' in such cases? What should practitioners do when a grown up child discovers that the person they have married or are living with is their half-brother or half-sister? What should they do about post-menopausal women who wish to become mothers? How should social workers respond to a post-menopausal woman who has post-partum depression?

The questions that arise and their attendant answers are complicated and complex for not only are they about responding to individual distress, but they are also about challenging currently existing fundamental understandings about all forms of family relationships. Social workers will be called upon to resolve disputes that emanate from these and need to be clear about how these impact on their personal value system, the values of the society they live in and the individual wishes of the children, women and men involved in a given situation. They will have to develop negotiation skills of a high order and a complex awareness of the issues to be addressed if they are not to pit the needs and interests of one party against another in seeking to establish a feminist win–win resolution to these conflicts. Social workers also have to be prepared to deal with their own and their 'client's' feelings when problems do not work out as anticipated.

Caring professionals' role in spreading reproductive technologies is unclear, although medical expertise is driving the discourses (Steinberg, 1997). Practitioners' responses to the moral and ethical dilemmas posed by the new reproductive technologies depend upon the definition of motherhood and framing of women's role in society. The rising use of IVF increases the likelihood that traditional arrangements and definitions of family life, motherhood and fatherhood will be found wanting. Contractual disputes are also augmenting as the parties to these arrangements dispute the outcomes. In the United States, several women who have contracted to deliver babies to prospective parents have been prosecuted for changing their minds once the child was born. Litigations involving practitioners caught in the cross-fire illustrate the complications emanating from disputes in this area. One woman in Canada has successfully sued her physician for not testing donor sperm for HIV/AIDS when she contracted the disease through this means. Social workers have to prepare for the possibility that they may be hauled before the courts too.

At the same time, the potential commercialisation of children and their becoming commodities for sale undermines their rights as human beings. Limitations on exploiting them in this way can carry unintended consequences. In Britain, women can cover their 'expenses', but are legally prevented from being paid to carry the foetus. This perpetuates the view that women undertake motherhood naturally and that it does not involve hard work. Women's experiences of the process challenge these assumptions. Kim Cotton, one of the first women to deliver a child through the use of these technologies and who went on to head an agency (COTS) that puts prospective parents in touch with possible surrogate mothers has argued that surrogacy provides a vehicle for giving women pleasure and validates the social role of mothering.

Feminist responses to these issues remain unclear and contradictory. Some feminists argue that paying women for their labour is recognition of its social worth (Ungerson, 1990). Others are concerned that going along this path reinforces hegemonic notions of women as breeding machines (Steinberg, 1997). The matter is complicated by the fact that *in vitro* fertilisation is considered a response to male infertility whilst surrogate motherhood addresses that of women. These options may devalue the contexts in which motherhood occurs. At the same time, they endorse the importance of giving birth to children and implicate women in the continuation of the human species.

Conclusions

Work with children and families provides sites in which patriarchial relations can be reproduced. Social workers engage in their perpetuation by enforcing women's roles as mothers and nurturers whilst excluding men from being involved in these. Social policies formulated around 'the family' endorse hegemonic definitions of the inegalitarian relationships that exist between women and men and children and their parents; children and the state; parents and the state. These help promote antagonistic gender relations which pit the interests of men and women against each other whilst ignoring the inalienable rights of the child. Despite the principle of practitioners' handling their interventions in accordance with 'the best interests of the child', there is no guarantee that this will be the outcome even within a liberal rights framework. At the same time, coupling women's roles as nurturers with their involvement in the waged labour market results in practices that enable one group of women with access to social resources to exploit the domestic labour of women who are less-well financially endowed with the potential for purchasing such services.

Feminist social work has sought to identify the inadequacies of this approach to women, children and men within family settings and provided principles on which more egalitarian relationships can be established. These are rooted in the recognition of children's human rights; women's rights to determine for themselves the lifestyle choices that they want to pursue; and the state's responsibility to embed these rights in socially supported obligations and resources for their realisation.

The new reproductive technologies raise new questions about social work interventions in family settings. For these question traditional assumptions about and definitions of the relationships between individuals, close relations and the wider community of people to which they relate. Additionally, these technologies are problematic for feminist social workers for while they increase the range of options open to women and highlight the importance of mothering as a social activity, they carry the danger of reducing the overall control that women retain over their fertility and reproductive capacities.

6

Working with Adults

Redrawing the Boundaries of Care in the Community

Working with adults is another major arena for social work practice. The bulk of these are older people who have been incapacitated through disease and physical infirmity. They constitute the major 'client' group covered in this chapter. Adults, unless they are disabled or mentally ill, are not normally expected to receive assistance from the social services (Zucchino, 1997). Rather, they are expected to meet their own welfare needs, although they may be instrumental in seeking help for children or older dependents.' In Britain, working with older people has traditionally been considered a Cinderella area because the work has low status and is done by women with little or no qualifications. Additionally, men wishing to rise rapidly through the ranks of practice have used residential care for older people as a springboard to child care and from there to rise up the career ladder to management (Howe, 1986).

Ageism is the oppression of people on the grounds of age, and is relevant to both dependent children and older adults. Ageism, however, is commonly expressed as a lack of respect for the specific needs of old age and discrimination against older people (Phillipson, 1982). Besides low social standing, poor health and poverty are other hardships encountered in old age (Ahmad, 1993). Ageist attitudes buttress the celebration of youth and depict older people as having restricted mobility, being mentally incapacitated and dependent on others. The popular view that older people are relatively worthless results in inadequate provisions catering to their specific needs, particularly those relating to disease management and ambulatory issues. As more and more people live beyond the 'threescore years and ten' that Westerners have defined as the expected lifespan of an individual, their societies have construed older people as problems (Bornat *et al.*, 1997). There are too many of them; they impose a burden upon the rest of society; the list goes on. New terms have been coined to (re)define a natural process – 'the ageing phenomenon', 'the greying population', and amongst others, 'wrinklies' (Doress and Siegal, 1987). This latter epithet encapsulates a highly disrespectful regard for older people. It dehumanises them and suggests that they are expendable. It fails to appreciate the talents and wisdom that older people have acquired through a lifetime of living, devalues the contributions that they have made to society during their younger years, ignores the work many undertake as active members of informal networks and voluntary agencies until their dying day, and rules them out for consideration as having continuing socially useful roles.

The realisation that there will be a large number of elders when the current baby boomers reach old age has sent policymakers scurrying to save public money and ensure that society is not faced with masses of destitute people (Biggs, 1993). Their solutions have been two-pronged: make individuals responsible for their own care whether this is personal care or pensions to provide them with an assured income; and compel individual families to provide whatever is needed to as great an extent as possible (Hughes, 1995).

Discourses around the burden of an ageing population convey the erroneous impression that the state provides care for the majority of older people. This misrepresents reality as experienced by most elders who are cared for by their families (Higgins, 1989). In Britain, only 5 per cent of elders are looked after by the public care system. The Family Policy Studies Centre (1984) has calculated that if women's unpaid care of older people over 75 years of age were to be remunerated at the same levels as public care, it would cost £3.7 billions per year. This estimate is conservative because it contains built into it, the low rates of pay that women undertaking paid elder care receive (Hugman, 1998). A further under-rated dimension in the ageing debate is gender. Most older people are women, as are most poor older people (Millar, 1996).

This chapter focuses on ageism in social work as it impacts on elder care, particularly in the context of the current policies of caring for older people in their communities and the opening up of provisions for elder care to the market and private providers. It reveals that whether women are practitioners, carers or users of services, they are at the forefront of the changes that are being initiated, not all of which work to their advantage. Additionally, caring in the community presupposes, that 'adults' (a term that is usually ungendered in political discourses on the subject) are doing the caring. However, we will see below that both children and older adults can be looking after even older people, thereby complicating inter-generational and family relationships further.

Institutionalised Ageism and Creating a Society Fit for All Ages

Ageism has been portrayed as an individual's failure to respond appropriately to older people. This is only part of the problem as ageism affects both ends of the age spectrum and is both personal and structural. It draws on and feeds into institutional and cultural endorsements of individual attitudes and behaviours that deny elders human dignity and rights. Phillipson (1982) highlights institutional ageism when arguing that ageism in capitalist societies reflects older people's loss of productive capacity in waged labour markets. Western feminists exposed its gendered dimensions. Most older people living in poverty are women (Millar, 1996). Penury arises because women have undertaken unpaid care work all their lives and been unable to purchase private pensions or accumulate sufficient contributions. Women may have spent a lifetime in poorly remunerated employment without amassing the necessary pension credits because they enter a segregated waged labour market in low paid jobs, many of which are part-time. These rarely have pension provisions attached to them, or if they do, the contributions that women are able to pay are insufficient to take them out of poverty in old age (Pascall, 1986; Dominelli, 1991). These so-called personal arrangements are institutionalised through the state's unwillingness to recognise women's labour in the home by either paying pension contributions on their behalf or addressing the issue of low pay. Indeed, the state as a major employer of women is implicated in devaluing their waged work. In Canada, for example, women public sector employees had to fight a protracted court battle with the federal government to receive the same remuneration as men for work of equivalent value (*The National Post*, 20 Oct 1999). A crucial factor exacerbating older women's impoverished position is institutional and indicates another site in which public patriarchy fails to meet women's needs.

Besides identifying the institutional basis of penury in old age, feminists have challenged the view that old age is a state of physical and mental decline. During the 1970s in the United States, Maggie Kuhn, the founder of the Gray Panthers, argued that neither men nor women are finished and ready to be put to pasture just because they have reached a prescribed arbitrary age of retirement (Kuhn, 1991). In that country, her efforts and those of other organisations of older people have been crucial in passing legislation that terminated a mandatory retirement age for men and women (Doress and Siegal, 1987).

The social relevance of older people has been substantiated by other groups. Black people have consistently argued for recognition of the contributions that elders make to society (Patel, 1990). In cultures where old age is venerated, this point is more readily accepted. The impugned lack of social roles for older women have been discredited by ethnic minority groups demonstrating that older women have traditionally undertaken care of young children for their sons and daughters. This has been an important informal source of childminding that has also been unpaid and unrecognised (Collins, 1991).

Valuing older people does not automatically acknowledge the gendered nature of old age and the role of ageism in oppressing women. In some cultures, preference is given to older men rather than women. The feminist message can become a source of conflict in such situations by challenging male privileges. Also, in some cultures, old age can result in increased powers being held by older women over younger women (Kassindja, 1998), and unless challenged, the oppression of younger women by older women can continue to occur (Croll, 1978; Shah, 2001).

Older women have questioned ageism within the feminist movement itself (Doress and Siegal, 1987). Arguing that intergenerational solidarity is crucial to healthy societies, older feminists have increased interaction between older and younger women through several initiatives. They have formed groups that encourage activities in which both younger and older women participate (Doress and Siegal, 1987). Other endeavours have included mentorship schemes to facilitate exchanges across the generation gap and enable younger women to experience firsthand positive inputs from older women (Doress and Siegal, 1987). These ventures have also undermined myths that mental and physical decline automatically accompany old age and demonstrated that many of the infirmities of old age have been socially constructed (Doress and Siegal, 1987).

Slower mobility and physical impairment do not have to act as barriers to older people's participation in society. Nor do these make it any less valuable (Hughes, 1995). On this score, feminists have been able to draw on the messages of other social movements of which they have been a part. Amongst these, the disability movement has been especially important in messages affirming women's abilities (Morris, 1991; Begum, 1992).

Feminists have examined the complexities of caring for older people and revealed the hard work that carrying it out entails (Finch and Groves, 1983; Ungerson, 1987). They have included the needs of both the carer and the person being cared-for in their analyses and plans for action. Social divisions between those doing the caring and those receiving it can create difficulties for women wanting non-hierarchical feminist relations between different groups of women (Knijn and Kremer, 1997). But, they indicate the extensive variety in the complexities of 'difference' that feminists have to address before they can embark on egalitarian collective action amongst women on any issue.

Redefining Communities in Caring Situations

Communities are collective spaces in which a person expresses both individual and group identities (Bell and Newby, 1971). For me, these tend to be defined according to geographic locale, interests or identity attributes. Communities can be conceptualised as socially defined spatial organisations with fluid and contested boundaries in and through which individuals come together with like-minded others to realise specific goals in ways that transcend time and space. Those included within its borders become identified as insiders, those beyond them are outsiders. So, communities become signifiers of exclusionary practices that can be breached only with difficulty by outsiders. The multiplicity of individual identity means individuals can belong to more than one community at any given point in time.

Whether based on geographical proximity, shared interests or common identities, community boundaries can overlap (Bell and Newby, 1971). So, a community of older women will draw on identity attributes associated with ageing and gender. They share some common interests around age with older men. They have some commonalities with younger women around gender. They may share similarities across other divisions of 'race', ethnicities, class and sexual orientation. Since this community resides in a small geographic locale with others different from them, overlaps also occur on the spatial dimension. Feminists have a dynamic view of communities as socially constructed and varying over time and space as people negotiate their boundaries with one another and develop supportive networks (Mayo, 1977; Dominelli, 1990). For feminists, expanding community horizons becomes one way of building social solidarity between people. Their extension to old age enables young and old people to work together in developing support networks (Shah, 2001). Social solidarity facilitates gender parity between men and women if social resources provided through taxation are embedded in social contracts in which each member of a national community accepts responsibility for meeting the needs of another whilst being entitled to receive the same in return if and when required.

Communities as defined by politicians differ from those envisaged by feminists for these are portrayed as passive, fixed entities, ripe for political manipulation. Community care policies have been processed within an ontological framework that expects women to be available to care gratis, regardless of their actual circumstances – a presumption of Britain's National Health Service and Community Care Act (CCA), 1990. The public purse may be inelastic, but policymakers assume women are not. The links that tie an individual and his or her community together constantly undergo a process of creation and re-creation, with each shaping the other through interaction. Communities are also sites in which resources are exchanged or refused. Conditions of scarcity and availability affect these transactions. The increased number of older people and the community's capacity to support them has been cast in terms of scarcity through political, professional, gerontological and research discourses that call upon women to fill the gap.

There is a close connection between conceptualisations of old age and community, for old age is lived out and defined by actors in those communities in which people live. Community is a problematic concept and can mean a range of things to different people (Wilson, 1977; Dominelli, 1990). It can be used to add to the oppression of women rather than end it. We will see below how this can happen under community care, a policy governing the provision of services for older people in their communities as opposed to residential or institutional care (Finch, 1984). Under this policy, the increased burdens of unpaid care fall upon women's shoulders more than men's (Finch and Groves, 1983). Men contribute a substantial amount of spousal care – about 25 per cent, but women are the main source of caring labour for all groups requiring it (Fisher, 1997). The 'labour of love' as Graham (1983) calls it, is performed by women to members of their families – in the broadest sense of the term, often sacrificing their own chances for happiness and fulfilment whether by relinquishing a waged career or foregoing marriage and creating their own families (Bonny, 1984). Additionally, women employed to care for older people often give extra services at their own expense and in their own time because they are committed to service users (Dominelli, 1997).

The gender neutral language of community care can disguise that it is care by women (Finch and Groves, 1983). Thus, it perpetuates a division of labour that assumes that women are 'natural' carers who may be called upon to fill the gaps that exist between public care provisions and individual needs for care with little or no training. Men, as the heirs to other tasks are usually excluded from such considerations, although some men do caring work. In reproducing professional discourses through their practice (Bourdieu and Wacquant, 1992), social workers contribute to the perpetration of a sexist division of labour by assuming that older people will be cared for by their daughters (in-law) rather than their sons (in-law). If social workers do not facilitate men's involvement in the preparation and delivery of care for elders, this becomes another site in which social workers neglect the contribution that men can make to women's well-being. Despite their espousal of sexual equality, these practices ensure that women bear the brunt of caring work as is illustrated below:

Case Study

Sukhev, a man of Thai origins, has been caring for his seventy-five year old mother with learning difficulties for about thirty years. One day she fell, broke her leg and was taken to hospital. Her x-rays showed that she had a pelvic bone fracture and severe arthritis in the hip joint. Her doctors recommended a hip replacement. She was hospitalised for several weeks. Sukhev went to visit her everyday. Once, his sister who lived some distance away went to visit with him. At the hospital, they met the white woman social worker assigned to the case. She was leaving their mother when they went in and asked them to see her when they finished visiting. During the interview that followed, the social worker kept asking his sister to provide care for their mother and talked as if she had been doing this in the past. Sukhev felt extremely angry.

This example indicates that professionals can challenge institutionalised ageism and sexism by drawing on strengths that people already display. From the vignette, it is clear that the family, by its actions, had already made this leap, even if the social worker did not. Had she recognised and thereby validated Sukhev's strengths, i.e., contribution to his mother's care, the social worker would have made him feel appreciated and countered the view that caring is exclusively women's responsibility. That she did not may have reflected the racist and sexist view that black men do not care for their elders. The case above also illustrates how adults make decisions for other adults which ignore the complex relationships between them, and in the course of doing so, reinforce relations of dependency and deny another individual's right to agency. The processes of infantilising adults embedded these relationships rob all the persons involved of their dignity.

The debate about the locality in which the care of older people is conducted has been around for a while. In some respects, the division between care in their own homes (community care) or in a residential institutions is artificial (Finch, 1984). An institution can become the base for developing a community of people with like-minded interests.

People's shared experiences of living in one place and being subject to its prevailing regimes can foster a sense of community (Goffman, 1961). An institution, like a family dwelling, is located within a broader community with which it interacts, even if only to obtain utilities and provide communication avenues outward. Whether care is institutionally situated or not, if the boundaries between the two are permeable, they are constantly being constructed and reconstructed. If their permeability is poor, isolation is more likely to occur as barriers impede high levels of interaction between them. On the individual level, different experiences of those boundaries are likely. Institutional walls become obstacles if residents feel overcome by a lack of permeability and excluded by it. Equally, a person left in their own home without community networks and supports to tap into, may not feel part of a community, merely a fragment of one – the isolated individual. Despite this possibility, social policy emphasises community care. So, official policies and popular discourses depict residential care for older people as second best to home care. Yet, many problems in residential establishments can be traced to poor levels of resourcing, inadequate staffing and lack of training for their personnel (Wagner, 1988; Utting, 1991). Inadequate links between institutional care and life in the wider community contributes to this sorry situation.

Feminists argue that residential care need not be of poor quality (Finch, 1984). Properly resourced, staffed by competent individuals, and having good connections with its surrounding communities, residential care for older people can be creative and provide satisfying places in which individuals can end their days (see ASRA, 1981). But, to make such provision available, older people should be involved in designing and running the facilities in question as much as possible. I (Dominelli, 1980) describe the aspirations of a group of older people to retain links with their community and families by having small, local residential establishments near their former homes and easily accessible by public transport so that friends and relatives can visit regularly. Older people consider it important to have facilities for visitors to keep in touch with important others in their lives and maintain continuities by having people to stay, as they would have done previously in their own homes (Dominelli, 1980). Catering for visitors in these institutions requires alterations in the physical layout of many residential homes as well as a change in attitudes amongst policymakers, staff and residents. ASRA has developed such 'client'-centred facilities for older Asians. Their efforts reveal a preference for small-scale homes in their own communities so that family and friends can be involved in ongoing relationships with them (ASRA, 1981). In ASRA schemes, high quality elder care bridges a number of social divisions including age, gender, 'race' and class.

Community care policies have been initiated as gender neutral although the bulk of older people and their carers are women. This framing of the matter may change as the double shift of paid work and unpaid domestic labour takes its toll on women's health. Heart disease, for example, is increasing at a faster rate amongst women than men, thus raising the numbers of women to be cared-for while reducing the pool of available carers (Kosberg, 1992). Poverty in old age will further complicate the pressures emanating from these trends. But, community care policies are presented as if individual resources are unlimited or not an issue. The expectation is that like a sponge, a poor older person can absorb any deficiencies created through public policies. This approach also ignores the long-term impact of women's current position in the labour force which restricts their capacity to access caring resources independently of the state as they earn considerably less than men, even if located in the higher paid echelons of the workforce (AUT, 1999). Women cannot finance future care expenditure on the basis of pension contributions that flow from low-paid work. Limited job security and increasing labour market casualisation for women in work (Nelson *et al.*, 1995) are unlikely to change this picture quickly.

Women's inability to pay more for provisions in old age and their greater longevity has been used to argue that women do not deserve higher rates of pension entitlement or more access to personal social services because they get more than their fair share (McKnight, 1995). The suggestion that women get a better deal from the state than men because they live longer fails to acknowledge that poverty constantly shapes women's experiences and leads to a deterioration in their quality of life throughout the lifecycle. A longer life-span results in women drawing on pension finances for a longer period than men, but they also get less funds than men at any particular point (Glendinning and Millar, 1992). Women receive smaller pensions throughout the period of eligibility as their career patterns do not meet actuarial practices upon which pensions provisions are predicated: expecting women to have the same career pattern and wage levels as men (Pascall, 1986).

Defining the financing of women's pensions as an actuarial problem misses the point. It ignores the enormous contribution to others' welfare that women have made and continue to make throughout their lives in unpaid work, and the lower incomes they receive from paid employment. Addressing the issue of providing a living income for older women will require four fundamental shifts in social expectations: redressing the inequitable rates of pay for women in the waged labour force; re-organising the waged workday; recognising the work that women undertake in the unwaged domestic workplace of the home; and involving men in caring work.

Reorganising social relations in the waged workplace and unpaid arena of the home to respond to these points would have major implications for men's lives as they currently lead them. Making the necessary changes might require some time. But, acknowledging women's unpaid work would be a key step forward. Some countries, e.g., Canada, are beginning to do this by notionally acknowledging the contribution that women's unpaid work is making to the economy by adding it as a shadow total in the gross national product (Status of Women, 2001). Laudable although this step may be, it fails to challenge inequitable ways of organising work and (re)distributing social resources. And, it will not release more resources to end the feminisation of poverty in old age.

To reach a more equitable distribution of resources and secure recognition of women's unpaid work requires a reorganisation of gender relations in both the home and the workplace, and a reformulation of intergenerational solidarities to include all sections of society. It also has to recognise the interdependent nature of relationships between different groups of people. For example, the old people of today have been the carers of the children of today and yesterday (Maracle, 1993). Yesterday's children may be called upon to be the carers of older people in the present and future.

Our past, present and futures are wrapped up in each other's lives. Contributions to each other's well-being ought to acknowledge this interdependence. One way of realising this commitment across generations may be to institutionalise payment for other people's care by having waged adults contribute premiums to pension funds that are today's collection for expenditures incurred yesterday, today and tomorrow.

The social insurance system is predicated on this principle (Ginsburg, 1979). By paying premiums, each generation invests in other generations, but does so on the basis of reciprocity. One gives now and expects to receive in the future. Rethinking provisions for older people to underpin their rights as citizens involves a reconceptualisation of community obligations regarding the expectations that people have of themselves and each other, and the kinds of interactions that can occur amongst them. Ensuring publicly-funded quality care across the lifecycle encourages a more egalitarian restructuring of social relations across generational divides.

The restructuring of social relations caused by retrenchment in the welfare state, especially at the local level where women are primarily located whether as carers or recipients of services will impact heavily on older women. As the private market bites into the state provisions made available for older people, women may lose out on two levels. One is in reduced levels of service provisions; the other is in diminished employment opportunities. The withdrawal of or reduction in state services causes suffering and hardship to both carers and users (Bonny, 1984).

As the British experience of the late 1990s indicates, the impact of market imperatives on the residential arena has prompted changes in the staffing of homes. These have included turning public establishments into private ones. In the process, workers have been compelled to apply for jobs at reduced pay with fewer fringe benefits. Often jobs previously undertaken by qualified social workers have been turned over to workers without qualifications and at lower rates of pay (Kosberg, 1992). Thus, social work is being deprofessionalised at the same time that its status as a ghetto of lower paid women workers is being intensified (Dominelli, 1997). Although some establishments have sought to qualify residential workers following a number of public inquiries into the conditions that have existed in residential homes for children (Utting, 1991; Wagner, 1988), many have chosen to qualify workers at minimal levels rather than rush to train them in universities. Those caring for older people have yet to be prioritised as deserving of high status quality education. This trend is enforced through minimalist care being made available to older people, often focusing on their physical needs rather than the gamut of emotional and social needs (Tronto, 1993). Even in the United States, where social workers are qualified to higher levels than elsewhere, residential care workers are less well-trained than fieldworkers. And, their status is diminished accordingly.

Providing an array of services to respond to a complex range of needs requires more finances and better trained workers. Reminiscence therapies can be used by skilled practitioners to enable older people to value their previous contributions to society whether or not these have been linked to the wage labour market (Coleman, 1990). In these, practitioners have to ensure that ways of surviving 'bad' memories are also to hand. For women whose lives have been absorbed in caring for their children, husbands and elderly parents, the valuing of mundane contributions to sustaining the lives of others is as important as having a valued paid role to absorb current energies.

Another feminist preoccupation is to have those being cared-for exercise agency by determining the kind of care they receive instead of having it decided for them (Doress and Siegal, 1989). The public acknowledgement of carers' work and leaving control in the hands of the person receiving the care are feminist insights relevant to this matter.

Carers are mainly other women, many of whom are themselves caring for other family members. They may be older women with their own catalogue of unmet needs. And, they may have sacrificed careers and friendships to fulfill caring obligations at earlier points in their lives. Cutbacks may leave them and those they care for more vulnerable than ever if there is no prospect of accessing alternative sources (Ralph *et al.*, 1997). Thus, caring can intensify the burdens inherent in the work for poor adult women who have limited possibilities in obtaining further resources. Mary, a seventy-two year old carer of an eighty year old severely disabled man, commenting on a recent round of cuts, makes a number of these points:

Case Study

When I got the letter saying the home care worker was going to be stopped, I cried. My husband's bed-ridden. I'm crippled by arthritis. How can I manage lookin' after him, cookin' and cleanin' the house. He's a big man, I can't turn him over to wash him, though I make sure he takes his pills at the right time. The worst thing was the list of people (enclosed in the letter) that can provide these services for money. But we've only our pensions. We can't pay their high fees. I've written to appeal the decision, but don't hold much hope.

Older people also like to exercise their own decision-making capacities and look after themselves for as long as possible, whether or not they live in institutional settings. Maintaining their independence and not being a burden is key in structuring their lives (Bonny, 1984). But they need adequate resourcing to make this possible. In failing to provide these, the state is not enabling the capacities of either carers or those they care for to flourish.

Shifting Professional Boundaries and Deprofessionalising Social Work with Older People

The Community Care Act regulates elder care in the mixed economy of welfare in the United Kingdom and has substantially changed the nature of social work. It has shifted state provisions away from providing services through the development of a caring relationship between workers and 'clients', towards purchasing services through specifically designed budget-driven packages of care delivered by workers in other (non-statutory) agencies (Priestley, 1998). This change requires social workers to act as purchasers and managers of care rather than providers, and is known as the purchaser-provider split (Price-Waterhouse, 1990). This mode of organisation has reduced the role of human relationship building in 'client'–worker interactions. The loss of social workers' role as catalysts for individual change has resulted in even more bureaucratic forms of service provision (Khan and Dominelli, 2000). Redrawing professional boundaries between different professional jurisdictions has affected traditional professional and disciplinary rivalries, particularly health and social work. In some local authorities, the purchasing function is not undertaken by social workers (Neysmith, 1998). Consequently, social work's sphere of influence has been reduced substantially. Although basic grade workers find these changes unsettling, managers have not responded to their workers emotional needs for stability. And, in keeping with the regimes being established under the 'new managerialism' (Clarke and Newman, 1997), are insisting that more work is conducted through interdisciplinary and multidisciplinary teams which can further undermine social workers fragile sense of morale and professional integrity (Neysmith, 1998).

Developments that further fragment social work's professional space become contentious in the context of budget-driven resource allocations that favour the more powerful and better organised health and medical sphere (Borden, 1996). The most important shift across discipline boundaries has involved health professionals assuming a number of tasks previously done by social workers. A study undertaken by Borden (1996), has revealed that social work is considered such a vague discipline that in situations where either health or social workers can perform the same task, health professionals such as budget-holding General Practitioners (GPs) chose health workers over social workers because they feel that they know exactly what health workers would do in a given situation. Social work has to consider strategies that resist having its boundaries redrawn to its disadvantage. Addressing its own internal contradictions and inconsistencies can be a first step in (re)fashioning and (re)asserting its (new) professional identity.

Community care as a budget-driven form of care involves social workers in making tough decisions when there is a mismatch between the care assessed necessary through a needs assessment and what can be purchased through the budgetary resources available. Tight fiscal controls cause practitioners considerable role conflict and moral dilemmas as they ration resources (Dominelli, 1997). Their practice produces monthly variations in the numbers of people covered, makes entitlement a lottery contingent on funding and exacerbates geographical inequalities as budgets are locally administered (George, 1996).

Caring for the Carers

Community care policies and practices have historically neglected the needs of those who have undertaken caring work, mainly women carers. Feminists have highlighted the importance of taking carers' interests into account (Bonny, 1984; Ungerson, 1987). Feminists have recently recast the devaluing of caring and shortages of time and resources for caring as the right to care and be cared-for, to ensure that the risks and interests of those caring and being cared-for are not framed in oppositional terms (Knijn and Kremer, 1997). The provision of respite care to relieve carers of the unremitting burden of being constantly available to care for and about another human being has been amongst their concerns. An important contradiction to be reconciled in these situations is not to pit the needs of those requiring care against the well-being of those providing it (Knijn and Kremer, 1997). This has required the provision of community support services in partnerships involving caregivers in commercial, public, voluntary and domestic settings (Griffiths, 1988). Creating these packages, even in instances where short-term respite care is provided, requires careful, painstaking work that takes time – a commodity in short supply for overstretched social workers (see Balbo, 1987).

Time, for women, is a scarce commodity (Balbo, 1987), but one that rarely features in budgetary allocations. Managers simply expect social workers to find it somehow. And if they don't, they are considered unfit for the jobs they hold. So, many social workers put in the extra hours, giving their employers a hidden subsidy that comes off private time that could/should have been spent with family or friends or even in leisure activities. Small wonder then, that social workers as professionals have high levels of absenteeism and high levels of burnout (Thompson *et al.*, 1996). Interestingly, managers who have noticed these trends in their audits of workers' performance have redefined the problem as one of malingering workers who want paid time off, thereby creating a new category of scroungers, rather than examining the organisation of work and asking whether it is designed to safeguard the general health of workers (Francis, 1992; Daly, 1998).

Another significant element in feminist demands for a better deal for carers has been remuneration for work done. This stance is contentious and repeats some of the points made in the Wages for Housework Campaigns of the mid-1970s (see Dalla Costa and James, 1972). While promoting recognition of the social nature of caring work, payment cements it as a private transaction between individuals who know each other. The disability movement has added its voice to this debate and insists that the money is paid directly to the person requiring care. They advocate this position on the grounds that such payments increase control over day-to-day decisions that affect them (Wellard, 1999) by enabling the person being cared-for to choose and dismiss carers. Remunerating caring work may open up the gendered nature of caring if more men are drawn into its ambit.

Many caring professionals have consulted the carer rather than the cared-for, thereby adding to the oppression of elders being cared-for by infantilising them and enforcing dependency upon them (Leonard, 1984). Sam, a sixty-eight year old wheelchair user I interviewed highlights this issue:

Case Study

What made me really mad about my social worker was that after she'd say 'hello' to me, she'd ask my wife, who was pushing the wheelchair, about me and what I needed. Why didn't she ask me? I hadn't become a vegetable cause I sat in a wheelchair. If I employed her, I'd sack her.

Another feature of caring relations that feminist interventions in the caring debate have exposed is the age profile of carers. Many carers are older people taking care of even older ones (Parker and Lawton, 1994). On the intragenerational level, friends and spouses end up providing care. So, women who have just finished caring for their children might find that they have become responsible for caring for an elderly spouse or parents. The 'empty nest' syndrome has been overtaken by 'the full house' syndrome of commitments to elder care, and women may discover that the time of pleasurable adulthood that they had anticipated as being available to meet their needs has shrunk or disappeared altogether. Women who have been looking forward to time for themselves in their mid-to-later adult years become cheated of the opportunity to give priority to their own needs and look after their own interests for a change (Zucchino, 1997).

Additionally, young people, including children, are taking care of disabled parents (Twigg and Atkin, 1994). Thus, carers are working intergenerationally and intragenerationally. On the intergenerational level, children caring for their parents as an expression of their love for them may be denied the opportunity to pursue their own growth and may experience considerable stress as a result. This places young carers in particularly vulnerable positions. Greater longevity means that some young carers are providing care over considerable periods of time. Concern for carers opens a space for supporting children in their own development as well as allowing them to contribute to their parents' care. However, this support cannot be assumed. Betty, a 14 year-old who cares for her disabled father, recounts her story below:

Case Study

I was seven years old when mum got killed in a car accident. My dad survived, but was brain-damaged and confined to a wheelchair. At first, my aunt came and looked after both of us. After a couple of years, she got married and went to live in Australia. She phoned social services before she left. A social worker came to see us. She asked a lot of questions and then went away, saying that we would hear from her. We're still waiting, though we're not asking for nothing.

In the meantime, Clare, a neighbour, came to help. She was very good. She did the shopping and the cooking for a long time, although I was left with my dad through the night and he was on his own most of the day while I was at school. But she had her own family to attend to, so we couldn't expect more of her. Gradually, as I got older, I took on more and more. I'm grateful to Clare for what she offered, cause she got us through a tough time. And, I think that if she hadn't helped, I'd have been split from my dad. I still worry that a social worker will come and take me away from him, so I don't want one snooping round.

Clare still pops in occasionally, but I see to most of dad's needs now. The neighbour and I do the heavy shopping together. The rest, I get at the corner shop, a bit at a time, usually on my way back from school. I also keep the house clean as best I can. I feel really tired most of the time, and I will quit school as soon as I'm able. Looking after my dad is the most important thing in the world for me. He's all I have.

Betty shows us how difficult it is to be a child carer. Their caring is hard work and it allows little space for them to address their own needs. She sees the work as a real challenge and has defined it in terms of the sacrifice she is prepared to make to keep up her relationship with her father. Being fearful of being taken into care has been a constant worry for her and prevents her from asking for any assistance to which she is entitled. Betty's position exposes the violation of the rights of children and people in need in wealthy industrialised nations when they do not receive services that could enhance their well-being. Children carry the burden of care on their small shoulders as a result. The absence of personal social services at the point of need also negates expressions of community-based solidarity. The curtailment of the right of child carers to growth and development to their fullest potential (UN Convention) is exemplified by Betty feeling that all she can do is give up school and forego her own future. This predicament alone is sufficient reason for social workers to become advocates for universal personal social services available as a right to all people in need and adapted to the particular circumstances of the recipient. Betty's story also indicates the lack of social work intervention for children when their immediate 'protection' is not at stake.

Elder Abuse

Feminist scholars and practitioners have exposed the high incidence of elder abuse that has lain hidden in caring relationships (Pritchard, 1992) and turned it from a private problem into a public issue, thereby challenging a taboo that condemns older people to suffer in silence. Elder abuse can take a number of forms: financial, when people take control of their money to misappropriate or use it for purposes that have not been endorsed by the older person; physical assaults; and sexual abuse (Biggs, 1993). Biggs *et al.* (1995) shows that the levels of abuse are considerably higher than anticipated. Elder abuse can be committed by a spouse, family members, or carers regardless of whether they are paid for their services. At the same time, the legal safeguards against elder abuse are limited. Also, the possibilities for accessing those that exist are restricted, particularly as many disabled elders have to rely on others to advocate on their behalf and ensure that their right to a non-abusive existence is upheld (Biggs, 1992).

Another form of emotional abuse concerns the right of older people to express their sexuality. Older people are discouraged from overtly expressing sexual feelings and loving relationships, particularly if they are gay or lesbian (Doress and Siegal, 1987). Romance has flourished in residential homes, despite hostility towards sexual expression being an integral part of their environment. The control of older people's sexuality, particularly when they are living in residential care has also received feminist attention. Feminists have challenged the assumption permeating residential establishments – that older people are 'past it'. Older women who no longer fear pregnancy can feel more carefree than ever to enjoy expressing their sexuality (Doress and Siegal, 1987). The struggle to validate the right of older people to sexual expression regardless of where they live, is ongoing (Gamarnikov *et al.*, 1983).

Genuine difficulties in facilitating the expression of sexual feelings can occur even if the right to do so is acknowledged and formal policies exist to guide intervention. Proving the suspected sexual abuse of older people whose mental capacities have declined through disease can be extremely problematic as the following vignette demonstrates:

Case Study

Priscilla is a 73 year old white woman who lives at The Maples (fictitious name). The staff are concerned about alleged sexual abuse. At least, that is the worry. But since Priscilla suffers from dementia, the nature of her relationship with Douglas, a 77 year old white resident, is unclear. She seems to enjoy his attention at times. At others, she complains to the staff that he won't leave her alone. The staff have been unable to determine exactly what is going on. Douglas has been clever enough to avoid being sanctioned by them by claiming that all he has ever given Priscilla is a kiss and a cuddle because she likes it. The other residents have labelled Douglas a sexual predator. Apparently, he takes sexual advantage of any woman who cannot consent to sex. Another resident has reported that she saw Douglas rape another woman resident who has severe dementia. But the case against him could not be proven.

The dividing line between abuse and consensual relationships that forensic experts seek to establish is difficult to draw, especially if a woman is not in full control of her mental capacities. Priscilla's case demonstrates the inadequacy of a forensic-driven approach that requires externally validated proof for it fails to protect vulnerable individuals.

In shedding its responsibilities for older people in England, the British state has introduced another form of institutional abuse into their lives: the policy of requiring older homeowners to sell their homes to pay for personal care during old age. This policy is problematic in a number of respects. Given differentiated housing tenures, this policy promotes indirect racism because people of Asian origins are over-represented as owner-occupiers. On the individual level, the policy can destroy older peoples' pride in having saved enough during their lifetimes to own their homes so that they can leave them to their offspring when they pass away. For policymakers to declare that a person's home is a source of wealth is irresponsible. It is merely foregone personal consumption. But it symbolises older peoples' sense of personal independence, commitment to reciprocity and bonds of interdependence across generations. Leaving 'something' as they see it, for their children who are usually their unpaid carers can be seen as a 'thank you' note for a lifetime of caring. It is also a way that parents provide for their children from beyond the grave. With rising house prices making it virtually impossible for young people to buy housing locally, it is also a way of ensuring that they continue to remain connected to a homebase. Carl, an 81 year old man explained his predicament as a result of the policy thus:

Case Study

I've just had to sell my terraced house to pay for being in Greenacres (fictitious name). It will see me through for a few years. What will happen after that? I pray that I'll be too far gone to care or even notice. But what gets me hopping mad is that I poured my life savings into the place (his home). I'd wanted to leave it for my son (aged sixty-four) who's been looking after me since my wife died more than thirty years ago. He's had a heart attack and can't look after me any more. That's why I'm here. What choices do he and I have? I feel I've been abused by politicians or at best, misled. I paid my national insurance stamps all those years. And now I get nothing for them.

The state's policy is experienced by some elders as a form of emotional and financial abuse, albeit in institutional guise. The state's approach is also a breach of contract and negates older people's right to continue living in their homes without worrying about evictions or being unable to pay their bills. Moreover, the high costs of residential care, and the rapid turnover in the ownership and uncertainties over the continued existence of such establishments, means that it does not take long for the 'savings' locked in people's homes to be quickly spent, leaving them homeless as well as penniless. Preventing the chaos and hardship that would ensue in these circumstances can be more easily undertaken if the community accepts responsibility for publicly-funded elder care as part of the interdependence within and between generations. A policy that pools risks across the whole of the community would be a more citizenship-oriented way of ensuring that everyone contributes to the well-being of others so that those in need can receive help when it is required without being subjected to stigmatising means-tests or experiencing a social problem as an individualised one. An action group has recently been set up to challenge existing policy in this regard in Britain.

There are a number of outstanding matters to be addressed in relation to the abuse of older people. Legislative protection is one of them. British social workers do not have the same powers to intervene to protect elders that they do in suspected cases of child abuse. However, I suggest that the model to be advocated in dealing with these problems is not that of the child protection system. For it is founded on crises interventions and assumptions of dependency that are inadequate for children, and arguably even more so for adults. Preventative work, interdependence and choice should be the bases of elder care legislation. Increasing the availability of stimulating, publicly-funded alternatives to home-based care for those who wish it is another important principle. Finally, the notion of active citizenship should underpin the entire system. In it, professionals' role should be to provide information and resources in assisting elders to make their own decisions.

Conclusions

The welfare state has contributed substantially to redefining women's place in society within the bounds of public patriarchy. Retrenchment in its provisions is unleashing a restructuring of public patriarchy and its return to private patriarchy. In this context, women are being called upon anew to provide unpaid care at home despite their increased involvement in waged labour. Only this time, the demand is for elder care not child care. As the state sheds responsibility for looking after people from the cradle to the grave, women are asked to cover the ensuing gaps. Many of these carers may be older women with care needs of their own. Others are young children.

Social workers, as the state employees formally assigned the task of responding on behalf of society are caught in the midst of these changes. A commitment to meeting people's needs, inadequate resources, and instructions to contract for services with other agencies place them in the crossfire between being part of the problem and not the solution to arranging dignified care for all people requiring it. Social work as a professional activity is unlikely to survive this onslaught unless it can argue that its remit is the provision of high quality care. To do that effectively, it has to place the 'client' at the centre of holistic service provision and delivery, and argue for universal personal social services rooted in citizenship rights that validate collectively-funded responses to individual need at whatever age these arise.

In this brave new world, existing gendered relations have to be reconstructed as an integral part of this arrangement. Women are at the centre of elder care whether giving or receiving it. But, elder care should not remain a concern solely for women. It should involve men as equal partners in both roles. For this to happen, the organisation of work, the devaluing of caring, and the exclusion of caring from current masculine ideals have to be rethought. Caring, as an endeavour that brings together interdependence and intergenerational solidarities in the social domain, is central to this re-evaluation. A reconsideration of the needs of child carers is also required if their own growth and development is not to be jeopardised.

7

Working with Offenders

The place of probation practice in the social work arena has been a contested one. In Britain, probation began as an activity with an interest in helping offenders change their behaviour – a matter definitively within the social work domain. It has now become an occupation concerned primarily with controlling and containing offenders in the community (Sone, 1995). Current attempts to locate it within the 'corrections' industry are not coincidental. Neither is the removal of probation training from the Diploma in Social Work (DipSW) and the university setting in parts of the United Kingdom. These events have been timed to signal a shift of emphasis in probation practice: providing community containment facilities (Home Office, 1998).

Gender dynamics have provided another reason for this change. These have impacted primarily on two areas: altering the composition of the workforce and including victim perspectives in the work being done. Feminist scholars and probation officers have been crucial in promoting these changes in a male-dominated part of social work. Their endeavours and the subsequent gains have not been uncontentious. As Home Secretary, Michael Howard stated forthrightly that probation training had to be changed for admitting to its ranks too many black people and women, a number of whom were single parents (Sone, 1995). Although equal opportunities policies were being implemented throughout the Probation Service at that point, less than half of main grade probation officers were women and fewer than 10 per cent of those in the chief probation officer grades were white women. The proportion of black people were considerably less – 3 per cent at basic grade level and none at chief probation officer level (NACRO, 1994).

In the debate over the role of probation services in modern society, the state declared these entrants unsuitable for the job (Dews and Watts, 1994). And, the failure of the Probation Service to deal adequately with offenders was placed at their door. Though laughable on one level, this complaint exposed the then Home Secretary's fear that white women and black people were 'soft' on offenders and responsible for shortchanging the presumably white male public. At the same time, this politician draw upon

144

gendered views of 'tough' white men as the protectors of vulnerable populations in their care. Demanding that probation officers protect the public, the Home Secretary replaced the Probation Service's unreliable (as he deemed them) recruits to the profession with more appropriate ones – strong white men (Sone, 1995). Consequently, he insisted upon the employment of former army personnel who could show offenders the tough side of the law. By placing offenders in the care of seasoned army men, punishment rather than rehabilitation would become the rule (Sone, 1995). Toughness was quickly adopted by magistrates and the prison population rose accordingly (Greenhorn, 1996).

In this chapter, I examine the context in which the state redefines probation practice as a corrections activity with an intensified social control function instead of a branch of social work committed to rehabilitating offenders. In official discourses, offenders are constructed as outside society when they live both within and outwith it. I also consider the importance of gender in work with offenders and use feminist criminological research to identify issues to be addressed in a just penal system. I conclude that: tackling the causes of crime are crucial elements within feminist jurisprudence; rehabilitating offenders is an important safeguard for victims; and working with offenders is part of the domain of social work practice.

Probation: Rehabilitation or Punishment?

In Britain, probation has had a longstanding interest in assisting offenders during the sentencing process and rehabilitation (Jarvis, 1976). The balance between protecting the public and rehabilitating offenders has been a precarious and constantly shifting one. Whilst the state has claimed to protect victims from the predations of offenders, increasing rates of crime, particularly of house burglaries and violent offences including those against women and children have prevailed (Mirlees-Black *et al.*, 1996). The criminal justice system has been accused of failing to protect society. A number of high profile cases of people wrongly charged and convicted has contributed to the perception that it is not dispensing justice and yielded public disenchantment with its capacity to do so. These have included prosecuting young people with learning difficulties who were poorly placed to defend themselves and those wrongly accused of terrorist offences whose cries of innocence went unheard for years e.g., the Birmingham Six (Young, 1999).

Probation, as part of this system, has its own credibility problems. It has recently been accused of being 'soft' on offenders and supporting their interests at the expense of those of the victims and the public (Sone, 1995).

Concern with its failure to side with victims led a Home Secretary to order probation officers to alert victims of violent crimes when their attackers were being released from prison. Its implications for practice were poorly thought out, resulting in women being informed that men who had raped them twenty-five years earlier were coming out. Without other forms of support, the repercussions of this policy can be horrific for victims, particularly when women victim–survivors of rape and other sexual assaults have been painfully and slowly attempting to rebuild their lives. Rather than helping, its implementation has caused women endless anguish as they suddenly realise their vulnerability to unwelcome callers. The cruder aspects of this policy did not last long, though a concern with responding to the needs of victims rightly remains (Tapley, 2000). However, the work continues to be marginalised and can be executed with little sensitivity. A Victim Support worker told me:

> I could not believe that I was being asked to cold call (i.e., arrive unannounced) on this woman who'd been sent a letter saying that the man who'd sexually assaulted her years ago would be released next month.

In another situation, a woman came across her former assailant in the High Street before she heard about it officially (Tapley, 2000). One reason for the policy's inadequate implementation has been lack of funding for victim-led services. Another has been that the state resorts to volunteers who are often not trained to support victims and have little clout in the courts (Tapley, 2000). However, debates favouring victims' concerns have shifted discourses on offenders more firmly towards punishment with little or no attempt at rehabilitation. Rehabilitative measures within probation services are not usually well-funded or resourced with appropriately trained personnel. But, they signal society's wish to do more with persons serving probation orders or prison sentences than contain them.

An orientation towards 'risk assessments' or attempts to calculate the dangerousness of a particular offender (Kemshall and Pritchard, 1996) intensifies the probation service's emphasis on controlling behaviour and replaces its concern to change it in significant ways. Discourses about the danger offenders pose separate them from 'normal' people who do not offend and reinforce the view that crime is caused by individual inadequacies.

Probation has lost much ground to the prison service in the credibility stakes as successive Home Secretaries have announced that 'prison works' (Williams, 1997). This approach has been constructed as a truism because a prisoner cannot inflict further damage upon the public whilst being physically removed from contact with its members. Research regarding 'what works' is more ambiguous. Probation practice can be effective (McIvor, 1996). The American experience on which the British one is modelled, demonstrates that prison as a way of dealing with offenders does not work. With 1 out of 37 adults under correctional supervision, the USA spends more on prisons than education while violent crime rates continue to soar (Young, 1999).

Furthermore, this facile position ignores a number of important considerations. One of these revolves around maintaining discipline within a prison as a total institution (Goffman, 1961) that houses a high concentration of men who seek to assert their power over others (Priestly, 1981). Maintaining discipline in such circumstances requires a system that commands obedience without having those who obey lose face so that they can continue to score high on the masculinity scale of bravado (Whitehead, 2000).

A well-worn method of reducing the number of inmates that misbehave while serving sentences is to offer the carrot of early release for 'good' behaviour. Those running prisons consider this a reasonable price to pay for retaining control and discipline over an unruly population. From victims' point of view, it is deplorable that an opportunity to really change men's behaviour, through specific programmes designed to enable them to treat others with respect rather than as objects to manipulate at their pleasure, has been bypassed (Young, 2000). For the lessons that a prisoner learns about the operation of power within custodial walls ensure that in any power struggle for supremacy, he must be victorious (Whitehead, 2000). Once learnt, this knowledge will serve him as well outside the prison as within it. As a number of people who have been imprisoned have testified, prisons are 'universities of crime' so that incarceration teaches them to become even more clever and hardened criminals (Boyle, 1977).

The expansion of the market within the interstices of the welfare state has also penetrated the British criminal justice system and strengthened its preoccupation with custody as the preferable form of punishment. Even the prison service, firmly ensconced within the public sector and cacooned until recently by a general consensus around the immorality of having private entrepreneurs amass profits from the incarceration of human beings, is now subject to privatisation. Private prisons now operate in the United States, United Kingdom and Australia (Logan, 1996). These developments raise important ethical questions, not least linked to the treatment of offenders within prison walls, because to make these institutions profitable, the welfare-oriented facilities that private entrepreneurs make available to prisoners have been reduced (Kassindja, 1998). Instead of investing in people through the provision of educational programmes and other measures aimed at rehabilitating offenders, money has gone instead into high-tech surveillance equipment that can monitor and control inmates more efficiently (Logan, 1996).

Feminists have identified for some time the failure of prisons to focus on changing prisoners' behaviour during their period of incarceration and prepare them for life post-release. A key element in the feminist repertoire has been to demand the rehabilitation of violent offenders, particularly those who have been imprisoned for physical and sexual assaults against women before their release into the community (Dominelli, 1989). Securing changes in men's behaviour has been crucial to ensuring women's well-being and right to live in their homes and walk the streets whenever they choose without fear of violence (Dworkin, 1981). This goal has yet to be achieved. Meanwhile, a group of male sex offenders in Kingston Penitentiary in Canada has sued the federal government for neglecting to provide them with educational programmes that would enable them to change their behaviour in preparation for life outside the prison gates.

Growing numbers of people in prison as a result of policies demanding higher rates of incarceration have strained available facilities and devoured substantial amounts of resources that could have gone elsewhere (Young, 2000). Reducing prison expenditures should make punishment in the community a politically popular alternative method of controlling offenders, but this is not happening. In theory, community-based sentences might provide probation officers with the opportunity to undertake rehabilitative work with offenders, but rising caseloads and inadequate resources for intensive one-to-one work with seriously damaged people curtail their potential to do so to any appreciable extent. Despite these limitations and the pessimism of 'what works' theorists, probation has been remarkably successful in keeping offenders on the straight and narrow, especially during the period of surveillance covered by a probation order (McIvor, 1992).

Feminist Criminologists Highlight the Link Between Masculinity and Crime

Feminist criminologists have made a substantial contribution to understanding offending behaviour in both men and women. They were amongst the first modern criminologists to highlight the importance of differentiating between men and women offenders, proceeding to identify the different patterns of crime, causes of crime, responses to men and women offenders and gendered punishments (see Smart, 1976; Smart and Smart, 1978; Dominelli, 1983; Morris, 1987; Carlen and Worrall, 1987). Their work on domestic and sexual violence against women has been instrumental in changing prevailing practices in the criminal justice system to take more notice of women victim–survivors' perspectives and experiences (Mullender, 1997).

Building on the analyses of 'black' and white anti-racists, feminists have also considered the impact of racism on offending behaviour and the treatment of 'black' men and women who are disproportionately represented within custodial settings (Dominelli, 1983; Cook and Hudson, 1993; Dominelli *et al.*, 1995). Racist stereotypes about 'black' offenders and fears of being considered racist for operating in contexts that they have not understood have resulted in white probation officers abrogating their responsibility to comment on appropriate disposals for black offenders in pre-sentence reports (PSRs). In failing to make recommendations on appropriate sentencing for black offenders to the courts, white probation officers increase the likelihood of magistrates passing harsher sentences than is warranted (Whitehouse, 1986; Denney, 1992). In a previous piece of research into community service orders in the early 1980s, a white male magistrate told me:

Case Study

I take SERs (Social Enquiry Reports, now PSRs) very seriously and I always ask for one if I haven't got it. If I get a clear SER without a recommendation for disposal, I take it to mean the probation officer thinks he can't work with the offender and change his ways. So, a lighter sentence like a probation order or community service order will not work. In these circumstances, I am more likely to go for a custodial sentence than I would have otherwise. Only the stiffest of sentences will do.

If this magistrate's actions are replicated throughout the country, the over-representation of women first-time offenders and black men in prison can be seen as the logical consequence of the intersection between a probation officer's reluctance to put certain offenders at risk through stereotypical approaches to identity attributes, and in the context of offending behaviour, a magistrate's interpretation of that reluctance as indicating a serious problem in the offender's responses to non-custodial sentencing. White probation officers also handle badly the provision of support made available to black offenders post-sentence (Dominelli *et al.*, 1995). And black offenders in prison experience racist treatment at the hands of white prisoners and officers (Cowburn, 1998).

Fortunately, black people working within the criminal justice system have orchestrated a range of initiatives in the private, public and voluntary sectors explicitly seeking to address questions of racism on the Bench, in the probation office and the prison setting. In Britain, the Association of Black Probation Officers (ABPO), the National Association of Asian Probation Officers (NAAPO) and the National Association of Probation Officers (NAPO) have made anti-racism a key feature of their contributions to national probation policy and practice. Their endeavours have created policies, codes of practice, mentoring schemes and publications that promote anti-racist probation practice on a national level.

Black feminists within these organisations have covered a range of issues around training and staff development, including organising black probation officers to support black students being victimised through institutional racism on training courses (Pillay, 1995). These activities have been crucial in assisting black students to have a positive experience of their education and prevented some from failing by having their energies consumed in responding to racism. Black people's initiatives on the training front have also resulted in 'benchmarking', that is, setting standards that improve the quality of educational life not only for black students, but also for white ones (Pillay, 1995).

Similarly, gains made in improving working conditions for black probation officers can be transferred to other personnel. Support networks developed in black organisations for black workers have provided role models for white practitioners to emulate in tackling the racism they both perpetrate and encounter, e.g., the White Collective for Anti-Racist Social Work (Dominelli, 1988). Such support groups or networks can be influential and play a crucial role in building and sustaining confidence, clarifying issues, and creating new egalitarian relationships across racial divides. These are particularly useful in realising good practice and checking out how to address the complex dilemmas that arise when addressing racism and handling offending behaviour in anti-oppressive ways.

Racism and its role in denying justice to black victims has been raised recently in a poignant way by the McPherson Report (1998) into the murder of Stephen Lawrence. After years of defying the racism of a police force that refused to take seriously his parents' complaints and bring his assailants to court, the Lawrences' allegations of racist treatment have been vindicated. The Report also affirms the structural connections between institutional racism and personal racist behaviours identified by anti-racists some time earlier (see Hall *et al.*, 1978; Dominelli, 1988; Solomos, 1989).

Feminists (Dominelli, 1991; Hanmer, 1994; Newburn and Stanko, 1994) and pro-feminist men criminologists (Jackson, 1995; Mac an Ghaill, 1994) have probed the link between masculinity and crime. Much of this work examines how masculine discourses legitimate violent crimes against women and children. Masculine rites enabling young men to be initiated into manhood play their part because crime becomes one site in which these dynamics are played out (Graef, 1992). The conjunction between masculinity and crime convinced feminists such as Andrea Dworkin (1981) and Susan Brownmiller (1976) to argue that masculinity provides the bond between offending men whom the criminal justice system has convicted of violent assaults against women, and 'normal' men whom it has not (Hanmer, 1994). Moreover, feminist research has highlighted ordinary men's potential to commit such acts (Russell, 1984), thereby undermining criminologists' divisions between normal men and bestial offenders (Mac an Ghaill, 1998). As Hanmer (1994) claims, 'Mr Anyman' is 'Mr Deviant'.

Masculinity has been exposed as normalising crime for all men. So, Roger Graef (1992) can write that in the United Kingdom, one in three men have been *convicted* of non-motoring offences before the age of 30. Antony Whitehead (2000) makes even stronger claims in his research into a British prison by demonstrating that men construct and re-construct themselves as men within the routine activities of their daily interactions. The exercise of power as *power over* others to cajole and terrorise people into behaving in particular ways becomes part and parcel of the masculine project of creating men and manhood as a continuous process of *social* reproduction. Crime, because it has an implicit critique of authority, simply provides one site in which masculinity is (re)created. Men, to become or be men, need to prove that they can control their own destiny and that of others (Whitehead, 2000). The irony of crime is that it both confirms and challenges their power to do so simultaneously. For while undermining the authority of other men, it reinforces hegemonic patriarchal relations between men (Whitehead, 2000).

Some feminists have difficulty accepting that although few in number, women sex offenders exist and have caused considerable damage and distress to children (Saradjian and Hanks, 1996). Others have argued that gender is not the only dynamic that operates in sexual assaults against children. I (Dominelli, 1986, 1989) have focused on adultist power relations as a way of understanding child sexual abuse by women. Feminists must pay more attention to the needs of women who have committed sexual offences and work to end such behaviour. Feminist principles that seek to ensure egalitarian relations between all people are against women oppressing others as much as they are against men doing so. Feminists do not aim to replace rule by one group of people with another.

Feminist perspectives on masculinity and crime have proved extremely controversial. Even after two decades of research that have demonstrated the ordinariness not the bestiality of men who are convicted of physical and sexual assaults against women and children, the National Coalition of Free Men in the United States claims in its website that all men are not potential rapists. It does so not by examining hegemonic masculinity and its legitimation of men's drive to control others and exercise *power over* them, but by distancing the 'good' men who have not been convicted of such crimes from the 'bad' men who have. In pursuing this line of argument, they disregard: self-report studies that indicate high numbers of men willing to commit violent offences if they know they can escape detection (Sim, 1994); feminist arguments and empirical evidence showing a high incidence of crime against women (Kelly, 1988; Graef, 1992); and the under-reporting of sexual and physical assaults against women and children (Newburn and Stanko, 1994). Anti-feminist men's groups also believe that the inclusion of violent women offenders alongside men offenders negates the relevance of gender dynamics. Besides, neglecting to account for the fact that the number of women committing such crimes are small (although their behaviour is also *un*acceptable), they miss the point that feminity is not linked to the dynamics of exercising gendered control as is masculinity. Women's identity is more rooted in their caring and mothering capacities (Belotti, 1975). These differences indicate that there are other reasons why women commit such crimes and these have to be addressed.

Women Offenders

Men and women offenders engage in some crimes specific to their gender (Smart, 1976); others, are committed by both, e.g., burglary and motoring offences tend to be dominated by men; prostitution and shoplifting by women (Smart, 1976; Dominelli, 1983). The two genders commit drug offences in approximately similar proportions. Yet, despite the less serious nature of their offences, women first-time offenders are more likely to end up in prison than men first-time offenders (Dominelli, 1983; NACRO, 1994). In Britain, this includes imprisonment for allegedly victimless crimes that in theory cover those to which both parties have consented and in which neither has been hurt, as in some cases of prostitution. Women can be incarcerated for failing to pay fines imposed upon them for soliciting. Once in prison, women are more likely than men to be given drugs to control their behaviour and are seen as particularly problematic (Worrall, 1990).

The criminal justice system is oriented primarily towards meeting the needs of men offenders. This slant is also reflected in the criminological literature which treats women offenders as anomalies (Smart, 1976, 1984). One reason for this has been the lower numbers of women offenders than men (Dominelli, 1983; Gelsthorpe, 1989).

Black feminists have unpacked white feminists' conceptualisation of men as a homogeneous category by identifying how racist constructs have differentiated black offenders from white ones. Their efforts have exposed as racist white feminists holding 'Reclaim the Night Marches' in communities where primarily black people live, for these contribute to public stereotypes of black men as violent aggressors, particularly as rapists and muggers (Bryant *et al.*, 1985). Black feminists have also identified how immigration policies silence the voices of black women victim–survivors of domestic violence (Mama, 1989; Bhatti-Sinclair, 1994) and sexual abuse (Wilson, 1993).

The roles women play and their place in society have carried implications for the processing of women offenders (Dominelli, 1983; Farringdon and Morris, 1983). Women's role as nurturers has been taken to mean that women will offend less than men, and they are punished severely when they transgress these norms. Women offenders experience double jeopardy because they are sentenced for their offences and for having broken the social taboo against women becoming criminals and socialising others, particularly their children, into similar anti-social habits. Consequently, women offenders are deemed 'mad, sad or bad' (Worrall, 1990). They have been depicted as hangers on to the more daring male criminal, goaded into crime by their menfolk, or suffering from mental illness, mental incapacity or hormonal imbalance (Pollack, 1978). These images deny women offenders agency in the commission of crimes. For women who have been sentenced, these stereotypes have yielded: stiffer penalties leading to over-representation in prison for first-time offenders, more medication being used to control them when serving custodial sentences, and a gendered use of probation to 'help' them become better mothers and wives when sentenced to community disposals.

These characterisations of women offenders apply largely to white women. My research (Dominelli, 1983) has revealed that even the category 'bad' does not reflect the threat that white racists believe black women offenders pose to the existing social order. Black women offenders, especially Afro-Caribbean ones, are more likely to be considered *dangerous* than 'mad' or 'sad'. Thus, they are more likely than white women to be over-represented in custodial settings and for less serious offences (Dominelli, 1983). Less emphasis is placed on rehabilitating them than controlling them through drugs that have considerable side-effects (see Kassindja, 1997). Gloria, an Afro-Caribbean woman who had served six months for her first offence had been involved in an affray that resulted in differential sentencing. Each black woman involved was given six months in custody and each white woman, a twelve month probation order. She maintains:

Case Study

I was sentenced unfairly. So were my mates. We had gone to this club in Midtown [fictitious name] and it was nearly closing time. We were having fun laughin' with each other, larkin' about. These white girls come up and started mouthing off. One of them hit my friend, Kristy. We went to help pull her away and suddenly, the white girls started hitting the rest of us too. We were kicking away when the cops arrived. They didn't wanna know that it weren't us who started the fight. We were all taken to the police station, but the white girls went home long before we did. I was really scared because although I'd done nothing, I didn't think anyone would believe me. As it turned out, they didn't. I got done.

As far as I'm concerned, the white girls got off scott-free ... Probation's nothing. You should try prison and see what it's like. Then, you'll know what I mean. The screws [prison officers] treated us like dirt. They said we [the black friends she made in prison] were a menace to the prison service. They gave us all the dirty jobs to do.

Probation sentences have been passed mainly upon white female offenders to help them address their moral welfare (Chesney Lind, 1973). Even for women whose major need is that of maximising their incomes, probation officers have little to offer beyond a listening ear, a willingness to help them explore options that will keep them on the straight and narrow, and very limited material resources, usually those that can be accessed from other agencies (Dominelli, 1988). The focus on women's moral character and the less serious nature of their offences have meant that probation orders have been deemed more appropriate for (white) women offenders than white men (Dominelli, 1983; Worrall, 1990). Black and white women consider probation orders invasive because all aspects of their lives, including their housekeeping and mothering capacities are placed under surveillance for considerable periods. They argue that fines and community service orders are preferable ways of punishing them than probation orders (Dominelli, 1983).

Women's roles as mothers continue to be important to women offenders who either are pregnant and give birth whilst serving a prison sentence or have children outside. With giving birth inside comes the pain of living with a young baby within the prison setting of a mother and baby unit and, when the time comes, the difficulty of separation from their newborn child (Enos, 2001). Women miss dreadfully children left in the care of either friends, relatives or the local authority. They also worry that children may feel abandoned when they want nothing more than to be with them (Enos, 2001). Wanting to provide a better life for their children drives some women to offend in the first place (Dominelli, 1983).

Women's experience of prison is a more isolating one than men's. As so few women are in prison, there are not many custodial institutions to house them. This makes it hard for the specific needs of women offenders to be met (Faith, 1993). Women may be imprisoned a long way from home. Friends and kin who wish to visit may have to travel extremely long distances and at great expense, thereby cutting down on the number of visits that it is feasible for them to undertake (Faith, 1993). Lack of contact with close others increases women offenders' sense of isolation and despair.

Prison authorities have argued that their small numbers make it uneconomical to provide the wide range of educational and recreational services that are available in men's prisons (Faith, 1993). The lack of educational provisions for women in prison is serious for it reduces women's chances of rehabilitation in accordance with their needs. Having educational and vocational programmes that equip them for gainful employment once they are released is important to achieve the goal of overcoming low incomes and setting them on a more suitable path for life outside the prison (Dominelli, 1983). However, these programmes need to offer women choices other than the domestic labour and child care that prison regimes believe is most appropriate for women (Faith, 1993). Such options reinforce the dominant ideology that women should be good mothers and homemakers and opens up only low-waged job opportunities that are unlikely to raise them out of poverty (Glendinning and Millar, 1992). Also, channelling women in these directions does not necessarily coincide with the aspirations women have for themselves.

Feminists have also challenged the representation of women offenders as incapable not only by demonstrating their capacity to act as agents in their own right, but also by taking direct action against stigmatising treatment by the criminal justice system. The Campaign for the Reform of the Law on Soliciting (PROS) is a well-documented example of this (McLeod, 1982; Dominelli, 1986). PROS redefined women sex workers on the streets as women performing socially necessary work. PROS argued strongly against the labelling of these women as 'common prostitutes' and demanded the decriminalisation of soliciting and an end to the unfair pursuit of women involved in these activities. Moreover, women's actions in PROS redefined prostitution as an issue about the poor economic opportunities available to women and men's control over them rather than their sexuality. At the same time, McLeod's (1982) work has highlighted the difficulties men have in subscribing to hegemonic definitions of male sexuality. PROS successfully formed alliances with and networks across a wide spectrum of women – practitioners, policymakers, academics, streetworkers, and men sympathetic to their cause. PROS exemplifies how woman-centered feminist action can be crucial in questioning dominant definitions of crime, redressing the criminalisation of particular groups, and positing alternative ways of dealing with offending behaviour.

The Criminalisation of Young Offenders

Discourses about young offenders focus on the difference between the justice model and the welfare model of reacting to children in trouble with the law. The pendulum on this issue swings in different directions depending on who assumes the roles of key opinion-formers. In recent controversies on the subject, politicians keen to impose the 'prison works' philosophy have endorsed a hardening of attitudes against young offenders (Pitts, 2000). Consequently, incarceration rather than helping them become better citizens playing a valuable role in society has assumed prominence as the way of dealing with them. The media has assisted in this task by exacerbating fears of frustrated young children venting their anger upon their elders and each other, as occurred in the coverage of the James Bulger murder in Britain (Jackson, 1990) or the murder of children by their playmates in the school grounds in the United States (Lasseter, 1998).

Politicians have used parents' failure to socialise children into socially accepted norms as a rod with which to beat women. Their discourses focus on women, particularly lone mothers, as inadequate parents responsible for offending behaviour in children. This is particularly apparent in media portrayals of young offenders (Lasseter, 1998). Single parent women have been castigated as culpable in creating this state of affairs in Britain, Canada and the United States (Murray, 1990, 1994). In all three countries, young offenders have been demonised with the result that *society's* responsibility for safeguarding the rights of children to a healthy environment conducive to their growth and development is being neglected with impunity (Finer and Nellis, 1995). Politicians are reluctant to link offending behaviour with social issues (Stewart *et al.*, 1994) such as: living on 'sink estates'; poverty; youth unemployment; and the lack of status accorded to young people in capitalist patriarchal societies that are losing their mass manufacturing base.

Instead, young people and their parents are pathologised and blamed for what are defined as behavioural deficiencies amongst youths. In Britain, parents can now be threatened with fines and imprisonment if they cannot control their offspring, regardless of age, resources, or capacity to do so. The 'offences' for which they may be held accountable include their children being persistently late for, or truanting from, school as well as burglary, and violent offences. Legislative changes have been enacted to make these possibilities a reality and several parents have been taken to court and sentenced for the activities of the youths that they have parented (Brandon *et al.*, 1998). In Britain, even local authorities can be held responsible for crimes committed by young people in their care (Young, 1999). And, there are moves afoot in both England and Canada to lower the age of responsibility for young offenders so that those committing more serious offences can be moved into the adult court system more rapidly (Wagg and Pilcher, 1996).

Current constructions of juvenile crime neglect issues of masculinity and feminity as articulated in the lives of young offenders. Yet, gendered perspectives are evident throughout the juvenile justice system. Young men have traditionally been treated more leniently than young women for 'sowing their wild oats', whilst adolescent girls have been detained for doing likewise (Chesney-Lind, 1973; Campbell, 1984). Young women's morality has consistently been a matter of concern for probation officers and social workers whereas that of young men has not. Moreover, despite the higher levels of crime committed by adolescent boys, they are expected to 'grow out of it' once they acquire girlfriends, a home and a family (Graef, 1992).

Young women, on the other hand, are not given a period of licence in which they can explore their sexuality and form their personalities. They are condemned to always behaving properly. And when they don't, they are labelled 'difficult to work with' by practitioners who try to avoid working with teenage girls at all costs (Dominelli, 1983). Difficulties faced by the few, are used to amplify deviance across all categories of young women in care (Dominelli, 1983), even though most of them are not in care for offending behaviour, but for family reasons, including the breakdown of nuclear family relationships between their parents (Pugh, 1993).

Young women offenders are being castigated for becoming more like young men in the crimes that they commit (Campbell, 1984). Newspaper portrayals of girl gangs are used to fantasise about the prospects of women's criminal profiles becoming exactly like those of men (Adler, 1975). Official crime statistics continue to reveal that young men commit the bulk of offences, although young women's share is rising more rapidly. The amplification of deviance is at play here. For statistics indicating that the rate of growth in young women's offences exceeds that of young men's, ignore the fact that there are fewer young women offenders to begin with. Regardless of feminists' positions in this debate, the crucial point is to find out why young people commit offences in the first place and what can be done to ensure that they acquire the skills and resources necessary for proving themselves in or developing more constructive social roles and status.

Working with Offenders from a Feminist Perspective

Feminist scholars have highlighted the significance of a differentiated approach to offenders so that the differing needs of white women and black men and women can be respected and taken on board throughout the criminal justice system. At the top of their list is the importance of rehabilitation as an integral part of the punishment or sentences meted out to offenders. Next, is the requirement that punishment fits the crime, and the eradication of discrimination against white women and black people.

Meeting feminist aspirations in this regard requires a reconsideration of the role and purposes of incarceration. Prisons should no longer function as closed institutions geared simply to controlling people serving their time. Inmates should not be penalised in addition to the punishment of losing their freedom. Instead, the authorities should use imprisonment as an opportunity to re-educate offenders into new modes of behaviour – those that respect the right of other people to live in a crime-free society and theirs to receive help. Expecting offenders to reform requires the causes of crime to be addressed. These are many and diverse, ranging as they do from psychological inadequacies to socially institutionalised ones. Prison authorities can promote the realisation of egalitarian relations in interpersonal relationships by treating prisoners with dignity even when condemning their behaviour.

Realising citizenship as a two-way process exemplifies the integration of feminists analyses in practice. A critique of societal shortcomings as well as individual failures and linking these to personal and institutional change are integral elements in implementing citizenship rights. So, entitlement to rehabilitation is a right of citizenship and there is an issue about safeguarding the citizenship rights of offenders. Achieving personal change is the prisoner's contribution towards the implementation of a citizenship based approach to incarceration. Society's obligation to remedy its inadequacies sits alongside a prisoner's duty to change behaviour. Prisoners are a captive audience. Engaging them in behavioural change as part of a rehabilitation programme aimed at reintegrating offenders into society post-sentence is a goal that prison officers can concentrate upon from the moment prisoners walk through the prison doors. All those working in the criminal justice system have the duty of ensuring that society takes its responsibility to offenders seriously. This requires issues of 'law and order' to cease being a political football tossed from one political party to another and be considered in more measured tones.

A further dimension of feminist criminological initiatives is understanding the impact of masculinity and power relations on men's offending behaviour (Dominelli, 1991). These strands have come together in feminist attempts to end men's physical or sexual assaults against women and children (Dworkin, 1981, 1988). With regard to sexual violence, feminists' focus on masculinity has challenged biologism – the view that sex offences are caused by men's uncontrollable sex drives. This work has highlighted as problematic not biological urges but gendered power relations and their organisation within family settings (Rush, 1980). Gendered analyses of power relations explain why most sex offenders are men and most victims are women. This work has also been crucial in emphasising the voices of women victim–survivors (Rush, 1980). Moreover, in creating resources to meet the needs of women, feminists were amongst the first to legitimate a concern for the needs of victims and provide facilities to address these.

The project developed by women to respond to domestic violence in Duluth in the United States illustrates a feminist model of practice that has been modified for use in a number of English-speaking countries including Britain (Orme *et al.*, 2000). The popularity of the Duluth power wheel model can be attributed to its basic feminist template for dealing with violent men. The model exposes men's psychological desire to dominate others as an indispensable part of their social position as men in a society that accords them superiority. Workers using Duluth inspired interventions as in the CHANGE project in Scotland, have responded to the different needs articulated by men offenders and women victim–survivors (Cavanagh and Cree, 1995).

Changing men's abusive behaviour, against those they deem inferior, has proved incredibly difficult. Many men offenders deny their assaults and refuse to take responsibility for their behaviour. Progress in altering the nature of their interactions with others is impossible unless men take responsibility for what they do (Snowdon, 1980). Tackling their refusal to do this is a major task for practitioners undertaking work with violent men in either one-to-one or groupwork sessions (Dominelli, 1999). This work has to place masculinity and power relations as central considerations to be addressed in a consistent and systematic manner (Cowburn and Dominelli, 1998).

Feminists have also questioned the criminal justice system's responses to victims of sexual violence, particularly women who have been raped (Dworkin, 1981). Their efforts have identified the institutionalised rape of women whose sexual behaviour in general is subjected to interrogation in the courtroom. Feminists have dismissed the validity of a legal mandate that holds women responsible for men's behaviour (Dworkin, 1981). Besides challenging the legitimacy of these state-endorsed practices, feminists have created gender awareness training sessions where judges can learn how they contribute to blaming women victim–survivors rather than male attackers for sexual violence (Horley, 1990). Feminist analyses, insights and practice in working with offenders are relevant to all those involved in the criminal justice system.

Conclusions

As long as probation practice engages with the rehabilitation of offenders, it constitutes part of the social work arena. The pressures to divert it towards corrections must be resisted if offenders are to do more than serve their time in either prison or the community. Probation practice cannot treat all offenders as an undifferentiated mass. It has to gear its activities to the specific needs of individual offenders by situating them within specific contexts that integrate them into the broader social order in which they live and ensure that practitioners acquire the range of skills necessary for making the links between personal and structural conditions that impact upon behaviour. The criminal justice system has to recognise racism alongside sexism in responding to black women offenders and see them as both individuals and part of a collective entity if it is to avoid colluding with existing stereotypes of different types of offenders.

Particular constructions of offenders and their victims need to be unpacked for their specificity and related back to determining what forms of punishment and rehabilitation will meet their needs alongside those of the victim–survivors. The provisions used for these purposes have to be adequately resourced and its practitioners well-trained. In short, probation practice has to operate in a manner consistent with affirming offenders' rights to learn to behave in more socially acceptable ways and enhance the quality of life of victim–survivors. Reciprocated citizenship should underpin how the criminal justice system operates in handling offenders, responding to victim–survivors of crime and caring for its workforce. Rehabilitation needs to be at the centre of a citizenship-based approach to offenders. The rights of citizenship should extend to young offenders as well as adult offenders, whether male, female, black or white.

Re-entry to the community on completing a sentence is a predictable eventuality for most prisoners. Probation officers working with them should begin to plan for release from the beginning of their sentence if the terms 'protecting the public' and 'rehabilitating offenders' are to move beyond rhetorical phrases. The probation service can respond to feminists' demands for a safe environment where women, children and men can live by carrying out work that fulfills this aim. This would mean responding to women's needs as they express them rather than welfarising women for social control purposes.

8

Conclusions

Feminist social work theory and practice has been developing apace in the past two decades bringing many innovations into the discipline. It has both friends and enemies within the system. And it has a considerable distance to go in reaching its objectives in tangible forms that permeate the broader society. With regard to social work, feminists have highlighted the importance of gender dynamics in a profession begun by women. The preponderance of women within its borders has not guaranteed that women's interests as women are recognised and responded to. Thus, feminists have had to develop a theory and a practice that places women at the centre of its interventions. From there, feminists have ensured that their work ripples out to encompass all people, regardless of gender. Additionally, feminists have created theories and proposals for practice that respond to critiques from within women's ranks to encompass the rich diversity of social divisions that women embrace. Feminists have developed analyses and social action whilst living in insider–outsider roles. That is, they have to work against being oppressed and being oppressive simultaneously.

Moreover, the majority of women continue relating to men as fathers, husbands, brothers, sons or co-workers. So, feminists have formulated strategies for liberation whilst living in close proximity to their oppressors. This has called for a reconceptualisation of relationships as interconnected and interdependent. Exploring these requires what Ruth Brandwein (1986) terms 'both/and' interconnected logic rather than the either/or linear framework that describes men's and women's worlds as one of dichotomous or opposing entities. Feminists have achieved their insights whilst including men within their analysis and suggesting action with which men and women interested in working with them can engage. In this, they have upheld the feminist principle of integrating theory and practice and demonstrated the relevance of feminism to all people.

Feminism is committed to ensuring that social justice prevails across all social divisions. This acknowledges women's presence in all of them and desire to end all forms of oppression. Despite its broader relevance, feminists continue to see women as the starting point of their analyses and improving their social situation as the purpose of their endeavours. In achieving these goals, feminists are concerned with inputs, processes and outputs as part of a holistic approach to social change at both personal and structural levels. Social work, with its concern for social justice, commitment to initiating change in individuals and involving people in the processes whereby decisions about their future are made, shares a number of features with feminism. Hence, feminist social work provides a method that is in keeping with the profession's preoccupations with service provision and delivery to enhance well-being. However, feminist social work goes well beyond the profession's traditional confines as defined by legislation. Feminists have been critical of contemporary practice in many situations relating to its treatment of children, women and men. The proximity between them, therefore, is more an uneasy co-existence rather than incorporation.

Feminist principles relevant to practice and evident in feminist social work are:

1. Recognising the diversity of women;

2. Valuing women's strengths;

3. Eliminating the privileging of certain groups of women to prevent difference from becoming a basis for unequal power relations between different groups of women;

4. Considering women as active agents capable of making decisions for themselves in all aspects of their lives;

5. Locating individual women in their social situations and acknowledging the interconnections between the individual and collective entities relevant to them;

6. Providing women with the space to voice their own needs and solutions to problems;

7. Acknowledging that the principle 'the personal is political' is relevant at macro, meso and micro levels of practice;

8. Redefining private woes as public issues;

9. Ensuring that women's needs are addressed within the context of their being seen as whole human beings in which each area of life interacts with the others;

10. Recognising the interdependent nature of human relations and through that, realising that what happens to one individual or group has implications for every one else;

11. Recognising that women's individual problems have social causes and addressing both levels in each intervention; and

12.   Looking for collective solutions to individual problems.

These principles provide the framework for the integration of feminist social work theory and practice. Social policies form part of the context within which these are elaborated.

Feminist principles that apply in social work with men are:

1.   Recognising that gendered power relation have implications for men;

2.   Acknowledging that masculinity is predicated upon power dynamics that impose power over others who are deemed socially inferior or weaker;

3.   Recognising that men are privileged over women by virtue of their gender because society has been organised in ways that make this so;

4.   Recognising the diversity that exists amongst men;

5.   Appreciating that the diversity amongst men reflects differing levels of privileging amongst men and between different groups of men;

6.   Ensuring that men take responsibility for their behaviour in oppressing others;

7.   Acknowledging a connection between men who abuse their power to oppress women and children by committing indictable offences and those who do not challenge the social relations in which such behaviour is embedded;

8.   Celebrating the redefinition of masculinity in nurturing and egalitarian directions; and

9.   Acknowledging the connection between structural constraints and personal behaviour and (lack of) emotional growth.

These principles have been used by feminists to develop gendered analyses and forms of practice that are relevant to women, children and men. Feminists' concerns with the rights of children have focused on the significance of adultist power relations in oppressing children. These have to be deconstructed if children's voices are to be heard on par with those of adults. Doing so is part of a broader strategy whereby feminists endorse the rights of all oppressed groups to have their voices heard.

The messages that feminists have tried to convey to society have not always been appreciated. Men who fear losing their privileges have organised to subvert the implementation of feminist demands. Their opposition has been particularly important in the areas of women's sexuality, women's reproductive rights, women's roles as mothers and wives, and paid employment (Brooks, 1996). This has led to feminist gains being withdrawn or reduced, for example, Thatchers's attack on women's social security and employment rights in 1986 (Levitas, 1986; Dominelli, 1988a); the continuing challenges to affirmative action in the United States (Clark *et al.*, 1996).

Feminist social workers have to work within and outside state structures to enable women to play the insider–outsider role that provides a springboard for resistance to gender oppression and promotes feminists' commitment to building a better world for women, children and men. Feminist social work has to continue developing its theory and practice into the foreseeable future. An important dimension for future deliberation and action is using computer-based technologies to assist social workers in undertaking their tasks in ways that are consistent with feminist principles. Access to these technologies and questions about who controls them remain crucial topics for further discussion. Similarly, the new reproductive technologies will have a crucial impact on tomorrow's developments in social work (Sewpaul, 1997; Dominelli, forthcoming). Their enhancement of women's well-being cannot be taken for granted (Stanworth, 1988; Steinberg, 1997). Although their use can increase women's chances of becoming mothers, the process of their becoming so will not necessarily be carried out under their control or auspices (Stanworth, 1988; Steinberg, 1997). Women may be disempowered to advantage the medical profession and men interested in controlling women more generally (Stanworth, 1988). At the same time, women who have relied on reproductive technologies to solve problems of fertility in either themselves or their partners have advocated for their continued existence as publicly-funded resources available to all (Cotton, 1999) rather than being restricted to a wealthy few. These developments pose a number of serious ethical and practice considerations that social workers must address.

The new reproductive technologies including *in vitro* fertilization (IVF) and surrogacy have also begun to establish new relationships around becoming parents and raising children that require a rethinking of familial terminologies and dynamics. Who is encompassed within their remit? Should money change hands? What obligations exist amongst those involved? Who should be involved in these forms of procreation? When should the resulting offspring be told? These questions raise complex moral and ethical considerations that need careful thinking (Warnock, 1984). Additionally, these developments have recast the links between biological and social parenting in ways that reorganise the meanings of familiar concepts associated with kinship relations.

Finally, feminist social workers have to consider their own needs as workers. Responding to these requires practitioners to develop networks and systems of support that will enable them to continue working in difficult circumstances including poorly resourced offices, heavy workloads and hostile colleagues and/or 'clients'. Getting support from their managers and political rulers is necessary, but often difficult.

At the same time, feminist practitioners have to maintain their commitment to 'clients' and work hard to ensure that service users set the agendas to which they contribute as professionals who are at their service. Citizenship becomes a major way of reframing the relationship between social workers and 'clients' in egalitarian partnerships that fulfill people's needs. Feminist social work theory and practice promotes such developments.

Bibliography

Achilles, K. (1992) *Misconceptions: The Social Construction of Choice* (Toronto: University of Toronto Press).

Adams, R. (1998) *Quality Social Work* (London: Macmillan – now Palgrave).

Adams, R., Dominelli, L. and Payne, M. (1998) *Social Work: Themes, Issues and Critical Debates* (London: Macmillan – now Palgrave).

Adamson, N., Briskin, L. and McPhail, M. (1988) *Organising for Change: The Contemporary Women's Movement in Canada* (Oxford University Press).

Adamson, O., Brown, C., Hanison, J. and Price, J. (1976) 'Women's Oppression Under Capitalism', *Revolutionary Communist*, No. 5, pp. 1–48.

Adler, F. (1975) *Sisters in Crime* (New York: McGraw-Hill).

Ahmed, B. (1990) *Black Perspective in Social Work* (Birmingham: Venture Press).

Ahmed, B. (1992) *A Dictionary for Black Managers in White Organisations* (London: National Institute of Social Work).

Ahmad, W. (ed) (1993) *'Race' and Health in Contemporary Britain* (Buckingham: Open University Press).

Amann, R. (1996) Re: Social Work, Letter to Lena Dominelli dated 7 June 1996, responding to her query regarding the ESRC's failure to recognise social work as a discipline.

Appleyard, B. (1993) 'Why Paint so Black a Picture?', *The Independent*, 4 August.

Arat-Koc, S. (1995) 'The Politics of Family and Immigration in the Subordination of Domestic Workers in Canada', in Nelson, E. D. and Robinson, B. W. (eds) *Gender in the 1990s: Images, Realities and Issues* (Scarborough, Ont.: Nelson Canada).

Armitage, A. (1996) *Aboriginal People in Australia, Canada and New Zealand* (Toronto: McClelland and Stewart).

Armstrong, L. (1978) *Kiss Daddy Goodnight* (New York: Pocket Books).

Armstrong, P. (1984) *Labour Pains: Women's Work in Crisis* (Toronto: Women's Press).

Arnup, K. (ed) (1995) *Lesbian Parents: Living with Pride and Prejudice* (Charlottetown: Gynergy Books).

Asante, M. (1987) *The Africentric Idea* (Philadelphia: Temple University Press).

Asian Sheltered Residential Association (ASRA) (1981) *Asian Sheltered Residential Accommodation* (London: ASRA).

Ashurst, P. and Hall, Z. (1989) *Understanding Women in Distress* (London: Tavistock/Routledge).

Association of University Teachers (AUT) (1999) Pay Differentials in Academe.

Attlee, C. R. (1920) *The Social Worker* (London: Library of Social Service).

Badran, M. and Cooke, M. (eds) (1990) *Opening the Gates: A Century of Arab Feminist Writing* (Bloomington, IN: Indiana University Press).

Balbo, L. (1987) 'Crazy Quilts: Rethinking the Welfare State Debate from a Woman's Point of View', in Showstack Sassoon, A. (ed), *Women and the State: The Shifting Boundaries of Public and Private* (London: Hutchinson).

Banks, O. (1981) *Faces of Feminism* (London: Martin Robinson).

Barker, H. (1986) 'Recapturing Sisterhood: A Critical Look at 'Process' in Feminist Organisations and Community Action', *Critical Social Policy*, 16, Summer, pp. 80–90.

Barlett, D. L. and Steele, J. B. (1998) 'Corporate Welfare: Special Report', *Time*, p. 4.

Barn, R. (1993) *Black Children in the Public Care System* (London: Batsford).

Barrett, M. (1981) *Women's Oppression Today* (London: Verso).

Barrett, M. and McIntosh, M. (1981) *The Anti-Social Family* (London: Verso).

Barrett, M. and McIntosh, M. (1985) Ethnocentrism and Socialist Feminist Theory, *Feminist Review*, 20, pp. 23–47.

Barnes, M. and Maple, N. (1992) *Women and Mental Health* (Birmingham: Venture Press).

Basu, M. (1997) *The Challenge of Local Feminisms: Women's Movements in Global Perspective* (Boulder: Westview Press).

Bayes, M. and Howell, E. (eds) (1981) *Women and Mental Health* (New York: Basic Books).

Beechey, V. (1980) 'On Patriarchy', *Feminist Review*, 2, pp. 45–77.

Begum, N. (1992) 'Disabled Women and the Feminist Agenda', in *Feminist Review*, 40, Spring, pp. 71–84.

Begum, N., Hill, M. and Stevens, A. (1993) *Reflections: The Views of Black Disabled People on their Lives and on Community Care* (London: CCETSW).

Belenky, M. F., Clinchy, M. B., Goldberger, N. R., Tarule, M. J. (1997) *Women's Ways of Knowing: The Development of Self, Voice and Mind* (New York: Basic Books).

Bell, C. and Newby, H. (1971) *Community Studies* (London: Allen and Unwin).

Belotti, E. (1975) *Little Girls* (London: Writers and Readers Publishing Co-operative).

Benn, M. and Sedgley, A. (1984) *Sexual Harassment* (London: Tavistock).

Benston, M. (1969) 'The Political Economy of Women's Labour', *Monthly Review*, 21(4), Sept, 13–27.

Bhatti-Sinclair, K. (1994) 'Asian Women and Domestic Violence from Male Partners' in Lupton, C. and Gillespie, T. (eds) *Working with Violence* (London: BASW/Macmillan – now Palgrave).

Bhavani, K. K. (1993) 'Taking Racism and the Editing of Women's Studies' in D. Richardson and V. Robinson (eds) *Introduction to Women's Studies* (London: Macmillan – now Palgrave).

Biesteck, F. P. (1961) *The Casework Relationship* (London: Allen and Unwin).

Biggs, S. (1993) *Understanding Ageing: Images, Attitudes and Professional Practice* (Buckingham: Open University Press).

Biggs, S. with Phillipson, C. and Kingston, P. (1995) *Elder Abuse in Perspective* (Buckingham: Open University Press).

Bishop, A. (1994) *Becoming an Ally: Breaking the Cycle of Oppression* (Halifax: Fernwood Publishing).

Bishopp, D., Canter, D. and Stockley, D. (1992) *Young People on the Move* (Guildford: Department of Psychology, University of Surrey).

Blair, T. (1999) 'PM's 20 Year Target to End Poverty', *The Guardian*, 19 March.

Bloom, H. (1992) *The American Religion: The Emergence of the Post-Christian Nation* (New York: Simon and Schuster).

Bly, R. (1985) *Iron John: A Book About Men* (Reading, Mass.: Addison-Wesley).

Bonny, S. (1984) *Who Cares in Southwark?* (London: National Association of Carers and their Elderly Dependents).

Borden, C. (1996) *GP Fundholders and Social Work*: paper presented at the Future of Social Work Seminar, Sheffield University, 20 November.

Bornat, J., Johnson, J., Pereira, C., Pilgrim, D. and Williams, F. (eds) (1997) *Community Care: A Reader* (London: Macmillan and Open University Press).

Bourdieu, P. and Wacquant, L. (1992) *An Invitation to Reflexive Sociology* (Cambridge: Polity Press).

Bowl, R. (1985) *Changing the Nature of Masculinity: A Task for Social Work* (Norwich: University of East Anglia Monographs).

Bowlby, J. (1953) *The Making and Breaking of Affectional Bonds* (London: Tavistock).

Box, S. (1987) *Recession, Crime and Punishment* (London: Macmillan – now Palgrave).

Boyle, J. (1977) *A Sense of Freedom* (London: Pan Books).

Brandon, M., Schofield, G. and Trinder, L., with Nigel Stone (1998) *Social Work With Children* (London: Palgrave).

Brandwein, R. (1986) 'A Feminist Approach to Social Policy', in N. Van Den Berg and L. Cooper (eds) *Feminist Visions for Social Work* (Silver Spring, MD.: NASW).

Brandwein, R. (1991) 'Women's Studies' in V. Mehta and F. Yasas (eds) *Exploring Feminist Visions* (Pune: Streevani).

Brody, C. (ed) (1987) *Women's Therapy Groups: Paradigms of Feminist Treatment* (New York: Springer Publishing).

Brook, E. and Davis, A. (1985) *Women, the Family and Social Work* (London: Tavistock).

Brooks, D. (ed) (1996) *Backward and Upward: The New Conservative Writing* (New York: Random House).

Brown, E. B. (1990) 'Womanist Consciousness: Maggie Lena Walker and the Independent Order of Saint Luke' in Du Bois, E. and Ruiz, V. (eds), *Unequal Sisters* (New York: Routledge).

Brown, G. and Harris, T. (1978) *The Social Origins of Depression* (London: Tavistock).

Browne, C. (1995) 'A Feminist Life Span Perspective on Aging', in Van Den Bergh, N. (ed) *Feminist Practice in the 21st Century* (Washington, DC: NASW Press).

Brownmiller, S. (1976) *Against Our Will: Men, Women and Rape* (New York: Bantam Books).

Bruyere, G. (2001) 'First Nations Approaches to Social Work', in Dominelli, L., Lorenz, W. and Soydan, H. (eds) *Beyond Racial Divides: Ethnicities in Social Work* (Aldershot: Ashgate).

Bryant, B., Dadzie, S. and Scafe, S. (1985) *The Heart of the Race: Black Women's Lives in Britain* (London: Virago).

Bulmer, M. and Rees, M. A. (eds) (1996) *Citizenship Today: The Contemporary Relevance of T. H. Marshall* (London: University College London Press).

Burden, D. S. and Gottlieb, N. (eds) (1987) *The Woman Client: Providing Human Services in a Changing World* (London: Tavistock).

Burnham, L. and Louie, M. (1985) 'The Impossible Marriage: a Marxist Critique of Socialist Feminism', *Line of March: A Marxist-Leninist Journal of Rectification*, No. 17, Spring.

Cahn, S. (ed) (1995) *The Affirmative Action Debate* (London: Routledge).

Callahan, M. (2000) 'Best Practice in Child Welfare: Lessons from the Field' in M. Callahan, S. Hessle and S. Strega (eds), *Valuing the Field: Child Welfare in International Context* (Aldershot: Ashgate).

Callahan, M., Field, B., Jackson, S., Lundquist, A. and Rutman, D. (ed) (1999) *Misconceiving Mothers: Women, Pregnancy and Substance Abuse* (Ottawa: Status of Women).

Campbell, A. (1984) *Delinquent Girls*. (Oxford: Basil Blackwell).

Campbell, M. (1983) *Half-Breed* (Halifax: Formac Publishing Company). First published in 1973.

Cannan, C. and Warren, C. (1997) *Social Action with Children and Families: A Community Development Approach to Children and Families* (London: Routledge).

Carlen, P. and Worrall, A. (eds) (1987) *Gender, Crime and Justice* (Milton Keynes: Open University Press).

Cavanagh, K. and Cree, V. E. (1996) *Working with Men: Feminism and Social Work* (London: Routledge).

Central Council for Education and Training in Social Work (CCETSW) (1989) *Requirements and Regulations for the Diploma in Social Work. Paper 30* (London: CCETSW). Revised in 1991 and 1995.

Chaplin, J. (1988) *Feminist Counselling in Action* (London: Sage).

Chesney-Lind, M. (1973) 'Judicial Enforcement of the Female Sex Role: The Family Court and the Female Delinquent', *Issues in Criminology*, Vol. 8, pp. 51–69.

Chodorow, N. (1978) *The Reproduction of Mothering* (London: University of California Press).

Churchill, W. (1998) *A Little Matter of Genocide* (Winnipeg: Arbeiter Ring Publishing).

Clark, V., Higonnet, M. and Katrakik, K. (1996) *Anti-Feminism in the Academy* (London: Routledge).

Clarke, J. and Newman, J. (1997) *The Managerialist State* (London: Sage).

Clegg, S. R. (1989) *Frameworks of Power* (London: Sage).

Clinton, H. R. (1996) *It Takes a Village: And Other Lessons Children Teach Us* (New York: Touchstone Books).

Cochrane, A. (1993) 'The Problem of Poverty', in Dallos, R. and McLaughlin, E. (eds) *Social Problems and the Family* (London: Sage).

Coleman, P. (1990) 'Ageing and Life History: The Meaning of Reminiscence' in Dex, S. (ed) *Life and Work History Analysis* (London: Routledge).

Coll, C., Suney, J., Weingarden, K. (eds) (1998) *Mothering Against the Odds: Diverse Voices of Contemporary Mothers* (New York: Guilford Press).

Collins, P. H. (1991) *Black Feminist Thought: Knowledge, Consciousness and the Politics of Empowerment* (London: Routledge).

Compton, B. and Galaway, B. (1975) *Social Work Processes* (Homewood, Ill.: The Dorsey Press).

Connell, R. W. (1995) *Masculinities* (Cambridge: Polity Press).

Cook, A. and Kirk, G. (1983) *Greenham Women Everywhere: Dreams, Ideas and Action from the Women's Peace Movement* (London: Pluto Press).

Cook, D. and Hudson, B. (1993) *Racism and Criminology* (London: Sage Publications).

Corrigan, P. and Leonard, P. (1978) *Social Work Under Capitalism* (London: Macmillan – now Palgrave).

Cotton, K. (1999) *Surrogate Mothers* (Programme on BBC 1).

Coulson, M., Magas, B. and Wainwright, H. (1975) 'The Housewife and her Labour under Capitalism' *New Left Review*, 89, Jan–Feb, pp. 59–71.

Cowburn, M. (1998) 'A Man's World: Gender Issues in Working with Male Sex Offenders in Prison', in *The Howard Journal*, 37(3), pp. 234–51.

Cowburn, M. and Dominelli, L. (1998) 'Moving beyond Litigation and Positivism: Another Approach to Accusations of Sexual Abuse', *British Journal of Social Work*, 28(4), August, pp. 525–43.

Coyle, A. (1989) 'Women in Management: A Suitable Case for Treatment', *Feminist Review*, 31, pp. 117–25.

Craig, G. and Mayo, M. (1995) *Community Empowerment: A Reader in Participation and Development* (London: Zed Books).

Croll, E. (1978) *Feminism and Socialism in China* (London: Routledge and Kegan Paul).

Culpitt, I. (1992) *Welfare and Citizenship: Beyond the Crisis of the Welfare State* (London: Sage).

Daenzer, P. (1993) *Regulating Class Privilege: Immigrant Servants in Canada, 1940s–1950s* (Toronto: Canadian Scholars Press).

Dale, J. and Foster, P. (1986) *Feminists and State Welfare* (London: Routledge and Kegan Paul).

Dalla Costa, M. and James, S. (1972) *The Power of Women and the Subversion of Community* (Bristol: Falling Wall Press).

Daly, M. (1978) *Gyn/Ecology: The Metaethics of Radical Feminism* (New York: Beacon Books).

Daly, N. (1998) 'Care or Scare', *Community Care*, 30 July–5 August, p. 19.

Davion, V. (1994) 'Is Ecofeminism Feminist?' in Warren, K. (ed) *Ecologoical Feminism* (London: Routledge).

Davis, A. (1981) *Women, Race and Class* (London: Women's Press).

Deacon, B., Hulse, M. and Stubbs, P. (1997) *Global Social Policy: International Organisations and the Future of Welfare* (London: Sage).

De Sousa (1991) 'Black Students' in CCETSW, *One Small Step Towards Racial Justice* (London: Central Council for Education and Training in Social Work).

Denney, D. (1992) *Racism and Anti-Racism in Probation* (London: Routledge).

Department of Health (DoH) (1995) *Child Protection: Messages from Research* (London: HMSO).

Derrida, J. (1987) *Writing and Difference* (Chicago: The University of Chicago Press).

Devore, W. and Schlesinger, E. (1983) *Ethnic Sensitive Social Work Practice* (Boston: Allyn and Bacon).

Dews, V. and Watts, J. (1994) *Review of Probation Officers Recruitment and Training* (London: HMSO).

Dobash, R. and Dobash, R. (1992) *Women, Violence and Social Change* (London: Routledge).

Dominelli, L. (1978) 'The Welfare State and the Public Expenditure Cuts' in *Bulletin of Social Policy*, No. 1, Spring.

Dominelli, L. (1980) 'So Glad to See You, Dear' Unpublished Paper (Coventry: University of Warwick).

Dominelli, L. (1981) 'Violence: A Family Affair', *Community Care*, 12 March, pp. 14–17.

Dominelli, L. (1983) *Women in Focus: Community Service Orders and Female Offenders* (Coventry: University of Warwick).

Dominelli, L. (1986) 'The Power of the Powerless: Prostitution and the Reinforcement of Submissive Feminity', *Sociological Review*, Spring, pp. 65–92.

Dominelli, L. (1986a) *Love and Wages: The Impact of Imperialism, State Intervention and Women's Domestic Labour on Workers' Control in Algeria, 1962–1972* (Norwich: Novata Press).

Dominelli, L. (1986b) Father–Daughter Incest: Patriarchy's Shameful Secret', *Critical Social Policy*, No. 16, pp. 8–22.

Dominelli, L. (1988) *Anti-Racist Social Work* (London: Macmillan – now Palgrave). 2nd edition published in 1997.

Dominelli, L. (1988a) 'Thatcher's Attack on Social Security: Restructuring Social Control', in *Critical Social Policy*, 23, pp. 46–61.

Dominelli, L. (1989) 'Betrayal of Trust: A Feminist Analysis of Power Relationships in Incest Abuse and its Relevance for Social Work Practice', *British Journal of Social Work*, No. 19, pp. 291–307.

Dominelli, L. (1990) *Women and Community Action* (Birmingham: Venture Press).

Dominelli, L. (1991) *Gender, Sex Offenders and Probation Practice* (Aldershot: Avebury).

Dominelli, L. (1991a) "'Race', Gender and Social Work' in M. Davies (ed), *The Sociology of Social Work* (London: Routledge).

Dominelli, L. (1991b) *Women Across Continents: Feminist Comparative Social Policy* (Hemel Hempstead: Harvester/Wheatsheaf).

Dominelli, L. (1992) 'More than a Method: Feminist Social Work' in K. Campbell (ed), *Critical Feminisms* (Milton Keynes: Open University).

Dominelli, L. (1992a) 'Sex Offenders and Probation Practice' in Senior, P. and Woodhill, D. (eds), *Gender, Crime and Probation Practice* (Sheffield: PAVIC Publications).

Dominelli, L. (1996) 'Deprofessionalising Social Work: Equal Opportunities, Competence and Postmodernism', British Journal of Social Work, No. 26, April, pp. 153–75.

Dominelli, L. (1997) 'Feminist Theory' in M. Davies (ed), *The Blackwell Companion to Social Work* (Oxford: Blackwell).

Dominelli, L. (1997a) 'International Social Development and Social Work: A Feminist Perspective', in M. C. Hokenstad and J. Midgley (1997) *Issues in International Social Work: Global Challenges for a New Century* (Washington, DC: NASW Press).

Dominelli, L. (1997b) 'Social Work and Social Development: A Partnership in Social Change' in *Journal of Social Development in Africa*, Vol. 12, No. 1, pp. 29–39.

Dominelli, L. (1997c) *Sociology for Social Work* (London: Macmillan – now Palgrave).

Dominelli, L. (1997d) 'The Changing Face of Social Work: Globalisation, Privatisation and the Technocratisation of Professional Practice' in B. Lesnick (ed), *Change in Social Work: International Perspectives in Social Work* (Aldershot: Arena).

Dominelli, L. (1998) 'Globalisation and Gender Relations in Social Work' in B. Lesnik (ed) *Countering Discrimination in Social Work* (Aldershot: Ashgate).

Dominelli, L. (1998a) 'Women, Social Work and Academia' in S. Malin-Prothero and D. Malina (eds), *Speaking Our Places* (London: Taylor Francis).

Dominelli, L. (ed) (1999) *Community Approaches to Child Welfare. International Perspectives* (Aldershot: Avebury).

Dominelli, L. (2000) 'Empowerment: Help or Hindrance in Professional Relationships' in Ford, D. and Stepney, P. (ed). *Social Work Models, Methods and Theories: A Framework for Practice* (Lyme Regis: Russel House Publishing).

Dominelli, L. (forthcoming) 'Glassed-in': Women's Reproductive Rights' in Adams, R., Dominelli, L. and Payne, M. (eds) *Critical Practice in Social Work* (London: Palgrave).

Dominelli, L. and Gollins, T. (1997) 'Men, Power and Caring Relationships', *The Sociological Review*, Vol. 45, No. 3, Aug, pp. 396–415.

Dominelli, L. and Hoogvelt, A. (1996) Globalisation, Contract Government and the Taylorisation of Intellectual Labour' in *Studies in Political Economy*, 49, pp. 71–100.

Dominelli, L. and Hoogvelt, A. (1996a) 'Globalisation and the Technocratisation of Social Work', *Critical Social Policy*, Vol. 16, No. 2, pp. 45–62.

Dominelli, L., Jeffers, L., Jones, G., Sibanda, S. and Williams, B. (1995) *Anti-Racist Probation Practice* (Aldershot: Avebury).

Dominelli, L. and Jonsdottir, G. (1988) 'Feminist Political Organisation in Iceland', *Feminist Review*, No. 27, pp. 36–60.

Dominelli, L. and McLeod, E. (1982) 'The Personal and the Apolitical: Feminism and Moving Beyond the Integrated Methods Approach' in R. Bailey and P. Lee (eds), *Theory and Practice in Social Work* (Oxford: Basil Blackwell).

Dominelli, L. and McLeod, E. (1989) *Feminist Social Work* (London: Macmillan – now Palgrave).

Donnelly, A. (1986) *Feminist Social Work with a Women's Group*, University of East Anglia Monographs (Norwich: University of East Anglia).

Donovan, J. (1985) *Feminist Theory: The Intellectual Traditions of American Feminism* (New York: Frederick Ungar Publishing).

Doress, P. B. and Siegal, D. L. (1987) *Ourselves Growing Older* (New York: Simon and Schuster).

Drakich, J. (1995) 'In Whose Interests? The Politics of Joint Custody' in Nelson, E. and Robinson, B. (eds) *Gender in the 1990s: Images, Realities and Issues* (Toronto: Nelson Canada).

Durrant, J. (1989) 'Continuous Agitation', *Community Care*, 13 July, pp. 23–5.

Dutt, R. (1999) 'Racism in the Workplace' *Community Care*, 2–8 December, p. 32.

Dworkin, A. (1981) *Pornography: Men Possessing Women* (New York: Perigee).

Dworkin, A. (1988) *Letters from a War Zone* (New York: E. P. Dutton).

Dyer, R. (1993) *The Matter of Images: Essays on Representations* (London: Routledge).

Eagleton, T. (1996) *The Illusions of Postmodernity* (Oxford: Blackwell).

Echols, A. (1989) *Daring to be Mad: Radical Feminism in America, 1967–1975* (Minneapolis, MN: University of Minnesota Press).

Eichler, M. (1983) *Families in Canada* (Toronto: Gage).

Eisenstein, H. (1983) *Contemporary Feminist Thought* (Boston: G. K. Hall and Co.).

Epstein, B. and Ellis, D. (1983) 'The Pro-Family Left in the US: Two Comments', in *Feminist Review*, 14, pp. 35–50.

El Sadawai, N. (1979) *The Hidden Face of Eve: Women in Arab World* (London: Zed Press).

Enos, S. (2001) *Mothering from the Inside: Parenting in a Women's Prison* (State University of New York).

Essed, P. (1991) *Understanding Everyday Racism: An Interdisciplinary Theory* (London: Sage Publications).

Faith, K. (1993) *Unruly Women: The Politics of Confinement and Resistance* (Vancouver: Press Gang Publishers).

Family Policy Studies Centre (FPSC) (1984) *An Ageing Population* (London: FPSC).

Farrell, W. (1994) *The Myth of Male Power* (New York: Fourth Estate).

Farringdon, D. and Morris, A. (1983) 'Sex, Sentencing and Reconvictions', *The British Journal of Criminology*, Vol. 23, No. 3, pp. 229–48.

Fawcett, B., Featherstone, B. and Fook, J. (2000) *Practice and Research in Social Work: Postmodern Feminist Perspectives* (London: Routledge).

Fernando, S. (1991) *Health, Race and Culture* (London: Macmillan – now Palgrave).

Finch, J. (1984) 'Community Care: Developing Non-Sexist Alternatives' in *Journal of Social Policy*, 9, pp. 6–18.

Finch, J. and Groves, D. (1983) *Labour of Love: Women, Work and Caring* (London: Routledge and Kegan Paul).

Finer, C. and Nellis, M. (1995) *Crime and Social Exclusion* (Oxford: Blackwell).

Firestone, S. (1970) *The Dialectics of Sex: The Case for Women's Revolution* (New York: Cape).

Fisher, M. (1997) 'Man-Made Care: Community Care and Older Male Carers', in *British Journal of Social Work*, 24, pp. 659–80.

Flax, J. (1990) 'Postmodernism and Gender Relations in Feminist Theory', in L. Nicholson (ed), *Feminism/Postmodernism* (New York: Routledge, Chapman and Hall).

Flexner, A. (1915) 'Is Social Work a Profession?' in *Studies in Social Work, No. 4* (New York School of Philanthropy).

Foster, J. (1997) 'A Woman's Liberation', *Community Care*, 4–10 December, pp. 18–19.

Forster, J. and Hanscombe, G. (1982) *Rocking the Cradle: Lesbian Mothers* (London: Sheba Feminist Publishers).

Foucault, M. (1980) *Power/Knowledge: Selected Interviews and Other Writings, 1972–77* (New York: Pantheon Books).

Francis, J. (1992) 'Sick Staff Syndrome', *Community Care*, 30 August, pp. 18–19.

Frankenburg, R. (1997) *Displacing Whiteness: Essays in Social and Cultural Criticism* (London: Duke University Press).

Frankfort, I. (1972) *Vaginal Politics* (New York: Quadrangle Books).

Franklin, A. and Franklin, B. (1996) 'Growing Pains: The Developing Children's Rights Movement in the United Kingdom' in J. Pilcher and S. Wagg (eds) *Thatcher's Children? Politics, Childhood and Society in the 1980s and 1990s* (London: Falmer Press).

French, M. (1985) *The Power of Women* (Harmondsworth: Penguin).

Friedan, B. (1963) *The Feminine Mystique* (New York: Bell).

Frye, M. (1983) *The Politics of Reality: Essays in Feminist Theory* (Trumansburg, NY: The Crossing Press).

Furniss, E. (1995) *Victims of Benevolence: The Dark Legacy of the Williams Lake Residential School* (Vancouver: Arsenal Pulp Press).

Gamarnikov, E., Morgan, D., Purvis, J. and Taylorson, D. (eds) (1983) *The Public and the Private* (London: Heinemann).

Gastrell, P. and Edwards, J. (eds) (1996) *Community Health Nursing: Frameworks for Practice* (London: Balliere Tindall).

Gavron, H. (1966) *The Captive Housewife* (London: Routledge and Kegan Paul).

Gatens, M. (1996) *Imaginary Bodies: Ethics, Power and Corporality* (London: Routledge).

Gelsthorpe, L. (1989) *Sexism and the Female Offender* (Aldershot: Gower).

George, M. (1996) 'Cash on the Nail', in *Community Care*, 17–23 October, pp. 24–5.

George, J. (1997) 'Global Greying: What Role for Social Work' in Hokenstad, M. C. and Midgley, J. (eds) (1997) *Issues in International Social Work: Global Challenges for a New Century* (Washington, DC: NASW Press).

Gilder, G. (1981) *Wealth and Poverty* (New York: Bell Books).

Gilmore, D. (1990) *Manhood in the Making: Cultural Concepts of Masculinity* (New Haven, CT: Yale University Press).

Giddens, A. (1990) *The Consequences of Modernity* (Cambridge: Polity Press).

Ginsburg, N. (1979) *Class, Capital and Social Policy* (London: Macmillan – now Palgrave).

Glaser, D. and Frosh, S. (1988) *Child Sexual Abuse* (London: Macmillan – now Palgrave).

Glasser, B. and Strauss, A. (1967) *The Discovery of Grounded Theory* (Chicago: Aldine).

Glendinning, J. and Millar, J. (eds) (1992) *Women in Poverty in the UK* (Brighton: Wheatsheaf).

Goffman, E. (1961) *Asylums* (Harmondsworth: Penguin Books).

Gordon, P. and Newnham, A. (1985) *Passport to Benefits: Racism in Social Security* (London: Child Poverty Action Group and the Runnymede Trust).

Gottlieb, N. (ed) (1980) *Alternative Social Services for Women* (New York: Columbia University Press).

Graef, R. (1992) *Living Dangerously: Young Offenders in Their Own Words* (London: Harper Collins).

Graham, H. (1983) 'Caring: Labour of Love', in J. Finch and D. Groves (1983) *Labour of Love: Women, Work and Caring* (London: Routledge and Kegan Paul).

Greenhorn, M. (1996) *Cautions, Court Proceedings and Sentencing, England and Wales, 1995. Home Office Statistical Bulletin, 16* (London: Home Office).

Gregory, J. and Foster, K. (1990) *The Consequences of Divorce* (London: OPCS/HMSO).

Griffiths, R. (1988) *Community Care: Agenda for Action, The Griffiths Report* (London: HMSO).

Grimwood, C. and Popplestone, R. (1993) *Women in Management* (London: BASW/Macmillan – now Palgrave).

Haber, H. F. (1994) *Beyond Postmodern Politics: Lyotard, Rorty, Foucault* (London: Routledge).

Haig-Brown, C. (1988) *Resistance and Renewal: Surviving the Indian Residential School* (Vancouver: Tillicum Library/Arsenal Pulp Press).

Hall, S., Critchen, C., Jefferson, T., Clarke, J. and Roberts, B. (1978) *Policing the Crisis: Mugging, the State and Law and Order* (London: Macmillan – now Palgrave).

Hallett, C. (1991) *Women and Social Services* (London: Sage).

Hanmer, J. (1994) 'Men, Power and the Exploitation of Women' in J. Hearn and D. Morgan (eds), *Men, Masculinity and Social Theory* (London: Unwin Hyman).

Hanmer, J. and Statham, D. (1988) *Women and Social Work: Towards a Woman-Centred Practice* (London: Macmillan – now Palgrave).

Harding, S. (1990) 'Feminism, Science and the Anti-Englightment Critiques' in L. Nicholson (ed), *Feminism/Postmodernism* (London: Routledge).

Harrison, K. (1996) *Horrible Hybrids* (London: Open Mind).

Hartsock, N. (1987) 'The Feminist Standpoint: Developing the Ground for a Specifically Feminist Historical Materialism' in S. Harding (ed) *Feminism and Methodology* (Bloomington, IN: Indiana University Press).

Healy, K. (2001) *Critical Practice in Social Work* (Sydney: Hale and Iremonger).

Hearn, J. (1987) *The Gender of Oppression: Men, Masculinity and the Critique of Marxism* (Brighton: Wheatsheaf).

Hegar, R. and Greif, G. (1991) 'Parental Abductions Across International Borders', *International Social Work*, 34, pp. 353–63.

Heraud, J. (1979) *Sociology in the Professions* (London: Open Books).

Hester, M., Kelly, L., Radford, J. (eds) (1996) *Women, Violence and Male Power* (Buckingham: Open University Press).

Hester, M., Pearson, C. and Harwin, N. (2000) *Making an Impact: Children and Domestic Violence* (London: Jessica Kingsley).

Higginbotham, E. (1992) 'African American Women's History and the Metalanguage of Race', *Signs*, 17(2), pp. 251–74.

Higgins, J. (1989) 'Caring for the Carers', *Journal of Social Administration*, summer, pp. 382–99.

Hill, A. (2000) 'A First Nations Experience in First Nations Child Welfare Services' in Dominelli, L. and Soydan, H. (eds) *Beyond Racial Divides: Ethnicities in social work practice* (Aldershot: Ashgate).

Hokenstad, M. C. and Midgley, J. (1997) *Issues in International Social Work: Global Challenges for a New Century* (Washington, DC: NASW Press).

Hollis, F. (1964) *Casework: A Psychosocial Therapy* (New York: Random House).

Home Office (1998) *Probation and Community Sentences* (London: Home Office).

hooks, b. (1982) *'Ain't I a Woman?' Black Women and Feminism* (London: Pluto Press).

hooks, b. (1984) *Feminist Theory: From Margins to Centre* (Boston: South End Press).

hooks, b. (1990) *Yearning: Race, Gender and Cultural Politics* (Boston: South End Press).

hooks, b. (2000) *Where We Stand: Class Matters* (London: Routledge).

Hooper, C. A. (1992) *Mothers Surviving Child Sexual Abuse* (London: Routledge).

Horley, S. (1990) 'A Shame and A Disgrace', *Social Work Today*, 21 June, pp. 16–17.

Howe, D. (1986) 'The Segregation of Women and their Work in the Personal Social Services', *Critical Social Policy*, 15, pp. 21–36.

Howe, D. (1994) 'Modernity, Postmodernity and Social Work', *British Journal of Social Work*, 24(5), pp. 513–32.

Hudson-Weems, C. (1993) *African Womanism: Reclaiming Ourselves* (Troy, MI.: Bedford Publishers).

Hughes, B. (1995) *Older People and Community Care: Critical Theory and Practice* (Buckingham: Open University Press).

Hugman, R. (1998) *Social Welfare and Social Value* (London: Macmillan – now Palgrave).

Humphries, B. (eds) (1996) *Critical Perspectives on Empowerment* (Birmingham: Venture Press).

Ife, J. (1997) *Rethinking Social Work: Towards Critical Practice* (Sydney: Longman).

Jackson, D. (1995) *Destroying the Baby in Themselves* (Nottingham: Mushroom Publishing).

Jackson, S. and Nixon, P. (1999) 'Family Group Conferences: A Challenge to the Old Order' in Dominelli, L. (ed) *Community Approaches to Child Welfare: International Perspectives* (Aldershot: Ashgate).

Jaggar, A. (1983) *Feminist Politics and Human Nature* (Totowa, NJ.: Rowman and Allanheld).

Jaques, E. (1975) 'Social Analysis and the Glacier Project', in W. Brown and J. E. Brown (eds), *The Glacier Project Paper* (London: Heinemann).

Jaques, E. (1977) *A General Theory of Bureaucracy* (London: Heinemann).

Jarvis, F. (1976) *Probation Practice* (London: Allen and Unwin).

Jayawardna, K. (1986) *Feminism and Nationalism in the Third World* (London: Zed Press).

Jo, B. (1981) 'Female Only' in Hoagland, S. and Penelope, J. (eds), *For Lesbians Only: A Separatist Ideology* (London: Only Women Press).

John-Baptiste, A. (2001) 'Africentric Social Work' in Dominelli, L., Lorenz, W. and Soydan, H. (eds) *Beyond Racial Divides: Ethnicities in Social Work* (Aldershot: Ashgate).

Jones, C. (1993) 'Distortion and Demonisation: The Right and Anti-Racist Social Work Education', in *Journal of Social Work Education*, 12(3), pp. 9–16.

Kassindja, K. (1998) *Do They Hear You When You Cry?* (New York: Delta Books).

Kelly, L. (1988) *Surviving Sexual Violence* (Cambridge: Polity Press).

Kelsey, J. (1997) *The New Zealand Experience* (Auckland University Press).

Kempshall, H. and Pritchard, J. (1996) *Good Practice in Risk Assessment and Risk Management* (London: Jessica Kingsley).

Kendall, K. (1998) *IASSW: The First Fifty Years, 1928–78* (Washington, DC: IASSW/CSWE).

Kettle, A. (1998) 'Women and Collective Action: The Role of the Trade Union in Academic Life', in Malina, D. and Maslin-Prothero, S. (eds) *Surviving the Academy: Feminist Perspectives* (London: Falmer Press).

Kettle, M. (1994) 'Emerging Findings of the Inter-Departmental Scrutiny of the Government's Use of External Consultants' in *The Guardian*, 30 April.

Khan, P. and Dominelli, L. (2000) 'The Impact of Globalization and Social Work Practice in the UK', in *European Journal of Social Work*. 3(2), pp. 95–108.

Knijn, T. and Kremer, M. (1997) 'Gender and the Caring Dimension of Welfare States: Toward Inclusive Citizenship', in *Social Politics*, Fall, pp. 328–61.

Knijn, T. and Ungerson, C. (1997) 'Introduction: Care Work and Gender in Welfare Regimes', in *Social Politics*, Fall, pp. 323–7.

Kosberg, J. (ed) (1992) *Family Care of the Elderly: Social and Cultural Changes* (London: Sage).

Krane, J. (1994) *The Transformation of Women into Mother Protectors: An Examination of Child Protection Practices in Cases of Child Sexual Abuse*. Unpublished doctoral dissertation (University of Toronto).

Kuhn, M. (1991) *No Stone Unturned: The Life and Times of Maggie Kuhn* (New York: Ballantine Books).

Lacan, J. (1977) *Ecrits: A Selection*. Translated by A. Sheridan (New York: W. W. Norton).

Laird, J. (1993) 'Lesbian and Gay Families' in Walsh, F. (ed) *Normal Family Processes* (New York: Guildford Press).

Laird, J. (1994) Lesbian Couples and Families: A Cultural Perspective' in M. P. Mirkin (ed), *Treating Women in their Social Contexts: A Feminist Reconstruction* (New York: Guildford Press).

Langan, M. and Day, L. (eds) (1992) *Women, Oppression and Social Work* (London: Tavistock).

La Rossa, R. (1995) 'Fatherhood and Social Change', in Nelson, E. and Robinson, B. (eds) *Gender in the 1990s: Images, Realities and Issues* (Toronto: Nelson Canada).

Lasseter, D. (1998) *Killer Kids* (New York: Pinnacle Books).

Lawson, C. (1993) 'Mother-Only Sexual Abuse: Rare or Under-Reported? A Critique of the Research', in *Child Abuse and Neglect*, 17, pp. 261–9.

Leonard, P. (1984) *Personality and Ideology: Towards a Materialist Understanding of the Individual* (London: Macmillan – now Palgrave).

Leonard, P. (1997) *Postmodern Welfare: Reconstructing an Emancipatory Project* (London: Sage Publications).

Leonard, P. and McLeod, E. (1980) *Marital Violence: Social Construction and Social Service Response* (Coventry: Warwick University).

Levitas, R. (ed) (1986) *The Ideology of the New Right* (Cambridge: Polity Press).

Liebow, E. (1993) *Tell Them Who I Am: The Lives of Homeless Women* (New York: Penguin Books).

Lister, R. (1997) *Citizenship: Feminist Perspectives* (London: Macmillan – now Palgrave).

Lloyd, L. (1996) *Marketing Race Equality: A Study of Race Equality Policies and Community Care*. Phd. Bristol: Bristol University.

Lloyd, L. (1998) 'The Post and the Anti-Analysing Change and Changing Analyses in Social Work', in *British Journal of Social Work*, 28, pp. 709–27.

Lorde, A. (1984) *Sister Outsider* (New York: The Crossing Press).

Logan, C. H. (1996) *Private Prisons* (New Haven, CT: University of Connecticut Press).

Lorenz, W. (1994) *Social Work in a Changing Europe* (London: Routledge).

Lovenduski, J. and Randall, V. (1993) *Contemporary Feminist Politics* (Oxford University Press).

Lukes, C. and Land, J. (1990) 'Biculturality and Homosexuality', *Social Work*, Vol. 35, pp. 155–61.

Lyndon, J. (1992) *Men in Danger* (New York: Random House).

Lyons, K. (2000) 'UK Policy Designed to Combat Child Poverty' in Link, R., Bibus, A. and Lyons, K. (eds) *When Children Pay* (London: CPAG).

Mac an Ghaill, M. (1994) *The Making of Men: Masculinities, Sexualities, and Schooling* (Buckingham: Open University).

MacKinnon, C. (1993) *Only Words* (Cambridge: Harvard University Press).

Malina, D. and Maslin-Prothero, D. (eds) (1998) *Surviving the Academy: Feminist Perspectives* (Brighton: Falmer Press).

Mama, A. (1989) *Hidden Struggle: Statutory and Voluntary Responses to Violence Against Black Women in the Home* (London: Race and Housing Unit).

Maracle, B. (1994) *Crazywater: Native Voices on Addiction and Recovery* (Toronto: Penguin Books).

Maracle, L. (1993) *Ravensong* (Vancouver: Press Gang Publishers).

Maracle, L. (1996) *I am Woman: A Native Perspective on Sociology and Feminism* (Vancouver: Press Gang Publishers).

Marchant, H. and Wearing, B. (1986) *Gender Reclaimed* (Sydney: Hale and Iremonger).

Marshall, K. (1995) 'Dual Earners: Whose Responsible for Housework?' in Nelson, E. and Robinson, B. (eds), *Gender in the 1990s: Images, Realities and Issues* (Toronto: Nelson Canada).

Mathiesen, T. (1974) *The Politics of Abolition* (London: Martin Robinson).

Mayo, M. (1977) *Women in the Community* (London: Routledge and Kegan Paul).

McAdam, D. and Snow, D. (1997) *Social Movements: Readings on Their Emergence, Mobilization and Dynamics* (Los Angeles: Roxbury Publishing Company).

McIvor, G. (ed) (1996) *Working with Offenders: Research Highlights in Social Work, 26* (London: Jessica Kingsley).

McKnight, J. (1995) *The Careless Society: Community and its Counterfeits* (New York: Basic Books).

McLeod, E. (1982) *Women Working: Prostitution Now* (London: Croom Helm).

McPherson, W. (1998) *Report of the Inquiry Into the Murder of Stephen Lawrence: The McPherson Report* (London: HMSO).

Memmi, A. (1965) *The Colonizer and the Colonised.* Translated by H. Greenfield (Boston: Beacon Press).

Memmi, A. (1984) *Dependence: A Sketch for a Portrait of the Dependent* (Boston: Beacon Press).

Midgley, J. (1996) *Social Welfare in Global Context* (London: Sage).

Millar, J. (1996) 'One Parents and Poverty' in Hallet, C. (ed) *Women and Social Policy* (Brighton: Harvester/Wheatsheaf).

Millar, J. (1999) *Lone Mothers and the New Deal.* Paper presented at the Social Policy Seminar Series, Southampton University, October.

Millet, K. (1969) *Sexual Politics.* (Garden City, NY.: Doubleday).

Minushin, S. (1974) *Families and Family Therapy* (Cambridge, Mass.: Harvard University Press).

Mirlees-Black, C. Mayhew, P. and Percy, A. (1996) *The 1996 British Crime Survey, England and Wales* (London: Home Office).

Mishra, R. (1990) *The Welfare State in Capitalist Society. Policies of Retrenchment and Maintenance in Europe, North America and Australia.* (Toronto: University of Toronto Press).

Modood, T. (1988) ''Black' Racial Equality and Asian Identity', *New Community*, 14(3), pp. 397–404.

Modood, T., Beishon, S. and Virdee, S. (1994) *Changing Ethnic Identities* (London: Policy Studies Institute).

Mohanty, C. (1991) 'Cartographies of Struggle' in C. Mohanty, A. Russo, L. Torres (eds), *Third World Women and the Politics of Feminism* (Bloomington, IN.: Indiana University Press).

Mohanty, C., Russo, A., Torres, L. (eds) (1991) *Third World Women and the Politics of Feminism* (Bloomington, IN.: Indiana University Press).

Moraga, C. (1994) 'From a Long Line of Vendidas: Chicanas and Feminism' in Herman, A. C. and Stewart, A. J. (eds) *Theorizing Feminism: Parallel Trends in the Humanities and Social Sciences* (Boulder Colo.: Westview Press).

Moran, B. (1992) *A Little Rebellion: Welfare Neglect Exposed* (Vancouver: Arsenal Pulp Press).

Morgan, R. (1970) *Sisterhood is Powerful* (New York: Vintage Books).

Morris, A. (1987) *Women, Crime and Criminal Justice* (Oxford: Basil Blackwell).

Morris, J. (1991) *Pride Against Prejudice: Transforming Attitudes to Disability* (London: The Women's Press).

Morris, L. (1995) *Dangerous Classes: The Underclass and Social Citizenship* (London: Routledge).

Mullender, A. (1997) *Rethinking Domestic Violence: The Social Work and Probation Responses* (London: Routledge).

Mullender, A. and Ward, D. (1991) *The Practice Principles of Self-Directed Groupwork: Establishing a Value Base for Empowerment* (University of Nottingham, Centre for Social Action).

Murray, C. (1984) *Losing Ground: American Social Policy* (New York: Basic Books).

Murray, C. (1990) *The Emerging British Underclass* (London: Institute of Economic Affairs).

Murray, C. (1994) *Underclass: The Crisis Deepens* (London: Institute of Economic Affairs).

National Association of Probation Officers (NAPO) (1999) *Caseloads, Budgets and Staffing: Probation's Crisis. NAPO Briefing Paper, May* (London: NAPO).

National Association for the Care and Rehabilitation of Offenders (NACRO) (1994) *Statistics on Black People within the Criminal Justice System* (London: NACRO).

Nelson, S. (1982) *Incest: Fact and Myth* (Edinburgh: Stramullion Co-operative).

Nelson, E. D. and Robinson, B. W. (eds) (1995) *Gender in the 1990s: Images, Realities and Issues* (Scarborough, Ont.: Nelson Canada International Publishing Company).

Newburn, T. (1995) *Crime and Criminal Justice Policy* (Harlow: Longman).

Newburn, T. and Stanko, E. (1995) *Just Boys Doing Business: Men, Masculinity and Crime* (London: Routledge).

Neysmith, S. (1998) 'From Home Care to Social Care: The Value of a Vision', in Baines, C., Evans, P. and Neysmith, S. (eds) *Women's Caring: Feminist Perspectives on Social Welfare* (Oxford University Press).

Nicholson, L. (ed) (1990) *Feminism/Postmodernism* (New York: Routledge, Chapman and Hall).

Oakley, A. (1974) *The Sociology of Housework* (London: Martin Robertson).

Oderkirk, J. and Lochhead, C. (1995) 'Lone Parenthood: Gender Differences' in Nelson, E. D. and Robinson, B. W. (eds) *Gender in the 1990s: Images, Realities and Issues* (Toronto: Nelson Canada).

O'Hagan, K. and Dillenburger, K. (1995) *The Abuse of Women within Child Care Work* (Buckingham: Open University Press).

Oliver, M. (1990) *The Politics of Disablement* (London: Macmillan – now Palgrave).

Orme, J. (2000) *Gender and Community Care* (London: Palgrave).

Orme, J., Dominelli, L. and Mullender, A. (2000) 'Working with Violent Men from a Feminist Social Work Perspective', *International Social Work*, 43(1) pp. 89–106.

Pahl, J. (1980) 'Patterns of Money Management within Marriage' in *Journal of Social Policy*, 9, pp. 326–39.

Panet-Raymond, J. (1991) *Partnership or Paternalism?* (University of Montreal Publications).

Parker, G. and Lawton, D. (1994) *Different Types of Care, Different Types of Carer: Evidence from the General Household Survey* (York: Social Policy Research Unit).

Parmar, P. (1982) 'Gender, Race and Class: Asian Women in Resistance' in Centre for Contemporary Culture Studies, *The Empire Strikes Back* (London: Hutchinson).

Parton, N. (1996) *Social Theory, Social Change and Social Work* (London: Routledge).

Parton, N. (1994) 'The Nature of Social Work Under Conditions of (Post)Modernity', *Social Work and Social Sciences Review*, 5(2), pp. 93–112.

Parton, N. (1998) 'Risk, Advanced Liberalism and Child Welfare: The Need to Rediscover Uncertainty and Ambiguity', in *British Journal of Social Work*, 28, pp. 5–27.

Parton, N. (2000) 'Some Thoughts on the Relationship between Theory and Practice in Social Work', in *British Journal of Social Work*, 30(4), pp. 449–63.

Pascall, G. (1986) *Social Policy: A Feminist Analysis* (London: Tavistock).

Patel, N. (1990) *Race Against Time: Ethnic Elders* (London: Runnymede Trust).

Payne, M. (2000) *Teamwork in Multi-Professional Care* (London: Macmillan – now Palgrave).

Pease, B. (1981) *Men and Feminism*. Paper presented at Women and Social Work Seminar. (Coventry: University of War Wick).

Pease, B. and Fook J. (eds) (1999) *Transforming Social Work Practice: Postmodern Critical Perspectives* (London: Routledge).

Percy, A. and Mayhew, P. (1997) 'Estimating Sexual Victimisation in a National Crime Surgery: A New Approach' in *Studies on Crime and Crime Prevention*, 6(2), pp. 125–50.

Perlmutter, F. (1997) From Welfare to Work: Corporate Initiatives and Welfare Reform (Oxford University Press).

Phillips, A. (1993) *The Trouble with Boys: Parenting Men of the Future* (London: Harper Collins).

Phillips, M. (1993) 'An Oppressive Urge to End Oppression', *The Observer*, 1 August.

Phillips, M. (1994) 'Illiberal Liberalism', S. Dunant (ed) *The War of the Word: The Political Correctness Debate* (London: Virago).

Phillipson, C. (1982) *Capitalism and the Construction of Old Age* (London: Macmillan – now Palgrave).

Phillipson, C. (1998) *Reconstructing Old Age: New Agendas in Social Theory and Practice* (London: Sage).

Phillipson, C. and Laczko, F. (1991) *Changing Work and Retirement: A Social Policy for the Older Worker* (Milton Keynes: Open University Press).

Phillipson, J. (1992) *Practising Equality: Women and Social Work* (London: CCETSW).

Piercy, M. (1994) *The Longings of Women* (Harmondsworth: Penguin).

Pierson, C. (1998) *Beyond the Welfare State: The New Political Economy of Welfare* (Cambridge: Polity Press). First published in 1991.

Pillay, C. (1995) *Black Student's Voice 2: Meeting the Challenges of the 1990s* (London: ABPO).

Pinker, R. (1993) 'A Lethal Kind of Looniness', *Times Higher Educational Supplement*, 10 September.

Pitts, J. (2000) 'The New Youth Justice and the Politics of Electoral Anxiety' in Goldson, B. (ed), *The New Youth Justice* (Lyme Regis: Russell House Publishing).

Polikoff, V. (1992) 'Lesbian mothers, Lesbian Families: Legal Obstacles, Legal Challenges' in D. J. Maggiore (ed) *Lesbians and Child Custody* (New York: Garland Publishers).

Pollack, J. (1978) 'Early Theories of Female Criminality', in Bower, L. H. (ed) *Woman, Crime and Criminal Justice* (Ann Arbor: Michigan State University Press).

Price-Waterhouse (1990) *Implementing Community Care: Purchaser/Commissioner and Provider Roles* (London: HMSO).

Priestly, J. (1981) *Community of Scapegoats: The Segregation of Sex Offenders and Informants* (Oxford: Pergammon Press).

Priestley, M. (1998) 'Discourse and Resistance in Care Assessment: Integrated Living and Community Care' in *British Journal of Social Work*, 28(5), pp. 659–73.

Pringle, K. (1992) 'Child Sexual Abuse Perpetrated by Welfare Professionals and the Problem of Men', *Critical Social Policy*, 36, pp. 4–19.

Pringle, K. (1993) 'Gender Issues in Child Sexual Abuses Committed by Foster Carers: A Case Study for the Welfare Services?', in H. Ferguson, R. Gilligan, and R. Torode (eds), *Surviving Childhood Diversity* (Dublin: Social Studies Press).

Pringle, K. (1994) 'The Problem of Men Revisited', *Working with Men*, 2, pp. 5–8.

Pringle, K. (1995) *Men, Masculinities and Social Welfare* (University College London).

Pringle, K. (1998) *Children and Social Welfare in Europe* (Buckingham: Open University Press).

Pringle, K. and Harder, M. (1997) *Protecting Children in Europe: Towards a New Millennium* (Aalburg University Press).

Pritchard, J. (1992) *The Abuse of Elderly People: A Handbook for Professionals* (London: Jessica Kingsley).

Pugh, D. (1993) 'Understanding and Managing Organisational Change' in Mabbey, C. and Mayon-White, B. (eds) *Managing Change* (London: Paul Chapman).

Ralph, D., Regimbald, A., St-Amand, N. (1997) *Open for Business: Closed to People* (Halifax: Fernwood Publishing).

Ramazanoglu, C. (1989) *Feminism and the Contradictions of Oppression* (London: Routledge).

Reinhartz, S. (1992) *Feminist Methods in Social Research* (Oxford University Press).

Reitsma-Street, M. (1993) 'Canadian Youth Court Charges and Dispositions for Females Before and After Implementation of the Young Offenders Act', *Canadian Journal of Criminology*, Vol. 35, No. 4, pp. 437–58.

Richards, S., Bhatti-Sinclair, K., Borrill, W., Dominelli, L. and Waldman, J. (2000) 'Developing Partnerships in Social Work Education in Britain' in Callahan, M., Hessle, S., and Strega, S. (eds) *Valuing the Field: Child Welfare in an International Context* (Aldershot: Ashgate).

Richardson, D. and Robinson, V. (1993) *Introducing Women's Studies* (London: Macmillan – now Palgrave).

Robinson, L. (1998) *'Race': Communication and the Caring Professions* (Buckingham: Open University Press).

Rosenberg, H. (1995) 'Motherwork, Stress and Depression: The Costs of Privatized Social Reproduction', in Nelson, E. and Robinson, B. (eds) *Gender in the 1990s: Images, Realities and Issues* (Toronto: Nelson Canada).

Rothstein, B. (1998) *Just Institutions Matter: The Moral and Political Logic of the Welfare State* (Cambridge University Press).

Rojek, C., Peacock, G. and Collins, S. (1988) *Social Work and Received Ideas* (London: Routledge).

Russell, D. (1984) *Sexual Exploitation* (London: Sage).

Rowe, D. (1983) *Depression: The Way Out of Your Prison* (London: Routledge).

Roy, A. (1997) *The God of Small Things* (New York: Harper Collins).

Rubin, G. (1974) 'The Traffic in Women: Notes on the "Political Economy" of Sex', in M. Rosaldo and L. Lamphere (eds) *Women, Culture and Society* (Stanford University Press).

Rush, F. (1980) *The Best Kept Secret: Child Sexual Abuse* (New York: McGraw-Hill).

Rutherford, J. (1992) *Men's Silences: Predicaments in Masculinity* (London: Routledge).

Ruhui, L. (1998) *Maori Social Policy*. PhD Submission (Palmerston North: Massey University).

Saradjian, J. with Hanks, H. (1996) *Women who Sexually Abuse Children: From Research to Clinical Practice* (Chichester: John Wiley and Sons).

Schissel, B. (1997) *Blaming Children: Youth Crime, Moral Panics and the Politics of Hate* (Halifax: Fernwood Publishing).

Schlaffy, P. (1977) *The Power of the Positive Woman* (New York: Jove Books).

Schofield, G. and Thoburn, J. (1996) *Child Protection: The Voice of Children in Decision Making* (London: Institute of Public Policy Research).

Scott, J. (1990) 'Deconstructing Equality versus Difference. Or, the Uses of Poststructuralist Theory for Feminism' in Hirsch, M. and Fox, E. (eds) *Conflicts in Feminism* (London: Routledge).

Scull, A. (1979) *Decarceration: Community Treatment and the Deviant: A Radical View* (New Jersey: Prentice-Hall).

Scully, D. (1990) *Understanding Sexual Violence* (London: Harper Collins).

Seebohm, L. (1968) *Reports of the Committee on Local Authority and Allied Personal Social Services*. Cmnd 3703 (London: HMSO).

Segal, L. (1983) *What is to be Done about the Family?* (Harmondsworth: Penguin Books).

Segal, L. (1987) *Is the Future Female?* (Troubled Thoughts on Contemporary Feminism (London: Virago).

Sewpaul, V. (1997) *Social Work and In Vitro Fertilisation*. PhD (University of Natal-Durban).

Shakespeare, T. (1999) 'When is a Man Not a Man? When He is Disabled' in J. Wild (ed) *Working with Men for Change* (University College London Press).

Shanley, K. (1984) 'Thoughts on Indian Feminism' in B. Brant (ed) *A Gathering of Spirit: A Collection by North American Indian Women* (Ithaca, NY.: Firebrand Books).

Shah, Z. (2001) *British Pakistanis in Luton*. PhD (University of Southampton).

Sheffield, C. (1992) 'Sexual Terrorism', in Kourany, J., Sterba, J. and Tong, R. (eds) *Feminist Philosophies* (Englewood Cliffs, N.J.: Prentice-Hall).

Showstack Sassoon, A. (ed) (1987) *Women and the State: The Shifting Boundaries of the Private and Public* (London: Hutchinson).

Sidel, R. (1986) *Women and Children Last: The Plight of Poor Women in Affluent America* (New York: Viking Books).

Silvera, M. (1983) *Silenced* (Toronto: Sister Vision Press).

Sim, J. (1994) 'Tougher than the Rest: Men in Prison' in Newburn, T. and Stanko, E. (eds), *Just Boys Doing Business: Men, Masculinity and Crime* (London: Routledge).

Small, J. (1984) 'The Crisis in Adoption', in the *International Journal of Psychiatry*, 30, Spring, pp. 120–41.

Smart, C. (1976) *Women, Crime and Criminology: A Feminist Critique* (London: Routledge).

Smart, C. (1984) *Ties that Bind: Law, Marriage and the Reproduction of Patriarchal Relations* (London: Routledge & Kegan Paul).

Smart, C. and Smart, B. (1978) (eds) *Women, Sexuality and Social Control* (London: Routledge & Kegan Paul).

Smith, D. E. (1987) *The Everyday World as Problematic: A Feminist Sociology* (Toronto: University of Toronto Press).

Smith, D. E. (1990) *The Conceptual Practices of Power: A Feminist Sociology of Knowledge* (Boston: North Eastern University Press).

Snodgrass, J. (ed) (1977) *A Book of Readings for Men Against Sexism* (New York: Times Change).

Snowdon, R. (1980) 'Working with Incest Offenders: Excuses, Excuses, Excuses' in *AEGIS: Issue on Child Sexual Assault*, 29, Autumn.

Solanas, V. (1971) *Society for Cutting Up Men* (New York: Olympia Press).

Solomos, J. (1989) *Race and Racism in Contemporary Britain* (London: Macmillan – now Palgrave).

Sone, K. (1995) 'Get Tough', *Community Care*, 16–22 March, pp. 18–20.

Spender, D. (1980) *Man Made Language* (London: Routledge & Kegan Paul).

Stack, C. (1975) *All our Kin: Strategies for Survival in a Black Community* (New York: Harper and Row).

Stanley, L. and Wise, S. (1993) *Breaking Out: Feminist Consciousness and Feminist Research* (London: Routledge and Kegan Paul). First published in 1983.

Stanworth, M. (ed) (1988) *Reproductive Technologies: Gender, Motherhood and Medicine* (Minneapolis: University of Minnesota Press).

Staples, R. (1988) *Black Masculinity: The Black Male's Role in American Society* (San Francisco: Black Scholar Press).

Status of Women (2001) *Women's Economic Independence and Security: A Federal/Provincial/Territorial Strategic Framework from the Ministers Responsible for the Status of Women* (Ottawa: Status of Women).

Steinberg, D. L. (1997) *Bodies in Glass: Genetics, Eugenics, Embryo Ethics* (University of Manchester Press).

Steuter, E. (1995) 'Women Against Feminism: An Examination of Feminist Social Movements and Anti-Feminist Countermovements' in Nelson, E. and Robinson, B. (eds) *Gender in the 1990s: Images, Realities and Issues* (Toronto: Nelson Canada).

Stewart, J., Smith, D. and Stewart, G. (1994) *Understanding Offending Behaviour* (Harlow: Longman).

Stoltenberg, J. (1990) *Refusing to be a Man* (New York: Meridan).

Strega, S., Callahan, M., Dominelli, L., Ruttman, D. (2000) *The Experiences of Mothers in Government Care*. Paper Given at the 29th Congress of the International Association of Schools of Social Work, Montreal, 30 July–2 August.

Swift, K (1995) *Manufacturing 'Bad Mothers': A Critical Perspective on Child Neglect* (University of Toronto Press).

Tait-Rolleston, W. and Pehi-Barlow, S. (2001) 'A Maori Social Work Construct' in Dominelli, L., Lorenz, W. and Soydon, H. (eds) *Beyond Racial Divides: Ethnicities in Social Work Practice* (Aldershot: Ashgate).

Tapley, J. (2000) *Victims Rights: A Critical Examination of the British Criminal Justice System from Victims' Perspectives*. PhD (Southampton University).

Taylor, M. (1999) 'Family Group Conferences: A Co-ordinator's Perspective' in Dominelli, L. (ed) *Community Approaches to Child Welfare: International Perspectives* (Aldershot: Ashgate).

Teeple, G. (1995) *Globalisation and the Decline of Social Reform* (Toronto: Garamond Press).

Thomas Bernard, W. (1995) *Survival and Success: As Defined by Black Men in Sheffield, England and Halifax, Canada*. PhD Thesis (Department of Sociological Studies, Sheffield University).

Thompson, N., Stradling, S., Murphy, M. and O'Neil, P. (1996) 'Stress and Organisational Culture', British Journal of Social Work, 26, pp. 647–65.

Thompson, S. (1998) 'Who Goes There, Friend or Foe? Black Women, White Women and Friendship in Academia', in D. Malina and D. Maslin-Prothero (eds) (1998) *Surviving the Academy: Feminist Perspectives* (Brighton: Falmer Press).

Thorpe, R. and Irwin, J. (1996) *Women and Violence: Working for Change* (Sydney: Hale and Iremonger).

Tolson, A. (1977) *The Limits of Masculinity* (London: Tavistock).

Tong, R. (1989) *Feminist Thought: A Comprehensive Introduction* (San Francisco: Westview Press).

Trainor, B. (1996) *Radicalism, Feminism and Fanaticism: Social Work in the 1990s* (Aldershot: Ashgate).

Twigg, J. and Atkin, K. (1994) *Carers Perceived: Policy and Practice in Informal Care* (Buckingham: Open University Press).

Tronto, J. (1993) *Moral Boundaries: A Political Argument for an Ethics of Care* (London: Routledge).

United Nations Development Programme (UNDP) (1998) *The 1998 Report on Human Social Development* (New York: UNDP).

Ungerson, C. (1987) *Policy is Personal: Sex, Gender and Informal Care* (London: Tavistock).

Ungerson, C. (1990) *Gender and Caring Work and Welfare in Britain and Scandinavia* (Hemel Hempstead: Harvester/Wheatsheaf).

Utting, W. (1991) *Children in the Public Care* (London: HMSO).

Van den Bergh, N. (ed) (1995) *Feminist Practice in the 21st Century* (Washington, DC: NASW Press).

Wagg, S. and Pilcher, J. (eds) (1996) *Thatcher's Children: Childhood and Society in the 1990s* (London: Frances Pinter).

Wagner, A. (1998) *European Journal of Social Work*.

Wagner, G. (1988) *Residential Care: A Positive Choice. Report of the Independent Review of Residential Care*. (London: National Institute of Social Work).

Walby, S. (1990) *Theorising Patriarchy* (Oxford: Basil Blackwell).

Walby, S. (ed) (1997) *New Agendas for Women* (London: Palgrave).

Walton, R. (1975) *Women in Social Work* (Routledge and Kegan Paul).

Ward, D. and Lacey, M. (eds) (1995) *Probation: Working for Justice* (London: Whiting and Birch).

Warnock, M. (1984) *A Question of Life. The Warnock Report on Human Fertilisation and Embryology* (Oxford: Blackwell).

Waterhouse, L., Dobash, R. and Carney, J. (1994) *Child Sexual Abusers* (Edinburgh: Scottish Office).

Weber, M. (1978) *Selections from Max Weber*. Translated by W. C. Runciman (Berkeley: University of California Press).

Wellard, S. (1999) 'The Loss of Control', *Community Care*, 21–7 January, pp. 22–3.

Wendall, S. (1996) *The Rejected Body: Feminist Philosophical Reflections on Disability* (London: Routledge).

White, S. (1997) 'Beyond Retroduction? Hermeneutics, Reflexivity and Social Work Practice', in *British Journal of Social Work*, 27, pp. 739–53.

Whitehead, A. (2000) *Rethinking Crime and Masculinity*. PhD Thesis in preparation (Southampton University).

Whitehouse, P. (1986) 'Race and the Criminal Justice System' in V. Coombe and A. Little (eds), *Race and Social Work* (London: Tavistock).

Wilcox, C. (1990) 'Black Women and Feminism', *Women and Politics*, 10(3), pp. 65–84.

Wild, J. (ed) (1999) *Working with Men for Change* (University College London).

Williams, B. (1995) *Probation Values* (Birmingham: Venture Press).

Williams, B. (1997) 'The Prison', in Davies, M. (ed), *The Blackwell Companion to Social Work* (Oxford: Blackwell).

Williams, L. (1998) *Wives, Mistresses and Matriarchs: Asian Women Today* (London: Weidenfeld and Nicolson).

Wilmot, P. and Young, M. (1968) *Family and Kinship in East London* (London: Pelican). First published in 1957.

Wilson, E. (1977) *Women and the Welfare State* (London: Tavistock).

Wilson, M. (1993) *Crossing the Boundary: Black Women Survive Incest* (London: Virago).

Wilson, T. J. (1996) 'Feminism and Institutionalised Racism: Inclusion and Exclusion at an Australian Women's Refuge,' in *Feminist Review*, 52, Spring, pp. 1–26.

Winnicott, C. D. (1964) *Child Care and Social Work* (Hitchin: Codicote Press).

Wise, S. (1985) *Becoming a Feminist Social Worker: Monograph in Studies on Sexual Politics* (Manchester University).

Wittig, M. (1988) 'The Straight Mind' in S. Hoagland and J. Penelope (eds), *For Lesbians Only: A Separatist Anthology* (London: Onlywomen Press), pp. 431–8.

Wollstonecraft, M. (1975) *A Vindication of the Rights of Women* (Harmondsworth: Penguin).

Worrall, A. (1990) *Women Offending: Female Lawbreakers and the Criminal Justice System* (London: Routledge and Kegan Paul).

Young, J. (1999) *The Exclusive Society* (London: Sage).

Younghusband, E. (1978) *Social Work in Britain, 1950–1975* (London: Allen and Unwin).

Zaretsky, Z. (1976) *Capitalism, the Family and Personal Life* (London: Pluto Press).

Zucchino, D. (1997) *Myth of the Welfare Queen* (New York: Touchstone Books).

Author Index

Subject Index

welfare bureaucracy, 60

welfare recipients, 38, 61

welfare state, 1–2, 9, 11–2, 20, 28, 44–6, 54, 58–67, 134, 142, 147

well-being, 4–6, 13–4, 17, 37–8, 51, 52, 63, 65, 69, 72, 77, 82, 96–7, 101–7, 113, 119–20, 130, 133, 137, 139, 142, 148, 162, 164

White Collective for Anti-Racist Social Work, 150

white men, 89, 91, 93, 145, 154

white women, 4, 16, 29–30, 31, 74–5, 91, 100, 144, 153–4, 157

white women practitioner, 74

woman victim-survivor, 95

woman-blaming, 90

woman-centred approaches, 7

women, 1–138 *passim*, 140, 142–64

women first-time offenders, 149, 152

women offenders, 100, 148, 152–7

women public sector employees, 127

work, 1–10, 13–29, 32–50, 52–61, 65–9, 71–8, 80–8, 92, 94–115, 121–39, 142–51, 155–65

workfare, 59–61

working relations, 25, 35, 46, 82, 100

working with men, 15, 28–9, 86, 94–7

Working with Men Collective, 29, 87–9, 102

working class, 3, 17, 41, 69, 78–80, 93, 102, 107, 110–11, 117

workplace, 21–8, 42, 48, 77, 82–3, 87, 100, 106, 109, 133

workplace relations, 42, 48, 83, 106

worldview, 26, 77

young offenders, 119, 155–6, 160

young women, 1, 66, 91, 156–7

young women offenders, 157

youths, 32, 156

CPSIA information can be obtained
at www.ICGtesting.com
Printed in the USA
LVHW061430031219
639261LV00006B/117/P

9 780333 771549